LISTENING

LISTENING

A FRAMEWORK FOR
TEACHING ACROSS DIFFERENCES

Katherine Schultz

FOREWORD BY Frederick Erickson

Teachers College
Columbia University
New York and London

MT

Published by Teachers College Press, 1234 Amsterdam Avenue, New York, NY 10027

Library of Congress Cataloging-in-Publication Data

Schultz, Katherine.
    Listening : a framework for teaching across differences / Katherine Schultz ; foreword by
  Frederick Erickson.
      p. cm.
    Includes bibliographical references and index.
      ISBN 0-8077-4378-X (cloth : alk. paper) — ISBN 0-8077-4377-1 (pbk. : alk. paper)
      1. Effective teaching.   2. Listening.   3. Teacher-student relationships.   I. Title.
  LB1027.S36638 2003
  371.39—dc21   2003050771

ISBN 0-8077-4377-1 (paper)
ISBN 0-8077-4378-X (cloth)

Printed on acid-free paper

Manufactured in the United States of America

10   09   08   07   06   05   04   03   8   7   6   5   4   3   2   1

3/1/04

To L. John Trott (1927–2000), who led so many of us into teaching.

John Trott taught me to listen to the rhythms of nature and the stillness of silence. He taught me how to fill my teaching and life with stories.

Contents

Foreword

FREDERICK ERICKSON

> For everything there is a season
> and a time for every matter under heaven.
>
> A time to plant and a time to pluck up what is planted.
>
> A time to keep silence and a time to speak.
>
> Ecclesiastes 3:1; 2a; 7b

TEACHING REQUIRES CAREFUL LISTENING, that is, paying close attention to those we are trying to teach. Of course, a teacher must understand subject matter and some basic pedagogical techniques. But that is not enough. The teacher must be able to turn to her students to learn how to reach them. This requires listening to them as individuals, to their community, and to their society.

Really good teachers know this. They can hear in a student's voice interest or understanding or fear, can see in a student's writing, drawing, and math notebook pages evidentiary traces of that student's thinking, like rabbit tracks in the snow. They know how to read the faces, the arms, the shoulders, and the feet of those they teach, how to tell when their students are *voting* with their faces, arms, shoulders, or feet, and whether the votes of the moment are *yea*'s or *nay*'s. Really good teachers know what is going on—really going on, that is, in local particulars—in their students' lives outside of school. They also know how to listen to their students' parents, taking seriously what those parents say.

There is no substitute for this, no end run around the teacher's need to come to know those she is teaching. Trying to teach without that knowledge, treating the class as a whole batch, only works a little. It doesn't draw out the latent capacities of students to realize their full strengths as sense-makers. It doesn't help students become engaged, resilient learners, but leaves many of them by the wayside, needlessly confused and alienated, shut down on school.

What a waste, what squandering of human potential. And how boring and self-defeating it is to try to teach this way, on the cheap.

Here is the crucial point: Teachers must listen in order to know how to act pedagogically at the right times. Without the awareness that comes from listening, a teacher does not know how to recognize *teachable moments* when they are happening. These are the times of opportunity to which Ecclesiastes refers—the right times for tactical action. In Hebrew the word for this kind of time is *eyt*. The translators of the Hebrew Scriptures into Greek used the word *kairos* for *eyt*. In modern Greek one of the meanings of *kairos* is opportunity. It contrasts with the term *kronos*, which refers to time conceived as continuous—as undifferentiated duration, as clock time. *Kairos*, in contrast, is the nonchronological, discontinuous time of appropriateness for action.

The really good teacher knows subject matter *and* her students. "One moment" in the activity of this morning is not quite *kairos* yet for the next new idea in mathematics. At another moment we are just past *kairos* for that, and so it is better to wait until tomorrow. But at *this* moment, and especially because these particular students just said what they did, we are in *kairos*, and so we'll go for the new idea, the new skill. The teacher who knows how to ride the crests of these pedagogical waves with her students is worthy of their trust. With such a teacher, students will rise to the occasion and take the risks that always inhere in trying to learn something new.

The teachers whose practices are described in detail in *Listening* by Katherine Schultz are adept at the subtle tactics of listening and taking advantage of teachable moments as a means of moving learners where the teacher wants them to go. The teaching of Judy Buchanan, Lynne Strieb, Katherine Schultz, and the others portrayed here shows how that tactical work of teaching is done—how to be a teacher that students can trust to lead them. If you want to learn to listen in order to teach really well, and to find your teaching interesting from one year to the next, pay close attention to how these teachers do their daily work.

As our author shows us, listening to teach is not simply a technique that can be labeled traditional or progressive; it transcends those categories. It is a process, a continually evolving relationship with students that is fundamental for the kind of teaching our nation continues to say it wants—teaching that supports rich, robust learning among a wide variety of learners. This is the instrumental reason for listening to teach, listening across the divides of race, class, ethnicity, religion, disability, sexual orientation, and any other lines along which people become separated and stigmatized.

It is an important reason. Yet there is another reason for listening to teach, and I will conclude these remarks by mentioning it. The voice of a wise and experienced philosopher and educator, Patricia Carini, recurs throughout these pages. She reminds us that listening to teach accomplishes even more than the instrumental aim of getting the best kinds of learning out of every student. The quality of close attention—the respect for others—as it manifests in this kind of listening enhances the humanity of both the listener and the listened-to. In and through listening to teach, teachers and their students are being true to what is most human in each other. They grow in that and stand taller together.

As a teacher do not settle for less. Aim for this for yourself with anyone you are teaching. Read the book carefully and revisit it occasionally. Then in your teaching practice the arts of listening and acting pedagogically in the times of *eyt*, the moments of *kairos*.

FREDERICK ERICKSON is George F. Kneller Professor of Anthropology of Education, and is also Director of Research at the Corinne A. Seeds University Elementary School at the University of California, Los Angeles.

Acknowledgments

ALTHOUGH I HAVE ALWAYS *said* that writing is a collective process and that texts reflect the voices of many (and the responsibility of one), I now understand what that means in a lived sense. I owe enormous gratitude to so many people who have been intellectual mentors, supportive friends: patient, prodding, insightful, and honest. I have been fortunate to have had many fine teachers and mentors in my life. Each of you has played a role in shaping my ideas. And, of course, the students I have had the privilege to work with during the past 25 years have taught me the most, in so many ways. The people I mention in this formal list are only a part of the community that has inspired me to write this book and supported me through its production. I include the names of only those who directly helped me with the final manuscript. The rest of you know who you are; please accept my sincere thanks.

First, I'd like to thank the teachers and students who so generously invited me into their classrooms and schools. A researcher can never experience the same vulnerability a teacher feels by allowing another to document or interrogate her practice. I hope that seeing yourselves and your work in print will begin to repay this debt. Special thanks are particularly due to Judy Buchanan and Lynne Strieb, who talked through descriptions of their classrooms, reading countless versions of their chapters and generously sharing their own fine accounts of their teaching.

I made the decision to write a book as a result of my summers as a Carnegie Scholar. Through the wise leadership of Lee Shulman and the enormous generosity of the Carnegie Foundation, I was fortunate to be in the first cohort of K–12 teachers and teacher educators in the Carnegie Academy for the Scholarship of Teaching and Learning (CASTL). Ann Lieberman, together with my teacher educator colleagues—Marilyn Cohn, Christine Cziko, Nancy Lourie Markowitz, and Deb Smith—read early drafts of these chapters and helped to give the book its current shape. Ann's gentle/tough feedback inspired me to see the project as a whole. Several teachers in our group read pieces of the manuscript and gave me feedback at critical moments. Heidi Lyne was the first person to read the entire manuscript; her insights about teaching and writing were central. Other readers included Maureen Carter,

Evelyn Jenkins Gunn, Cris Gutierrez, Marsha Pincus, and Diane Waff. They, and the rest of our cohort, taught me so much about teaching, research, and listening.

Throughout the process my writing was nurtured by my writing group— Thea Abu El-Haj, Janine Remillard, and Ellen Skilton-Sylvester. Each has contributed immeasurably to this final text. In addition to this group, early on several people generously took precious time to read the entire manuscript. While on a sabbatical in Mexico, Nancy Barnes read chapters in Internet cafes, always raising questions and lending insight and tremendous support. Other early readers of the entire book included Thea Abu El-Haj, Margery Albertson, Mollie Blackburn, Bryan Brayboy, Patti Buck, Patricia Carini, Tamara Glupczynski, Galen Longstreth, Carlye Nelson-Major, Lisa Morenoff, David Paul, Lisa Smulyan, and Anne Burns Thomas (who may have read it more than five times). Each made a unique contribution to its final form, often providing invaluable advice. In addition, several colleagues read chapters along the way, giving me substantive feedback: Bob Fecho, Sarah Jewett, Marci Resnick, Dirck Roosevelt, Marvin Lazerson, Susan Lytle, and Jeff Shultz. In so many ways you taught me to write and think about teaching. Colleagues who have collaborated in the research for this book in critical ways include Thea Abu El-Haj, Judy Buchanan, Patti Buck, James Davis, Sarah Jewett, Alison McDonald, Tricia Niesz, Lynne Strieb, Katie Zimring, and members of the Philadelphia Teachers' Learning Cooperative. As early re- viewers, Tim Lensmire and Caroline Heller gave me critical feedback. I am enormously grateful for their wisdom, gentleness, and clarity.

Becca Steinitz has not only been an invaluable friend throughout the process of writing this book; she also was willing to put aside her own work at a crucial point to help me craft the text. Her editorial eye is unparalleled. In addition, Anne Burns Thomas is one of the most careful readers I know. She generously gave me hours of time and close reading of the manuscript. Lalitha Vasudevan helped me to track down references, among many other tasks.

The central ideas in this book have benefited from feedback at several conferences, and from several colleagues and friends, most notably from Glynda Hull, Frederick Erickson, and Michelle Fine. My colleagues at the University of Pennsylvania have been enormously generous with the time, support, and knowledge of educational practice. Countless colleagues across the country, including those at the University of Delaware and the University of California at Berkeley, those in the Council of Anthropology and Education, and teachers in Philadelphia including our teacher research group, Going Deeper, have played an important role in my writing. Along the way, several graduate students, especially student teachers, have read portions of the manuscript.

The research in this book was supported by several grants from the Spencer Foundation, which has been a critical source of funding for educational research. A grant from the MacArthur/Spencer Professional Development and Documentation Program funded the research for Chapter 3, a National Academy of Education/Spencer Postdoctoral Fellowship supported the research in Chapter 4, and a research grant from the Spencer Foundation partially funded the research in Chapter 5. Grants from the University of Delaware and the University of Pennsylvania Research Foundation provided additional support for the research described in Chapter 5.

Carol Collins at Teachers College Press has guided the book through this long process with enormous skill and consistent support.

My family, and especially my father, Frank Schultz, my late mother Jean Barnett Schultz, my stepmother Ginger Schultz, and my siblings Bill, John, and Caroline Schultz were my first teachers and central in so many ways to my life. I owe my deepest thanks to my children Nora, Danny, and Jenna Paul-Schultz. They are the future and my greatest source of pleasure. They have put up with my absence for far too many nights and weekends. Finally, my husband David Paul has read every single word many times, contributing insight and humor; his constant support and belief in me for over 25 years has sustained me as a teacher in so many ways. Heartfelt thanks to all of you.

1

Locating Listening at the Center of Teaching

> To teach in a manner that respects and cares for the souls of our students is essential if we are to provide the necessary conditions where learning can most deeply and intimately begin.
>
> (hooks, 1994)

There was a sudden silence in the classroom as the 10-year-old girl stood her ground, her eyes locked in battle with her teacher. Her face twisted in a scowl, she refused to budge. Her teacher's face, in turn, displayed anger and frustration. Exasperated, the teacher started to order the student to leave the classroom and sit in the hall, but stopped short. She paused, caught her breath, and calmly instructed the girl to write about the incident.

SUCH HIGHLY CHARGED SCENES occur daily in classrooms across the country: A student acts out, her teacher tells her to change her behavior, the student resists, the teacher gets frustrated. The next step seems inevitable: The teacher will deliver a punishment. However, the resolution of this particular interaction was different. Instead of immediately punishing the offense, this teacher decided to listen to the student's explanation for what had happened. Without interrupting the flow of the classroom activity or the academic focus of this class period, the teacher instructed the student to write a letter detailing what had transpired. After soliciting the student's perspective, the teacher was able to craft her rejoinder to reflect the student's own understanding of the events. Turning to letter writing, a practice she had introduced and carefully cultivated with her students, the teacher was able not only to maintain the rhythm of the classroom and reengage the student in academic activity but also to address the misbehavior constructively. Her response was improvisational in the moment and built upon established classroom practices; it demonstrates how listening to her students was key to this teacher's work.

1

This teacher and her coteacher had extensive pedagogical knowledge that guided their teaching, gained through years of experience and extensive study with teacher inquiry groups and work at various universities. In addition, there was a rich academic curriculum in the classroom developed over many years in collaboration with colleagues in this school and across the city. This knowledge of pedagogy and content was an essential component in the teachers' repertoires of strategies for teaching. At the center of this understanding of how to teach was the knowledge gained through active listening to the students. The letters that students wrote as a consequence of their (mis)behavior were just one of the ways that the teachers listened closely to their students in order to teach them. They developed projects connected to each of the academic subjects that allowed students to bring their interests and stories into the classroom. Teachers found frequent times to interact with students individually about academic and social issues. This knowledge guided their relationships with students and, most important, their teaching.

Listening to students is essential to teaching. This book, written for new and experienced teachers, as well as university- and school-based educators working with teachers, offers a conceptual framework for listening. Beginning with listening to know individual students, this book describes how teachers listen to the rhythm and balance of the whole class, the social, cultural, and community contexts of students' lives, and, finally, how teachers listen for silence and acts of silencing.

This conception of listening in order to teach assumes that teachers have knowledge of strategies to use in response to what they learn from paying close attention to students. Rather than teaching prospective and experienced teachers how to follow prescriptions or blueprints, I suggest that teachers learn how to attend and to respond with deep understanding to the students they teach. If a fundamental purpose of schooling in the United States is to prepare students to participate actively in a democracy, then teaching by scripts, with predetermined questions for teachers and answers for students, is not sufficient. Teachers need to bring into classrooms robust understandings about content, pedagogy, and children. It is only by engaging students in posing questions and critique—imagining the possible—that we educate students to participate in our pluralistic democracy.

WHO SHOULD READ THIS BOOK?

As a new teacher, I learned early on to listen in order to teach. A first-year teacher at 22, teaching in a mixed-age, fourth- and fifth-grade classroom, I knew I couldn't possibly know everything necessary to teach my students. I developed an exciting and complicated curriculum on ancient Greece. I adapted methods for structuring activities and learning based on my observations of other teachers and my experiences during student teaching. Still, it was clear that this knowledge wasn't enough. Although the students were interested in the material, they weren't deeply engaged in learning in a manner that lasts a lifetime. I knew that kind of learning was rare; I also understood that it was possible. So I turned to the students' curiosity and abiding interests as my guide. I listened to who they were as individuals and as a group and to the understandings they brought to the classroom. The students had plenty to communicate in both words and actions, and an endless number of questions. As I listened, I learned to teach. My classroom began to reflect both my own understandings and the growing knowledge of the students.

Years later, as a middle-class teacher educator raised in the suburbs and committed to preparing student teachers to teach in urban settings, I turned to students in urban schools as a source of knowledge about schools and schooling. In addition to teachers and texts, students in a range of contexts were a fund of information for how to teach. Students in an urban high school patiently taught me about what they cared about and needed to know and learn for their futures. I learned about the literacy practices that were valuable to them as parents, poets, hairdressers, athletes, adolescents interested in popular culture, and students with plans to continue on to college or pass tests to enter the military. As I reflected on my work in varied classroom settings, I realized that I had taken a listening stance in both my teaching and research. It wasn't always easy to listen or know how to respond to students. Often, I found myself failing to grasp the tenor of the classroom.

As an experienced teacher, I still find myself misreading individuals and groups, thinking that I've taken in what students say or need when I haven't understood the subtleties of the scene in front of me. I have come to appreciate the fundamental value of taking a listening stance in teaching, but I'm still learning to both hear the voices and read the signals of each class that I teach. The purpose of this book is to make explicit a framework for listening to teach so that new and experienced teachers can reflect on and deepen their practice, not just in individual classrooms but throughout their careers as teachers.

In my current position as a teacher educator, a focus on listening is central to how I structure my courses, my assignments, and field experiences for students. Learning to teach is a lifelong undertaking that has no beginning or ending point. Most of us cannot remember when we first began to learn to teach—for some it began by listening to or observing older siblings or adults—and many of us still consider ourselves engaged in the process of learning how to teach each time we encounter a new group of students. This book is written for everyone interested in reflecting on teaching: prospective teachers in teacher education programs; experienced teachers who have remained in the classroom for many years; educators working with new and experienced teachers; professors; educational theorists; and researchers seeking to document and articulate theories of teaching and learning.

I suggest that listening to teach offers a way to understand and reconceptualize teaching as an ongoing process of learning over time. A focus on listening highlights the ways in which learning to teach involves more than mastering a set of skills. It emphasizes how learning to teach is grounded in knowledge of content, child development, pedagogy, and curriculum, and is constantly mediated by interpretations made in daily interactions with students.

A scene from the first day of a teacher education seminar that I cotaught with my colleague Sarah Jewett illustrates the listening stance I take in my own teaching and introduces the concepts I outline in this chapter.

Sarah and I arrived breathlessly at our classroom. It was exactly 4:30, the time the class was scheduled to begin. As we paused for a moment in the doorway, we realized that the room was strangely silent. Instead of the excited chatter we were accustomed to hearing as we entered a classroom—especially on the first day of class—we heard the voice of a single student. We entered cautiously, lingering in the doorway. The group of nearly 40 student teachers was seated in desks sprawled across the room. With her blond bangs brushed across forehead and her entire body in motion, Julie, a student teacher in the program, stood in front of the classroom organizing her peers. Confident in her leadership role, she asked the group, "Do you agree that an eight- to ten-page assignment due next week is unreasonable?" Most of the crowd murmured assent. "We should get them to change this, right?" There was more agreement, although this time the voices were somewhat subdued as several student teachers eyed Sarah and me in the doorway. My heart sank as I surveyed the scene. The student teachers were clearly disgruntled. I wondered how we could claim the floor and start in the upbeat manner more typical of a first class. In the meantime, we listened and waited until Julie gestured for us to come into the classroom. Sarah went to the board to write the agenda for the class. I looked over at Julie, sizing up the mood of the class and the sway she held over the group.

I hesitated as I rethought my first words to the students for the semester. I ascertained that they were talking about an assignment from another class they had attended that afternoon, taught by an adjunct instructor. The instructor was hired at the last moment and did not coordinate her syllabus with the rest of the program. The student teachers in her section of the course detected the difference between that class and other classes in the program and labeled it as unfair. The complaints were pertinent to their experience in the teacher education program, but not to our class on that day. In a split second I decided that I could change the topic, move this conversation to the end of the class period, and begin on my own terms. Without apology, I greeted the class in an upbeat manner and announced that we would save time at the end of class for this discussion. I looked to Julie for approval. She gave it easily, smiled, and congenially sat down with her classmates. Some students looked annoyed at the change of topic; most followed Julie's cues and turned their attention to me. I asked the student teachers to move their chairs into a circle and together we began the course.

(field notes, 9/12/00)

Teaching involves hundreds of split-second decisions on the part of the teacher and learners. Whether the instruction occurs between teachers and their 10-year-old students, or between professors and graduate students, teaching is a transaction that is at once carefully planned and spontaneously improvised by all participants. As illustrated in the opening moments of this teacher education seminar, although teachers generally hold most of the power in teaching interactions, there are occasionally moments when teachers hand that power and control over to their students, as well as instances when they reclaim their authority.

To make a decision about how to begin the class, I had to listen to more than the words of the students. I had to read the landscape, including the tone of the group. I used this knowledge to carefully synchronize my first words so that they were in tune with the group. I could not know ahead of time how Julie or her classmates would respond to my move to shift the topic. Listening enabled me to cross the boundary between teachers and students to understand how the group might react to my decision to address their concerns at the end of class. Further, I had to create a context for the students to voice their displeasure if my teaching decisions were out of synch with them. At the same time, I needed assurance that I could address the curriculum plan I had for the day. These teaching moves exemplify the notion of teaching that is theorized in this opening chapter and elaborated through examples in later chapters of the book.

FOUNDATIONS OF THIS RESEARCH

Listening to teach is a stance I gravitated toward as a new teacher and researcher. As a new teacher, I learned about and participated in the work of Patricia Carini and educators affiliated with the Prospect Center for Education and Research described in Chapters 2 and 3. Their phenomenological approach taught me the value of close and careful description of children and classrooms in order to uncover children's capacities as a guide for teaching (cf. Carini, 2001; Himley, 2000; see also Greene, 1995).

My early research projects were focused on students' and adult learners' accounts of their education, especially how they learned to read and write in and out of school. Particularly useful for this work were the explanations by McDermott and his colleagues that illustrated how schools and institutions construct students as successes or failures (e.g., McDermott, 1987, 1993; McDermott & Varenne, 1995; Varenne & McDermott, 1999). The adult learners I interviewed in my initial research projects had "failed" at school because of standards external to them rather than internal traits. The judgment that they could not read did not take into account the sociopolitical and cultural contexts of their literacy practices. My reading of McDermott and Varenne (e.g., 1995) led me to look beyond individuals to social systems. Erickson's work (e.g., 1982, 1984, 1995) was also important in focusing my attention on the moment-to-moment interactions and the musical relationships embedded in talk and interaction. I sought to document "successful" teaching interactions in urban public schools even as I critiqued the ways in which success was defined by various social and institutional structures. The examination of both the macro- and micro-levels of schooling in order to understand students' experiences in schools led me to develop a methodology for listening to and with students.

In each of my research settings—which included elementary, middle, and high schools as well as workplaces and adult literacy programs—I entered with the following question: How can listening to students and documenting their perspectives and practices inform understandings of schooling, especially in relation to what teachers need to know to teach in urban public schools? At the same time that students were a rich source of new perspectives and information, I knew that I had to look beyond what they could articulate. To complement my learning from students, I read widely in education research, cultural studies, anthropology, sociology, and psychology. I focused my reading at the intersection of educational research with gender and race, pushing my growing understandings of how these perspectives could deepen my own analytic frameworks. Most recently, my 3 years of work with the Carnegie Academy for the Scholarship of Teaching and Learning (CASTL) gave me opportunities to document and reflect on my own teaching practice in a community of teachers and teacher educators. This work has supported me to identify and articulate the themes in this book.

TAKING A LISTENING STANCE

I developed a conceptual framework by focusing on the moment-to-moment interactions of teaching in a wide range of settings. With a broader focus on how education is organized by social structures and institutions, I looked across contexts—in adult literacy programs, circuit-board assembly plants, and youths' experiences in school and out—as I sought to understand the interplay of structure and agency (e.g., Giddens, 1979). In each of these projects, I investigated learners' accounts of their education and schooling with a focus on literacy practices. These research projects form the core of this book. Each focuses on literacy practices grounded in sociocultural theories of literacy and the New Literacy Studies (e.g., Gee, 1996, 2000; Street, 1993a, 1993b, 1995, 2001; for a review, see Hull & Schultz, 2002).

More recently, critical race theory (e.g., Delgado, 1995; Delgado Bernal, 2002; Guinier & Torres, 2002; Ladson-Billings, 1998; Ladson-Billings & Tate, 1995; Parker, 1998) has guided me to articulate the value of placing the stories of individuals and groups who have been marginalized in the center of discussions and analysis. Theorists working in this domain explain the ways in which stories help to construct reality. They insist on recognizing the salience of race and its interaction with notions of citizenship (e.g., Ladson-Billings, 1998). These ideas shape how I have listened to and represent the stories learners have told to me.

Placing listening at the center of teaching stands in stark contrast to the trend to hand teachers prescriptions or scripted texts from which to teach. Such pedagogies fail to take into account either the students or the context in which teaching occurs. As a result, prescriptive teaching offers information or words to teachers that do not engage students in learning. Locating listening at the center of teaching works against the notion that teachers talk and students listen, suggesting instead that teachers listen to teach and students talk to learn (Meier, 1996).

When student teachers stand in front of 30 children in urban public schools, they face challenging situations. Student teachers often demand answers from their instructors. Again and again they articulate their concerns about classroom management and want easy answers to address their sincere questions. They crave techniques and foolproof lessons (e.g., Bartolomé, 1994). In many school systems, the response to this complexity is to hand teachers—especially new teachers—scripts from which to teach. Too often, teachers are taught or encouraged to *deliver* instruction and *cover* curriculum.

In our urban-focused teacher education program at the University of Pennsylvania, we offer a different solution. We suggest that by taking an inquiry stance and listening carefully to students, colleagues, and more experienced teachers, student teachers will learn to teach. In our courses we introduce a framework for listening that initially focuses student teachers' attention on their students—both individually and collectively—as resources for deciding how and what to teach. Our student teachers are not always happy with our reluctance to give them ready-made solutions. For many, it takes several years before they understand our approach.

We continually remind student teachers that we are teaching them to become teacher leaders over the long term rather than simply preparing them to teach the next day. This reassures some, whereas others remain skeptical. Throughout their 10 months in our program, we balance practical discussions about strategies for responding in the moment with conversations that offer student teachers a conceptual framework for learning to teach over time. My claim is that taking a listening stance is fundamental to this process of becoming a teacher.

Why Listening?

Taking a listening stance implies entering a classroom with questions as well as answers, knowledge as well as a clear sense of the limitations of that knowledge (e.g., Cochran-Smith & Lytle, 1999; Lytle & Cochran-Smith, 1992). Such an approach suggests that teaching is improvisational and responsive to students. It requires confidence to enter into teaching as a learner as well as a knower. Too often, teachers believe they have to start with the answers rather than the questions and understand their primary role as telling (Freire, 1973). Students perceive their role as passively absorbing information. But when teachers talk rather than listen, they are unlikely to notice how and whether students truly understand the material.

A ubiquitous phrase in classrooms is "Listen up." Students are dubbed "good listeners" if they obediently follow directions without thinking. I want to turn this notion around by defining listening as an active, relational, and interpretive process that is focused on making meaning. The emphasis on teaching as telling ignores teachers' responsibility to ensure that students become engaged in the process of constructing their own understandings. A focus on listening highlights the centrality of students as resources for the moment-to-moment decisions teachers make as they teach.

I use the term *listening* to refer to more than just hearing. As used here, it suggests how a teacher attends to individuals, the classroom as a group, the broader social context, and, cutting across all of these, to silence and acts of silencing. Teachers listen for the individual voices and gestures in their classrooms; they also listen for the heartbeat or tenor of the group. Whereas educational literature often foregrounds the importance of observation, I purposefully choose to focus on listening, to highlight the centrality of relationships in teaching. Observation can be done from a distance; listening requires proximity and intimacy. The phrase "listening to teach" implies that the knowledge of who the learner is and the understandings that both the teacher and learner bring to a situation constitute the starting place for teaching. Listening encompasses written words as well as those that are spoken, words that are whispered, those enacted in gesture, and those left unsaid. It is an active process that allows us to both maintain and cross boundaries. When I listen to teach, I am changed by what I hear.

Listening as Connected to Action

Central to this theory of listening is the proposition that listening necessitates action. That is, the act of listening is based on interaction rather than simply reception. Freire (1973) explained that to become an integrated person means to understand the worlds in which we live and work and to take part in reshaping those worlds. He wrote, "There is no true word that is not at the same time a praxis. Thus to speak a true word is to transform the world" (Freire, 1970, p. 68). I would add that to become a listener is to participate in this transformation. Listening closely to students implies becoming deeply engaged in understanding what a person has to say through words, gesture, and action. Listening is fundamentally about being in relationship to another and through this relationship supporting change or transformation. By listening to others, the listener is called on to respond.

The notion of listening to teach focuses on what to listen *for* as well as *how* to listen. It emphasizes both the act of listening and the actions that result from paying close attention to another. This kind of listening requires the teacher to become an active inquirer into her own pedagogy. Duckworth (1987) connects teaching to inquiry and research in her explanation of what she means by the term *teacher*:

> By "teacher" I mean someone who engages learners, who seeks to involve each person wholly—mind, sense of self, sense of humor, range of interests, interactions with other people—in learning. And, having engaged the learners, a teacher finds his questions to be the same as those that a researcher into the nature of human learning wants to ask: What do you think and why? While the students learn, the teacher learns, too. (p. 134)

Conceptualizing teaching as listening suggests that the teacher is always learning and that this learning shapes decisions in the moment and contributes to the teacher's growth as a professional.

The conception of listening in this book includes close observation and interaction. This framework for listening is based, in part, on the ethnographic notion that everyone makes sense all of the time and, further, that the teacher's task is to understand, as much as it is possible, students' understandings as a starting place for teaching. For instance, the patterns of errors a student makes as he reads aloud are often evidence for what that student needs to work on in reading. When a student explains her own algorithm in math that led to a series of miscalculations, her teacher gains insight into her mathematical thinking (e.g., Ball, 1993, 1997). Hearing and making sense of the student's words, reading and analyzing the student's writing, and close observation: All are essential to teacher decision making.

Foregrounding listening highlights the ways in which teaching is based on relationships between and among teachers, students, and texts (Schultz, 1991). Learning to teach is a complex and multilayered process. Although the received wisdom is that elementary teachers focus on pedagogy and high school teachers and university professors focus on content or subject matter, I suggest that all teachers weave into teaching the knowledge of their students that comes from listening. Teaching as listening, in bell hooks's (1994) words, respects the soul of the learner.

Listening Across Difference

We live at a historical moment characterized by rapid changes. Increased access to technology and information distinguishes what is sometimes referred to as the "era of globalization." In the United States, the recent waves of new immigrants add to the growing linguistic and cultural diversity of the country. At the same time, there is a widening gap between the rich and the poor. Increased racial and ethnic segregation is endemic to both communities and schools. The social and demographic changes in the United States are perhaps most visible in its public schools (Nieto, 2000). Paradoxically, while students are becoming increasingly diverse, and the content of popular culture that permeates students' lives outside of school is changing rapidly, there has been a press for standardization and uniformity inside of schools. These trends toward uniformity in pedagogy and curriculum ignore the rapid changes in demography and the changing content of students' lives.

The demographic changes in U.S. schools mean that teaching always involves crossing lines of difference, whether these are generational or based on gender, race, social class, sexuality, ethnicity, or culture. To cross boundaries of difference requires listening, not to erase the boundaries but to understand and use them as a resource. Erickson (1997) distinguishes between cultural boundaries and borders, writing that cultural boundaries are politically neutral with similar rights and obligations, whereas cultural borders are politically charged. (See also McDermott & Gospodinoff, 1979, for an elaboration of these ideas.) Learning to teach students different from oneself always requires that teachers begin with listening and learning. It also requires that students learn to listen to each other to grow in their understanding and reframe their differences as strengths.

Teachers have the responsibility to listen closely enough to understand students' perspectives. Geertz (1973) explains that anthropologists cannot represent what others see and understand. Instead, they describe lenses others see *through* or their interpretive perspectives on their own experiences. Like-wise, teachers can never fully understand the experiences of students or their communities; they can learn only as much as students articulate. The responsi-bility of teachers is to create the conditions for students to give words to their perspectives and understandings so that their teachers can respectfully teach them.

It has become a common practice for teacher educators to ask students to write cultural autobiographies. Educators use personal narratives as the starting point for student teachers—especially new teachers from White, mid-dle-class backgrounds—to learn how to teach across lines of difference (e.g., Bullough & Gitlin, 2001; Cochran-Smith, 2000; Ladson-Billings, 1994; Nieto, 1999, 2000). Assignments such as these emphasize the importance of begin-ning with an understanding of oneself. Raising questions about this direction for teacher education programs, Sheets (2000) warns that a focus on White identity should not replace what she calls "equity pedagogy" (e.g., Hollins, 1996; Ladson-Billings, 1994). Sheets suggests that without knowledge of cultural groups from the perspectives of those groups themselves, autobio-graphical approaches "might encourage narcissistic educational philosophies rather than advanc[ing] inclusive multicultural positions" (p. 19). Sheets urges teacher educators who work with White, middle-class student teachers—the predominant group in most teacher education programs—to focus on learning about students in their classrooms from the students' own perspectives. I con-cur with Sheets's proposal to teach student teachers about how to use the students in their classrooms as the primary resource for learning how to teach, with one reservation. I worry that student teachers often spend too much time focused on themselves and their performance rather than on their students. Nonetheless, I see the value of asking student teachers to explore their cul-tural biographies in order to claim their own ethnic and racial background, so that they, as well as the students, enter classrooms from racialized and class positions.

In my teacher education classes I encourage student teachers to listen to students across cultural divides. I ask student teachers to look outside of them-selves at the same time that they use their own histories and knowledge of their cultural lenses to uncover blind spots and biases. When new teachers enter the classroom, they often focus on themselves as teachers (asking ques-tions such as, "How did I do?"), or they focus on experienced teachers (asking, "How can I do what she does?"). Although these are important questions, I suggest that preservice teachers turn instead to the students themselves, to discover who the students are as learners and members of the class. In doing so they might replace questions about their own performance with ones such as the following: "How can I draw on this student's strengths to engage her in learning?"

Listening across lines of difference raises the challenge of understanding what students mean in their words, pictures, gestures, and tone as they express themselves in ways that may differ from what their teachers expect. The listening I describe includes listening beyond an individual frame of reference. It encompasses listening to be caught off guard and surprised, or listening beyond what a person expects to hear. Thompson (1998) describes the difficulty of this kind of listening when she explains:

> While our bodies, histories, culture, and situations are too central to who we are for men to be women-identified in the way that women can be, or for whites to be Black-identified in the way that African Americans can be, it is nevertheless important for cultural outsiders to study and learn as much as possible about what it would mean to address others in these terms. Otherwise, we risk treating those unlike ourselves as, at best, mirror images of ourselves, and at worst, as inferior, exotic, or instruments for our own purposes. (p. 542)

Learning to listen is key to bridging the divide teachers often face as cultural outsiders. To listen in this way implies retaining the authority teachers bring to their classrooms. It requires that teachers use their expertise as educators and members of the classroom communities they create to make sense of what they hear.

In contrast to the image of teaching as delivering content or covering material, my argument here is based on the notion that teaching involves hundreds of decisions each day and depends on "quick instinctive habits and behavior, and on deeply held ways of seeing and valuing" (Clark, 1988). It is in this context that I advocate learning to teach by emphasizing listening with the knowledge and capacity to act upon what is heard. This manner of teaching requires subject matter knowledge, understanding of child development, and cultural understanding. It also demands that teachers reach beyond what they know. As Ball and Cohen (1999) explain:

> Learning to attend to one's students with insight requires expertise beyond what one gathers from one's own experience. What one enjoyed, thought, or felt as a child may afford helpful speculation about one's students, but is insufficient as a professional resource for knowing learners. (pp. 8–9)

People have a tendency to assume likeness between their experiences and those of others. We often want to bridge social distance by assuming a common humanity that unites rather than divides us. How can teachers learn to see and understand differences, reframing those differences as potential resources rather than deficits? At the same time, how might teachers look for common ground from which to build understanding?

Nieto (1994) reminds us of the importance of going beyond "giving students voice" or simply hearing what students say:

> But listening alone is not sufficient if it is not accompanied by profound changes in what we expect our students to accomplish in school. Even more important than simply *listening* is *assisting* students to become agents of their own learning and to use what they learn in productive and critical ways. (p. 421)

The stance of listening proposed in this book is precisely *not* "listening alone." Rather, it is a reconceptualization of listening as multifaceted, and broader than hearing, shaped by moment-to-moment interactions, interpretations, and always including response or action.

Creating Conditions to Listen to Students

> Democracy, we realize, means a community that is always in the making. Marked by an emerging solidarity, a sharing of certain beliefs, and a dialogue about others. It must remain open to newcomers, those too long thrust aside. This can happen even in the local spaces of classrooms, particularly when students are encouraged to find their voices and their images. (Greene, 1995, p. 39)

Many classrooms are dominated by teacher talk; few are the democratic spaces filled with dialogue that Greene (1995) asks us to imagine. Often students assume a stance of silence either to take in information or to produce answers for teachers. What are the conditions or classrooms that enable teachers to listen to teach? How can we create the openings for conversation and exchange that are essential to learning and democracy? All too frequently when we assign student teachers in our program to study individual children in their classrooms, they inform us that they have no opportunities to talk with the children individually—either formally or informally—during the school day. If teachers value and want to develop the disposition, proclivity, and inclination to listen to students and the class as a whole, what kind of environment is necessary to support both listening and talking in the classroom across the day? This may involve reallocating time and reconfiguring classroom dynamics so there are more opportunities for talk and interaction. A focus on how to create an environment that supports listening allows us to imagine the possibility of changing the context of schooling rather than grooming students to fit classroom expectations.

Historically, educators have thought of their goal as changing children to fit what is considered the "norm." In an effort to move away from this deficit model, which casts blame on children and families, researchers in the 1970s and 1980s described how children's ways of learning might differ from the expectations of schools (Gilmore, 1983; Gilmore & Glatthorn, 1982; Heath,

1983). This research resulted in an exploration of the discontinuities between home and school. Despite the benefits of this approach, however, in practice, students of color are frequently treated as people who need special accommodation; ultimately, most children are expected to fit the norm.

For example, as a result of desegregation mandates of the kind I report on in Chapter 5, when students of color entered White schools, they were often forced to adapt to their new environment. In response to the Coleman report (1966), proponents of desegregation argued that by attending White schools, Black students would learn White, middle-class ways of acting that would improve their academic achievement and their chances to attain economic success in a White society. With rare exceptions, little effort was made to change the school culture to respond to the new students entering them (Foster, 1997; Walker, 1996). In many of the instances where a small number of students were chosen to desegregate previously all-White institutions—such as the highly publicized example of Central High School in Little Rock, Arkansas—the children and their families chosen to desegregate the school were those who were willing to adapt or accommodate to the majority culture. Although on the surface the United States has made some progress since that time, in many schools there remains the assumption, often held by teachers across race lines, that students of color must adopt the White, middle-class ways of acting and learning in order to succeed in school. The notion of listening to teach assumes that the teachers and students will shape the classroom culture together. In addition, it presumes that there is a climate of trust that supports both students and teachers to take risks in what they say and how they listen.

TRANSFORMING THE TEACHER'S ROLE

The dominant paradigm that guides teaching is telling; a focus on listening alters the role of the teacher and the nature of pedagogical interaction. Listening shifts the locus of activity away from the teacher, without taking away the responsibility to teach. Building on the work of Dewey and other progressive educators, researchers and teachers have described how to develop curriculum by listening to students' interests (Levy, 1996; Skilton-Sylvester, 1994). Progressive educators, in particular, have described ways to develop themes from students' interests and their lived realities (e.g., Meier, 1996; Perrone, 1991, 2000; Skilton-Sylvester, 1994). Those curricular changes can be coupled with the moment-to-moment interactions that shape teacher decision making in the midst of teaching. It is essential, but not always enough, for classrooms to reflect students' lives with books and materials that build on their deeply felt interests and heritage. The kind of listening to teach I describe in this book goes beyond provisioning classrooms or embracing a set of progressive education strategies. I offer a framework to guide teachers' daily actions as they translate pedagogy and curriculum into classroom teaching.

There has been a growing interest in listening to and understanding students' understandings in order to know how to teach them (Ball, 1993, 1997). Educators and researchers have described how to respect children and the knowledge they bring to school tasks, and what it might mean to take this stance in teaching. For instance, Duckworth (1987, 2001) illustrates how to probe a student's understanding in a clinical-type interview in order to discover the depth and complexity of her knowledge. Likewise, Ball (1993, 1997) demonstrates the ways that children's explanations can push mathematical understanding and serve as a guide for pedagogy and curriculum. Classrooms filled with student talk and explanations follow these teaching methodologies. Yet, even in classrooms characterized by researched-based teaching models, such as Success for All (Slavin & Madden, 1999), that emphasize direct instruction and choral response, teachers can find moments in the day to listen carefully to students to guide their teaching. This book is written for all teachers: not only those who find themselves in classrooms that are built around the voices and interests of the students but also those who are struggling to find moments in their days to bring students' voices into their classrooms.

Perhaps better than anyone else, Vivian Paley (1986) has described what happens when teachers stop teaching the prescribed curriculum or preplanned lesson. She explains her own process of learning to listen to children, which mirrors the theoretical and empirical discussion in this book:

> When my intention was limited to announcing my own point of view, communication came to a halt. My voice drowned out the children's. However, when they said things that surprised me, exposing ideas I did not imagine they held, my excitement mounted. I kept the children talking, savoring the uniqueness of responses so singularly different from mine. The rules of teaching had changed; I now wanted to hear answers I could not myself invent. Indeed, the inventions tumbled out as if they had been simply waiting for me to stop talking and begin listening. (p. 125)

Paley explores the ways in which her teaching was changed by listening to children and hearing what they said. These moments are sometimes the dominant mode of interaction during the day and in other contexts saved for rare moments between activities. The listening Paley articulates is based not only on profound respect but also on deep knowledge of children and an understanding of how to listen.

PLAN OF THE BOOK

The central chapters of this book elaborate a conceptual framework for listening to teach based on my research projects in elementary, middle, and high schools over the past 12 years. This conception of teaching for all grade levels includes listening to know particular students; listening for the rhythm and balance of a classroom; listening for the social, cultural, and community contexts of students' lives; and listening for silence and acts of silencing in classrooms and social institutions. Taken together, these four components of listening provide a conceptual framework, grounded in practice, for new and experienced teachers to reflect on how to teach. (See Figure 1.1.)

The first kind of listening, described in Chapter 2, is listening for the particularities or the unique ways of learning and interacting that different individuals bring to the classroom. This listening enables teachers to adapt their teaching and classroom practices to each student, rather than assuming that the student must fit the classroom. This form of listening includes listening closely enough to learn how to teach to students' capacities or strengths. Focusing on a large, urban, elementary school classroom, this chapter illustrates how teachers used writing to listen and respond to individual children even as they maintained their attention on the class as a whole.

Moving outward from a focus on the individuals, Chapter 3 describes how a teacher listens for the rhythm and balance of a classroom, reading the landscape of the class. Teachers often enact rituals to assess or listen for the ethos of their classroom. Listening for the rhythm and balance of a group allows teachers both to lead and to follow the distinctive direction of each

Figure 1.1. *Conceptual Framework for Listening to Teach*

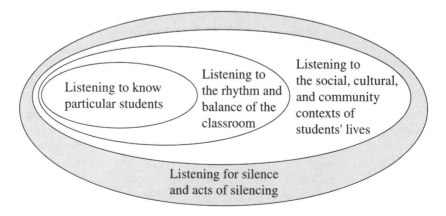

class. This chapter uses the whole-class discussions in a first-grade classroom to demonstrate how one teacher listens and responds to the rhythm and balance of her students as a whole. Two extended examples of classroom conversations—the first about leaves, the second about how children interact with one another—illustrate this stance.

Chapter 4 elaborates how teachers listen to the larger picture of who students are and the social, cultural, and community contexts of their lives. Listening to the broader contexts of students' lives suggests that teachers reframe teaching and assessment to include an understanding of students' learning in and out of school. It includes listening beyond students' learning during the school day. Listening to students in this manner means taking into account the vast resources and relationships students bring to the classroom and adding that knowledge to the assessment of what students know and are learning at any given time. This chapter is based on findings from a research project located in a multiracial urban high school. The literacy practices of three high school seniors illustrate the dilemmas and possibilities for including students' out-of-school writing in the school curriculum.

The concept of listening for silences and the ways in which students are silenced, as described in Chapter 5, intersects each of the other forms of listening. The articulation of listening in this manner helps teachers to learn how power works in the classroom and to recognize and bring out students' voices that may have been silenced. Listening for silence and acts of silencing highlights the importance of actively inquiring into what is not said in a classroom or school and noticing absences as well as what is said and done at individual and institutional levels. Building on research conducted in a postdesegregated middle school, this chapter offers portraits of three eighth graders to illustrate silencing at the institutional level, silencing by peers, and silencing by teachers.

The final chapter, Chapter 6, describes the implementation of these four kinds of listening in a teacher education program. I describe the ways I listened—and at times failed to listen—to students in a teacher education seminar. With an extended vignette of my interactions with student teachers in the seminar, I illustrate the complexity of listening to teach.

During the last class for the literacy course I teach to preservice elementary teachers, a group of student teachers were engaged in an activity to recall, in various categories, what they had learned during the semester and the questions and concerns that remained. One group raised the question: "How can we brainstorm topics for writing with students so that they don't all write the same thing." In many ways, I see the challenge of listening to teach as addressing a similar dilemma. How can teachers learn to listen to students and to respond to them in individual yet collective ways? How can teachers learn to move beyond the mandates that require them to teach everyone the same way so that the "products" or outcomes are identical? What kind of listening and teaching does this require? How can teachers trust that they will learn enough about who the students are in order to know how to teach them yet still hold on to their familiar methods? As a society, how can we learn to respect teachers enough so that we can entrust them with the responsibility of developing standards for and high expectations *with* the students in their classrooms rather than taking on and implementing the curriculum external experts provide?

It is the details of what happens in the moment-to-moment accounts of listening to teach, placing the students at the center of teaching, that I describe in the following chapters. Through my conceptual framework of listening, I attempt to articulate how teachers listen to students and respond to what they hear. The aggregate of these informed responses constitutes teaching. Through discussion and analysis of empirical research, a response to these questions emerges in the following chapters. I argue that taking a listening stance toward teaching is key to reconceptualizing pedagogy that is responsive to students living and learning in a pluralistic democracy.

2

Listening to Know
Particular Students

Slowness: to pause. Slowness: to linger. Slowness: to practice acts of attention. Attending, to learn to see in the child's dancing, the child's storytelling, the child's painting, the child's construction—in the child's play—how this child particularizes and selects the world, learning it actively and in the process of that making, making her own self as well.

(Carini, 2000, p. 21)

IN 1976—HER THIRD YEAR OF TEACHING—many new families from Southeast Asia entered Judy Buchanan's urban elementary school. Over a short period of time, the numbers of students from Vietnam, Laos, Cambodia, and Thailand had grown exponentially in what had been a predominantly African American school (Buchanan, 1994). Judy began to understand how to teach this new group of students by paying close attention to the children as individuals. She reached out to their families, collecting children's drawings and providing opportunities and materials in the classroom for students to engage in crafts to learn more about students' lives and approaches to learning. In Carini's words, she gave them a range of opportunities to display how they "particularize[d] and select[ed] the world" (Carini, 2000, p. 21). With few resources and little knowledge or information about how to teach this group of students, Judy then turned to her colleagues for support in addressing the challenges posed by these students whose cultures and life experiences were unfamiliar to her.

Though Judy's approach was successful with the majority of her students, Phia, a fourth grader, perplexed her. Specifically, she wondered how to support Phia in learning to read. Although other Hmong students she taught had struggled in various ways, she had never before had such difficulty teaching reading to a fourth-grade student (Buchanan, 1994). In order to learn how to teach Phia, Judy had to understand who he was as an individual beyond his membership in a group of new immigrants. To do so, she paid close attention to his learning as a means of listening to his individuality. For instance, she noticed the words he could not read and also the patterns of his reading. She discerned the ways in which he interacted with materials in the classroom, including his enjoyment of copying words and figures. She paid attention to his spoken words, and also to his gestures and tone. She listened for what she could hear easily and also for what was more opaque and difficult to discern; she drew upon her own knowledge of children and teaching. I call these practices listening to know particular students.

With the information she had gained from listening to Phia, Judy turned to her colleagues in a group called the Philadelphia Teachers' Learning Cooperative (PTLC). Begun in the early 1970s, this group was formed by teachers who had met regularly at a teachers' center funded by the School District of Philadelphia. From the beginning, the group of 15 to 20 teachers developed important and sustaining professional relationships with each other and with Patricia Carini, founder of the Prospect Center for Education and Research. They decided to continue to meet on their own when the school board discontinued funding for teachers' centers. Since 1978, they have met voluntarily for 2½ hours every Thursday afternoon during the school year, sharing responsibilities for all aspects of leading the group (Philadelphia Teachers' Learning Cooperative, 1984). The group uses a set of structured oral-inquiry processes developed with Carini to describe children, children's work, classroom practices, and educational issues that grow out of the daily work of teaching (Himley, 2000, 2002). These teachers are committed to working together to develop their own knowledge of teaching and learning through a close examination of practice that begins with listening to particular students.

When Judy presented Phia to the group, her question was how to support this 10-year-old child as a beginning reader. She presented a detailed description of his reading, and the group listened to and described what they heard as they paid attention to an audiotape of the student's reading. Judy framed learning to read as larger than decoding text. For instance, she presented a detailed portrait of Phia, including a description of the work he did with his hands and his enjoyment of copying. Her colleagues listened carefully to her description and made recommendations about how to teach this struggling reader. First-grade teachers mentioned books that might be more engaging than the early reading books in her classroom that relied on sight words. Others suggested that Judy build on Phia's interest in copying to provide him with opportunities to practice reading. They gave detailed descriptions of specific ways to use his skills and interest in drawing to teach sounds as well as comprehension.

Judy attended to Phia in this comprehensive manner in part because there were no ready answers in the mandated curriculum or standard texts for how to teach Phia and countless other children in her classroom. She was unwilling to relegate children to the familiar categories of success and failure, or to generalize about them on the basis of their ethnic backgrounds. She and her colleagues were determined to teach the individual children in their classrooms by listening, describing what they saw to their colleagues, sharing their insights and knowledge, and imagining new practices.

What I refer to as listening and Carini (2000, 2001) calls the close attentiveness to the particular can also be understood through philosopher Isaiah Berlin's (1996) description of the importance of observation as the salience of experience and knowledge for garnering an understanding of what lies beneath the surface. He writes that qualities including "a sense of timing, [and] sensitiveness to the needs and capacities of human beings" are essential for understanding a social setting. As he elaborates,

> But there is an element of improvisation, of playing by ear, of being able to size up the situation, of knowing when to leap and when to remain still, for which no formulae, no nostrums, no general recipes, no skill in identifying specific situations as instances of general laws can be a substitute. (p. 33)

In this description of observation, Berlin invites us to pay attention to particularities and finely tune our responses or our teaching to this understanding. Although Berlin wrote these instructions to politicians, they are apt for thinking about teaching as a relational practice that is responsive to the unique qualities children bring to the classroom. They provide a way to understand the decisions teachers make on a daily basis about how and what to teach the students in their classrooms. My focus on listening includes this kind of observation or attention and emphasizes the interactions or relationships between the listener and the one who is speaking, acting, or writing.

The discussion of teaching in this chapter focuses on listening to children through their writing and by paying close attention to their gestures and ways of being in the classroom with others. I suggest that teachers pay close attention to *how* the individual child approaches school: what captures his attention, his preferences, and his ways of making meaning. With this understanding, a teacher can shape pedagogy that responds in the moment to students as individuals and as a group. I describe teaching as improvisation based on knowledge of content, pedagogy, and listening in order to come to know children. Through two case studies of teaching, the chapter illustrates how an elementary teacher, Judy Buchanan, fashioned a way to teach based on deep knowledge of her students' academic and social strengths—knowledge gained through interaction, writing, and talk. I illustrate how Judy and her coteachers discovered and created ways to engage resistant children in learning by listening together and reimagining a teaching practice that responds to individuals as members of a classroom community.

RESEARCH CONTEXT

At the time of this research, 1988 through 1989, Judy Buchanan was teaching in a small neighborhood public school a few blocks from her home. Although Judy cotaught with a colleague, Katie Zimring, during my research in her classroom, I focused on Judy's interactions with her students and her pedagogical decisions. I conceptualized my project as collaborative and regularly shared my findings with both teachers and students, asking both groups to join me in the research process (Schultz, 1991, 1994, 1997b). Judy Buchanan's own writing about her practice (Buchanan, 1994), our numerous interviews and discussions, and records from the Philadelphia Teachers' Learning Cooperative (Abu El-Haj & Schultz, 1998; Philadelphia Teachers' Learning Cooperative, 1984) add to the classroom portrait I describe here. Although the preponderance of my discussion is based on observations from the time I spent in Judy and Katie's classroom, the teaching practices described here reflect Judy's long history of teaching in urban public schools and her close work with teacher colleagues in several teacher networks. Her membership in the Philadelphia Teachers' Learning Cooperative (PTLC) and groups such as the Philadelphia Writing Project and the Urban Sites Network of the National Writing Project, as well as close collegial relationships inside her school, supported her to take a listening stance in learning with and from her peers how to teach the particular students in her classroom.

During the 1988–1989 school year, Judy's combined third- and fourth-grade class included two White teachers and 57 students. The racial and ethnic mix of the class reflected its location in a multiracial, urban neighborhood of mostly African American and White families from working-class and professional families. As a desegregation magnet school, the school drew students from adjacent neighborhoods to maintain a racial balance. The School District of Philadelphia initiated several waves of curricular reform during Judy's teaching career, from 1974 until the time of this study. One of the reform efforts during that time period found a small number of teachers in the district hired as "open classroom" teachers. At this school, one class at each grade level was designated as an open classroom and staffed by one of those teachers. Judy was able to transfer into the school, which had an excellent reputation, because of her status as an open classroom teacher.

Consistent with her knowledge and commitment to open classroom teaching, Judy's classroom offered students many choices. At the same time, she closely followed the pacing schedules mandated by the district, which specified when each subject or curriculum area should be introduced and completed. Each day in the classroom began with a class meeting that included a discussion of current events and the reading aloud of a book that was connected to the current social studies or science theme. Judy and Katie, the two teachers, used this whole-group instructional time to prompt discussions about a range of topics, often connected to the thematic study. An extended language arts period usually followed the class meeting. During this time, both teachers met with small reading or literature groups, while other students worked independently on assigned and open-ended projects—mostly related to the current theme—in their assignment folders. Each day one teacher read aloud to the whole class. Throughout the morning there were varied groups of students: Children met in math groups, read and wrote in small teacher-led groups, and occasionally collected peers to initiate their own projects, such as writing a play.

Much of the teaching and learning in this classroom was connected to thematic units or projects that lasted from 1 to 3 months. There were school-wide themes—ancient Greece, China, and Africa—that all teachers taught on a 3-year cycle. In addition, the librarian organized a school-wide project on biographies each January. During the rest of the year, teachers chose their own topics in line with the citywide mandated curriculum. The two teachers believed that given opportunities to explore their own interests in depth, students would become engaged in learning. The curriculum was thus shaped by the teachers' knowledge and experience accumulated over their many years of teaching, students' interests, school-wide social studies themes, and citywide mandated curricular guidelines.

This kind of curriculum demanded that the teachers know their students well in order to formulate appropriate choices for them and guide them through their days. Judy and Katie achieved this knowledge by listening closely to their students: attending to their talk, reading their writing, noting their choices, and paying close attention to their interactions. During the first month of school, Judy and Katie established modes of engagement and interaction with the 57 students so that they had the opportunity to hear each child's voice. They read individually with students, worked with them in small groups, observed their choices, and assigned them projects that gave them chances to bring their lives into the classroom. Drawing on their extensive knowledge of teaching and children, Judy and Katie thus crafted methods that challenged students to become learners who initiated and sustained their engagement in school.

RODERICK: LISTENING TO A STUDENT THROUGH DRAWING

Judy and Katie used students' work to gain insight into how they constructed knowledge, their interests, and their capacities for learning. This section focuses on how they built a curriculum for teaching Roderick, a 10-year-old African American fourth grader from a working-class background, through careful study of his drawing and writing. This attention to a child's work in a sustained and systematic manner is an illustration of listening to the particulars of a student.

During the year I observed him, Roderick was spending his third year in Judy and Katie's combined third- and fourth-grade classroom. He had struggled academically the previous year and was not yet writing more than a sentence at a time. His teachers and his mother worried that he would get lost in middle school because of its large size; teachers would be more likely to focus on his deficits rather than on his considerable strengths and talents. He had finally begun to make progress in all aspects of his learning at the end of his first year in fourth grade, and they hoped that an extra year in this classroom would give him the edge he needed to succeed in middle and high school. Holding him back a year increased the stakes: This was his last chance to gain the requisite knowledge and skills for middle school.

Throughout his time in elementary school, Roderick thought of himself, and was recognized by his teachers and classmates, as an artist. He approached each of his class assignments, including his writing, through drawing. A close look at his work reveals his considerable talent. His peers admired his drawing, enjoyed his inventiveness, and appreciated his offbeat sense of humor. Often a group of students surrounded his desk, looking through his collection of *Mad* magazines, reading and working with him on his own *Rad* magazine, or sharing his prized fluorescent markers. Although he usually relished their attention, occasionally they overwhelmed him and he would tell them to leave him alone.

Despite Roderick's generally agreeable demeanor, he occasionally got into fistfights with other students. Adults sometimes described Roderick as a "defiant" student with an "attitude," in part because of his fierce independence. Roderick insisted that he decide how and when he would accomplish various classroom tasks. For instance, rather than following the suggestions or rituals of his teachers or his peers, Roderick turned his writing folder into a *Rad* magazine—a parody of *Mad* magazine—which was filled with drawings and humor. Nearly everyone else used the writing folder in a more traditional manner, writing short stories and personal reflections. His substitution of drawing for writing placed him outside of the class norm.

Roderick began the year as a reluctant writer. The process by which Judy and Katie helped him to transform his *Rad* magazine writing into appropriate academic writing took a long time and depended on attentive listening and careful nurturing. They had to pay close attention to Roderick's work in order to find ways to entice him to engage with them and the classroom's academic curriculum. Roderick explicitly wrote for a peer audience, assuming that teachers would not be interested in its content and wouldn't "get" the humor of the magazine. His early versions of the *Rad* magazine were composed almost entirely of pictures. Fewer than 2 weeks after the school year began, Roderick had filled all of the pages of his initial writing folder. Each page was covered with an elaborate cartoonlike drawing with scattered words woven into the pictures.

When she saw the folder filled with pictures, keeping her exasperation in check, Judy made a new folder for him and explained sternly that it was time for him to begin to *write*; he had drawn plenty of cartoons. Although Judy and Katie encouraged students to choose their own topics for their writing folders, Roderick was hardly writing at all, and though his teachers wanted him to be able to go his own way at his own pace, they also needed to hold him to standards and expectations based on what he would need in future years. This constant push and pull required close attention and listening to Roderick through his work. For the next several months, nearly every day that the students wrote in their writing folders, the teachers reminded Roderick that he needed to write, not draw. At times, they would listen to him and then demand that he stay in from recess until he had written the requisite one or two sentences. There were occasional standoffs; he would refuse to write and they would refuse to let him *not* write. Sometimes he wrote nearly incomprehensible sentences. Most often, after a brief period, he complied and wrote something they all found acceptable. Thus their listening involved both respecting the student's starting point and nudging the child forward. The timing for each of these moves was critical; it was essential for the teachers to be closely attuned to their students.

As the year progressed, the *Rad* magazines in Roderick's writing folder continued to appear to have little connection with the "school writing" introduced by the teachers in the assignments connected to the thematic projects. Most of the stories in Roderick's folder rambled for pages and were difficult to decipher. Interspersed between stories were a series of lists and drawings, fold-ups, and comic strips. A careful reading of the stories revealed both Roderick's comfort with and reliance on oral language. He wrote stories to be read *to* rather than *by* his peers. Slowly, however, the components of the teachers' curriculum began to appear in Roderick's work.

Incorporating Lists and Structure

One of the teachers' goals for the fourth graders was for them to write a story or report that had a clear beginning, middle, and end. This seemed to be an essential skill for success in later grades (interview, 7/11/89). At the beginning of the year, Roderick struggled with this challenge, and his more formal or assigned school writing often had the same rambling quality that characterized the stories in his writing folders. However, in November, when the teachers introduced outlines and other organizational heuristics for structuring the students' writing, Roderick began to practice these skills in his *Rad* magazines. For instance, after the introduction of outlines, Roderick included an elaborated table of contents at the front of his *Rad* magazines. Roderick interspersed various other lists throughout the magazines, including a list of rap singers and a list of sneakers. His teachers delighted in his clever drawings, which reflected his sophisticated, and sometimes cynical, perspective. Although they urged him to elaborate these whimsical drawings and lists in his writing folder, they encouraged him to write in more conventional formats for the more formal class assignments. Roderick recognized that his teachers respected and appreciated his work, especially when it matched their expectations for a particular assignment. Over the years, Judy and Katie were able to establish a relationship where their instructions to him displayed both firmness and understanding, reflecting their close listening, so that he was willing to hear them and respond to their suggestions and demands.

In his work in the *Rad* magazines, geared to an audience of peers, Roderick learned to create order, to sequence, and to establish categories (Schultz & Buchanan, 1990). In these instances, Judy's listening and teaching were nearly invisible to the outside observer. She taught the class strategies for writing, gave them numerous and varied opportunities to compose texts, and paid close attention to how Roderick was using these strategies. Because Roderick often maintained his distance from teachers, he appeared to learn on his own. Yet, through constant interactions and quiet but firm support, Judy taught him. Erickson (1987) writes about the importance of "legitimacy, trust, and assent" (p. 354) for students to learn from teachers. Judy listened to Roderick, and through that attention established trust and legitimacy over time. Roderick, in turn, finally assented to learn.

In response to an assignment to write an autobiography as part of a unit on biographies, Roderick initiated the idea to generate a list to organize his writing. Composed halfway into the school year, this piece of writing was pivotal for Roderick. Up until this point, Roderick's writing in his *Rad* magazines and for official assignments had mostly been difficult to follow and filled with meandering sentences that appeared disconnected to each other. For this assignment, he brainstormed three themes for his autobiography—art, sports, and games—in order to create a list and write the following story about his own life. (Note: This piece was partially edited by the teachers.)

> When I was small I used crayon's to draw. Now I use marker's. I also couldn't reach the McDonald's order conter. Now I'm taller. when I was littel i didn't like sport's Now I play soccer.
>
> I won a Art contest when i was in 2nd Grade. Teacher Rhoda entered me in it. i Had to draw what i thought was the spirit of Philadelphia. I drew a picture of down town from Penn's Landing to City Hall for Channel 10. I didn't think I woud win.

This composition has a clear structure that follows the outline Roderick constructed. It is more coherent and better organized than any of his previous writing. The list, a strategy introduced by teachers earlier in the year and one Roderick decided to use on his own for this assignment, seemed to help him to stay focused on his topic and write in a sequence.

As Roderick developed these strategies for structuring and sequencing stories, internalizing and interpreting the teachers' directions, his teachers patiently attended to his development and guided him, giving him the time and space he needed to work out his own process for learning to write. They applauded his decision to use a list, maintaining a low profile so that he could retain control and authority. In this instance, listening entailed providing him with opportunities, direction, and encouragement. In addition to recognizing the strengths in his initial work, listening also meant holding high standards and expectations for Roderick that were particular to him. The teachers not only listened to Roderick's constant claim to want to do things his own way; they also listened to understand and follow his rhythm and pace for learning to write.

Composing an Elaborated Story

Toward the end of the year, the class read several Greek myths and hero tales, including the story of Jason and the Golden Fleece, which captured the students' imaginations. Judy and Katie read versions of the stories aloud to the entire group and students read their own versions in reading groups and on their own. The classroom was filled with literature and storytelling. Although Roderick enjoyed hearing the stories, he initially resisted the assignment to write a story of his own. After a considerable amount of prodding and support from his teachers, Roderick announced that he had finished a Greek story at home. The following day he bounded into the room and with tremendous excitement showed the story to his classroom teachers. This hero story provides an example of the kind of conventional writing Judy and Katie knew Roderick would need to master. Roderick was willing and even excited about writing in this format because his teachers allowed him to make choices about how to tell the story.

JASON AND THE GOLDEN CHAIN
BY RODERICK

Jason was going to the mall and he saw people walking down the street with gold chains. He wanted one of his own. He asked someone and they told him to go to the corner of Canal St. So he went into the store and there were stereos, car radios, radios, T.V. everything electronic and more. He asked the owner for a gold chain and the owner said, "I'll be right back." The store owner got away just in time because the stuff there was stolen and Jason didn't know. But the cop thought he did so they arrested Jason for stealing. Jason tried to tell them about the man that told him about the store owner and the cops believed him and they let him go. But the cops wanted a favor. They wanted to find the man. They asked if there was anything they could do for him. "Yes, could you get me a gold chain?" So Jason got some help from the gods. They gave a rock to help him. The rock will light when the men are around so it will be easy to find them. It worked and the cops gave Jason a chain.

This hero tale represents one of the first times that Roderick wrote a story with both adults and peers as his intended audiences. After showing it to his current teachers, bursting with pride, he took the composition to his teacher from second grade. Previously he had composed intricate narratives in pictures. His teachers guided him to attempt a longer, more complex story on a topic they chose—Greek gods and heroes. At the same time, they listened to and heard his need to connect this writing to what he knew and enjoyed—imagining scenarios in an urban landscape like his own. Although initially somewhat resistant to the Greek theme, Roderick was able to find a bridge between his own interests and style of writing and the assignments given to him by his teachers. Through this theme Roderick connected his rambling adventure narratives with the stories he was asked to write as part of a thematic project about ancient Greece.

Roderick's developing abilities as a writer emerged out of numerous sources, including the explicit curriculum developed by the teachers and his own course of study built on his particular interests and talents. Listening closely to who Roderick was and what he needed to develop into a confident and successful writer, Judy allowed him to move into writing through drawing, with a minimal amount of teacher interference. This was true even when his writing looked unconventional and was hard to locate among the drawings. The adaptability or permeability in the curriculum and the flexible time frame allowed by his teachers enabled Roderick to learn numerous skills, which supported his growth as a proficient writer. Without opportunities for children to write in their own styles about topics they cared about, Judy would not have been able to gain knowledge about this student that was critical for moving him toward grade-level expectations.

After he mastered writing for his first audience of peers, Roderick was ready to write for his teachers. He was able to move from imagining stories through pictures to thinking them through in words. Although his teachers supported him to use his talents as an artist to learn how to write, they continued to hold high expectations for his achievement in their classroom. This was translated into the moment-to-moment decisions Judy made each day and the larger picture she held of who Roderick was and what he needed to succeed in the school system. Her close listening allowed her to see that Roderick was making progress even when his talent in writing was hidden and difficult to discern. Working with and listening to colleagues over time supported Judy's decision to take a long view of Roderick's growth as a writer. Her attention to detail allowed her to teach to his strengths and hold high expectations for him based on deep knowledge of his capacities.

KENYA: LISTENING TO A STUDENT THROUGH WRITING

Judy also used close listening to establish a working relationship with Kenya, an African American girl in this same class. Whereas Roderick wrote primarily for himself and his peers, much of Kenya's writing was to and for her teachers. This case illustrates how Judy used writing to listen to students across academic and social dimensions.

Over the years Judy had developed the practice of asking students to write "behavior letters" when they acted in ways that did not fit her expectations. The students also wrote letters to defend or justify their positions when there was an argument with peers that could dissolve into a fight. These letters were then used to mediate the disagreements. This practice allowed the students, and not incidentally the teachers, time to reflect on what had happened and to offer an explanation outside of the heat of the moment. It also gave the teachers the opportunity to respond when they were not as enmeshed in the incident. The letters lengthened the time of the interaction and they allowed the teachers to come to know their students better. Although the students resisted other assignments, in general they readily took the opportunity to explain and defend their positions. Teachers were able to listen to their students in this large classroom through relationships developed in this exchange of writing. At the same time, students who might have resisted academic writing grew proficient arguing their cases in letters. Letter writing thus provided a critical opportunity for literacy learning with authentic audiences and purposes for writing. Students wrote because they felt an urgency to deliver a message. For many students, this practice provided them with the knowledge and strategies they needed to become skillful writers.

Kenya's oppositional behavior gave her numerous opportunities to practice writing letters to her peers and teachers. Nearly every day the teachers asked her to write at least one letter explaining her behavior. These letters allowed Judy and Katie to begin a dialogue with Kenya. By listening carefully to her immediate concerns as expressed in the letters, and discerning who she was and what she valued, they learned how to interact with this student around academic learning. Kenya gravitated toward letter writing. She extended her growing proficiency in this genre to classroom assignments and chose to write letters in response to literature and to correspond with a pen pal in the suburbs. Rather than viewing Kenya as "deficient" or even as "resistant" to school, the teachers listened carefully to who Kenya was through these letters so they could come to know her strengths, interests, capacities, and approaches to learning. Over time, they built a trusting relationship that fundamentally shifted Kenya's willingness to learn from and with them (Erickson, 1987).

Writing About Conflict

One morning there was a misunderstanding between Judy and Kenya because Kenya had left the room to get a drink of water without permission. After Judy reprimanded her, Kenya became extremely angry and spoke harshly to her teacher. Ending the verbal dialogue before it escalated further, Judy told Kenya to write about the incident. The following dialogue took place over the course of the morning between academic lessons. Notes were passed between Judy and Kenya.

> Dear Teacher Judy
> I wanted some water but I Thout that you wer going to line us up in line. The End.

> Dear Kenya,
> I'm sorry we didn't understand each other. You were extremely rude to me and you may not speak to me that way.

> Dear Teacher Judy
> That's all you had to say ok The [reason] I got mad is [because] I did get no water. Kenya

> Dear Kenya,
> The point is that you cannot be rude even when you are angry. Are you ready to apologize?
>
> Teacher Judy

> Dear Teacher Judy
> I am ready to apologize to you Teacher Judy, Kenya

Sensing that Kenya's emotions were out of control and too heightened for a verbal exchange, Judy convinced her to work toward a resolution of their conflict on paper through letters. The letter format allowed Kenya to negotiate with her teacher by reasserting her position and thus save face. At the same time, she was able to apologize for her inappropriate behavior, an action that might not have been possible face-to-face. Through numerous exchanges like this, Kenya and her classmates also learned more about formulating arguments, gathering evidence to support their assertions, posing questions, and articulating critique. For her part, Judy was able to apologize and assert the rules and behavioral expectations of the class without involving the whole group. It is important to remember that Judy wrote these responses in the midst of managing a classroom of 57 students. Yet, although sometimes brief and without a signature, the letters Judy wrote nearly always reflected careful thought. Grounded in a prior relationship, this written exchange contributed to a growing understanding and respect between them and allowed Judy to learn to listen to and teach Kenya.

Although the teachers had originally introduced the genre of writing behavior letters, students such as Kenya adapted this genre to initiate their own communication. The ability to write letters on her own, to an audience that she chose, enabled Kenya to begin to take charge of her own learning in both academic and social domains. She wrote letters to her teachers to ask for their help, and she wrote to her mother to describe the first chapter book that she completed, a biography of Martin Luther King.

Writing to Ask for Help

Over time, Kenya used letter writing to ask Judy for help in becoming a successful student. In her first letter, she explained to Judy that she didn't want to go to one of the specialist's classes because she hadn't done her homework and was afraid of receiving a zero (letter, 10/21/88). Judy acknowledged Kenya's concern and gave her an alternative solution. Perhaps emboldened by this positive response, the following day, when asked to write about why she was so upset, Kenya wrote a letter, which resulted in the following exchange with her teacher.

> Dear Teacher Judy can you help me understand what you mean by being good. I can't do it I tried to do it and it did [not] work. I try to be good but I can't. I get no bad marks on my report card but I think I am [bad]. Because I am a bad little girl to be in the four grade. You say I am doing much better and I don't think so. Because the same way I am now I was [from] four[th] grade up. I like the class but I just can't do it. Teacher Alison [my teacher from last year] says I am much better but I don't think so.
>
> By KENYA 11–22–88

Dear Kenya,
Could you tell me what you think being bad means.

[Dear Judy]
It means you can't believe in yourself in school you get sent to [the principal] like me.

Dear Kenya
You've had a lot of good things said to you this year. I think you've seen [the principal] twice. Once for the [Baring] peso [a reward initiated and given out by the principal for exemplary behavior] and once to talk about a problem.

   One thing about trying to be good that might help you is this: You have to try and understand things before you hit or lose your temper. I thought you handled getting paint on your shirt very well. You changed your shirt and went back to painting. Some things will always upset you or make you angry, but you have to try not to let them keep you from doing what you want to do. Let's keep writing about this.

Judy's response to the student was grounded in specifics that were a result of careful listening and noticing. She not only listened to Kenya's words, she also paid attention to her relationships with peers and adults. By prodding Kenya to articulate and elaborate her feelings, Judy also helped her to develop reasoning and writing skills critical to her academic success. Judy listened for patterns of interaction in Kenya's work across content areas and genres of writing and reflected them back to Kenya in her letters.

   At the same time that Judy occasionally got angry with Kenya, she realized that Kenya was "struggling with something that [she] could help her with" (interview 7/11/89). The letters gave her assurance that they were working together. She felt strongly that she needed to do more than help Kenya learn to be a "good" student; her goal was to teach her academic and social skills that would be critical to her success as she continued on to middle school the next year. As Judy explained her strategy for helping Kenya with her anger:

   I think my overall feeling was that if she couldn't find a way to handle
   her anger with us in the fourth grade, she really was going to have a
   hard time making it through school because people just weren't going
   to put up with outbursts. My idea for helping her handle her anger was
   sort of this long slow process of writing and talking and figuring out and
   trying to make sense and that always directly meeting her with confron-
   tation wouldn't necessarily help.

                                                                      (interview, 7/11/89)

While she taught the mandated curriculum and managed a classroom of 57 students, Judy allowed time to listen and for her relationship to develop with Kenya and each of the students in the classroom. She saw this listening as integral to academic learning. A recurring theme for Judy was how to help students "make it through school" (Buchanan, 1994). By providing Kenya with opportunities to learn through an exchange of letters, Judy fashioned a curriculum for Kenya that united the social and academic dimensions of learning and built on her considerable interests and strengths. According to Hicks (2002), "What is required for critical literacy teaching is not just the right kinds of discourses but the right kinds of relationships" (pp. 151–152). Hicks explains that forming relationships such as these requires patience, reflection, and learning to see—and I would add hear—those who are different from us. Letter writing gave Judy this opportunity to listen to form a relationship with and come to know Kenya.

At the end of the year Judy reflected, "Kenya was really struggling with something in herself and with others and she didn't always keep it together but she really acknowledged the struggle" (interview, 7/11/89). Judy had joined in this struggle in a particular way by providing Kenya with the opportunities to reveal and articulate her concerns. She took the time to hear beyond Kenya's actions to understand what she was saying. She understood Kenya to be an individual with both a rich culture and history as a student and a particular disposition and stance in this classroom. She listened to make deep connections with Kenya and invite her into learning. She listened beyond the surface to understand her as a talented and questioning student. And through the processes of listening and communicating through letters, Kenya gained confidence in her writing and reading. She came to view these literacy practices as critical to her ability to communicate and assert herself in the classroom. In doing so, she gained proficiency and confidence in writing. As Kenya composed letters to make herself heard, she became a writer.

LISTENING TO PARTICULARITIES IN CONTEXT

Judy faced countless dilemmas as she made decisions about how to teach Roderick and Kenya. Many of these decisions were carefully orchestrated and planned ahead of time in the projects, assignments, and experiences she offered Roderick, Kenya, and their classmates. Others were made in the moment when she confronted pages that Roderick filled with drawings or incomprehensible strings of words, or Kenya's refusal to read a chapter book. Rather than completely following the child's lead or, conversely, holding Roderick and Kenya to external standards alone, she relied on her professional judgment, stayed in contact with their parents, consulted colleagues, and, most important, listened to them as learners. She listened to how much time they each needed, carefully calibrating that time to her goals for the class and for them as individuals.

Initially, Roderick made sense of the world through drawing; later his understandings were revealed in his words. Judy was able to listen to and guide this student through distinct and particularized knowledge of him in relation to others. A resistant and sometimes difficult student, Kenya could easily have been written off by Judy. If Kenya had been taught in a prescriptive manner, it is possible that she would have tuned out and disengaged from learning. In contrast, Judy formed a relationship with her based on trust and knowledge formed through interaction and writing. This was not accomplished in isolation or through a single set of actions. Rather, Judy, Katie, and the students in the classroom were part of a large and complex system that shaped their actions, as they worked together to create the culture of their class. For instance, Judy's stance as a listener was supported by Kenya's willingness to communicate in several different modalities—through writing and gesture, and by initiating and responding to interaction.

It is not always easy to know how to listen to or hear students. Each of the interactions with students documented in this chapter involved crossing racial and cultural boundaries for Judy as a White teacher working with students of color. She could not presume to know how to teach her students without taking an inquiry stance and carefully listening to them. And, even as she listened and learned from each student, she knew that there was more for her to learn. In each case, Judy listened to the student through writing, using a set of descriptive practices that enabled her to read closely, looking for nuance and the person in the writing (Carini, 2001; Himley, 2000, 2002). In schools and school districts, teachers can sometimes turn to their colleagues, particularly those who might have insider knowledge of the dominant culture of the school, in order to learn to listen to their students. As a team, the two teachers in this classroom had each other to consult—as well as colleagues at their school and in the professional networks to which they belonged—as they made sense of what they heard from students. They also had many years of experience to sift through as they thought about choices and possibilities. They had each formed numerous relationships with parents and members of the community surrounding the school. Too often, teachers' personal and professional networks include only people whose backgrounds are similar to their own. This suggests the difficulty and importance of stepping outside of familiar contexts to learn and grapple with unfamiliar perspectives. It is both difficult and necessary to learn to listen outside and beyond what is familiar.

Judy was able to set up a classroom and establish relationships with children that allowed her to help them. She was supported in her decisions and work with children by close collegial relationships at her school and across the district. Although they are wonderful teachers in many ways, Judy and her colleagues are not unique. What is exceptional is to include the stories of their teaching and the students they taught as part of the story of urban schooling. By providing detailed descriptions of teaching that many teachers will recognize, my aim is to lend the same kind of support to teachers who attempt to go beyond scripted pedagogy and mandated curriculum to fashion a way of teaching that puts children's capacities at the center of teaching. This vision of teaching, which recognizes that the humanness of every child is closely tied to notions of democracy, values each person's contribution.

Listening to know particular students suggests noticing the humanness of every child and recognizing what Carini (2001) refers to as children's "widely distributed capacity" (p. 1) to be creators, builders, and actors in their education and their lives. This noticing, honoring, and teaching embodies the democratizing potential of public education. As Carini explains, "Human complexity, the complexities of learning, the complexities of teaching resist systemization" (p. 9). It is only by holding onto the complexity, by listening closely and deeply, that teachers can craft ways to teach students such as Phia, Roderick, and Kenya, whether they are inventing curriculum, following a packaged program, or abiding by district mandates. Taking a listening stance implies that teachers place students' humanity alongside their own at the center of the classroom and curriculum.

When teachers listen for the specificity of who students are, they recognize the multiple and often tightly intertwined identities and cultures students draw from as they enter classrooms. This notion of teaching extends the ideas developed and articulated by educators such as Gloria Ladson-Billings (1994) and Sonia Nieto (1994, 1999) who offer methods for teaching particular groups or categories of students (cf. Banks, 1984, 1994; Delpit, 1995; Gay, 2000; Sleeter 1991; Valdés, 1996). These descriptions of culturally relevant pedagogy are critical for teaching to become more inclusive. A focus on listening within these categories as a way to understand the variation each child represents supports pedagogy and curriculum based on what each individual child brings to the classroom as a member of multiple and diverse communities. Listening to know particular students draws our attention to the relationships that shape students' positions in classrooms.

Culturally responsive pedagogy is too frequently translated by teachers and diversity trainers who deliver professional development to teachers as activities or methods for teaching single groups of students. Although it is critical to know about the multiple cultures students bring to the classroom, it is also important to understand individual children within these categories and in relationship to each other, their teachers, and texts. This does not mean that teachers should or can develop individual plans for each child in the class. Knowing children well means learning about their heritage and communities, their particular stories and entry points into learning, and their relationships to others. This entails folding their knowledge into plans for teaching the class as a whole. As I describe in Chapter 3, at the same time that a listening stance suggests that teachers focus on the particularity of the individual child, it also provides a way for teachers to listen to the whole class and each child's position within the larger group. Knowledge of a single child can be the basis for understanding and teaching a class. Further, by listening to one child closely, teachers gain a habit of mind (Dewey, 1902/1956; Meier, 1996) and information useful for teaching other, even all, children in their classroom.

In their book, *Successful Failure*, Varenne and McDermott (1999) warn of the dangers of focusing attention on individual students to explain what transpires in school. They argue that a focus on the success or failure of an individual turns our attention away from the ways in which social institutions such as schools are structured to create students as successes or failures. Too often the focus on an individual leads to attempts to "fix" that individual, as if the "problem" is located in the person rather than in the institution or culture that produced the child as a particular kind of person or student. Similarly, students' identities—as raced, classed, or gendered, for instance—are often treated as if they were internal rather than socially produced.

Listening for the particularities of students in a classroom highlights the importance of going beyond unitary categories such as race, class, gender, sexuality, ability, and (dis)ability. Listening to particular qualities of a student accounts for the larger context that privileges or disenfranchises because of these social identities. When Judy listened to the Hmong student, Phia, she listened beyond his membership in a group of new immigrants to the United States, to hear who he was as a learner in her classroom and a member of that community. She listened for his strengths and the particular ways he could be invited into learning to read and entering into academic learning as an individual. Likewise, as she fashioned a way to draw him into the classroom, she was aware of the sociopolitical context that surrounded his entry into her school and the settlement of his family in the neighborhood. Racial tensions were great as this new group moved into the school community. Judy saw her job of teaching Phia to read as intricately tied to both the macro- and microcontexts of his learning.

Educational reform in the United States can be characterized by its mercurial changes. In recent years, policymakers and educators have implemented several series of reforms, rarely giving any one idea or program time to develop and flourish. Too often, discussions of these reforms are framed by polarities: whole language versus phonics; a focus on the child's interests versus mandated, standardized, or subject-centered curriculum. At the turn of the century, Dewey (1902/1959) argued against this oppositional way of thinking, suggesting instead that both the child and the content of the curriculum should define instruction. In her classroom, Judy worked toward the balance of the child and the curriculum Dewey (1902/1956) described in his book by that title. A listening stance enabled her to teach in this manner.

The time to listen to who individual children are in order to know how best to teach them has become a scarce commodity in public schools across the United States. Listening occurs in fleeting moments as teachers struggle to keep pace with a growing number of demands. Children are often not known well by their teachers; most teachers simply do not have the time to gain intimate knowledge of all the children in their classrooms. By necessity, they turn their attention to mandated curriculum programs and preparation for high-stakes testing.

In several school districts across the country, teachers are handed texts and teaching materials that not only mandate what they teach but also prescribe *how* they teach the material. Outsiders—people far removed from the lives of the particular children engaged in learning—determine the topics and also the words with which to teach. Teaching manuals prescribe specific language and predetermine the answers teachers should expect from all students. Teachers are encouraged to simplify their teaching to limit the possible answers their questions might elicit. They are prompted to cover material quickly. Strict accountability measures calibrate their success. Often promoted in the name of equality, curriculum delivered in this manner is purported to provide the same education for all students. Under this regime there is no rationale for close attention; teaching and learning are based on standardized assessment, rather than on the strengths and interests of individual children.

In contrast to this notion of a prescribed curriculum, many teachers hold on to the goal of beginning with the particularities of the children in their classrooms. Even as schools require students to wear uniforms, wiping out the status differences that often accompany choice in clothing and accessories, many teachers look past the uniformity for the uniqueness of each child in their classrooms. The events in the classroom described in this chapter occurred at a time when teachers were given pacing schedules that required them to cover material during specified time periods. Principals checked lesson plans. Citywide tests assessed teachers' complicity as well as student learning. Even under these circumstances, which are similar to the climate many teachers face today, Judy and her colleagues found ways to teach to the strengths and particular interests of the students in their classrooms. Judy was able to do this by coming to know each student through listening and paying attention to his or her work.

Teachers like Judy set up their classrooms so that listening is at the center of the activity. They provision their classrooms with a wide variety of materials and offer students opportunities to make choices about how they learn and represent that knowledge. Holding students to high standards, they are able to build relationships with children that allow them to listen for and begin to understand the particularized ways students approach learning. Through teaching in this manner, teachers are able to hold large and critical visions of democracy, education, and change, while always beginning with the child.

3

Listening to Classrooms: Rhythm and Balance

My hope is to remind people of what it means to be alive among others, to achieve freedom in dialogue with others for the sake of personal fulfillment and the emergence of a democracy dedicated to life and decency.

(Greene, 1988, p. xii)

IT WAS PROJECT TIME. Thirty-two second graders fanned out across the classroom, talking and bumping into one another as they claimed tables and began working on their chosen activities. Several children needed reminders to begin their projects without delay. Along with the opportunity to move around came conversations held in check all morning. Toys from home were pulled out of pockets, shown or exchanged, and hastily put away before they were spotted by an adult.

Their teacher, Lynne Strieb, was familiar with this scene and walked purposefully around the room monitoring the children's actions and inviting them to begin their projects. She directed, cajoled, encouraged, explained, and scolded. Lynne balanced her time between working closely with a few children—showing them how to begin a weaving project or record their work—and surveying the whole group. She made careful choices about whether and how to enter a conversation, synchronizing her responses with the rhythm of students' words. At times she simply reacted, "George, get to work. What *are* you doing?" Despite the wide array of activities—students were learning about patterns by weaving, using Dienes blocks to explore place value, building marble track mazes to experiment with motion, observing and writing about the classroom snake, and reading in pairs—there was an order and purposefulness in the room.[1]

Walking into a classroom such as Lynne's second-grade classroom, one becomes aware of the complexity of teaching a large group of children. Teaching is most often described as a dialogue or a series of interactions between a student and teacher (Erickson, 1996). Alternatively, teaching is characterized as the interaction between a teacher and a classroom group speaking in uni-son. Teaching individuals—either singly or in the aggregate—requires the kind of listening to particularities that I explore in Chapter 2 and is a central aspect of teaching and learning. The dynamic nature of many classroom inter-actions—which often involve several students speaking with each other and with their teacher, contributing contrasting viewpoints, contradicting each other, or building on one another's ideas—requires a different set of skills and knowledge.

Theories of learning as socially situated (e.g., Vygotsky, 1962, 1978) and language as "populated—over populated with the intentions of others" (Bakh-tin, 1981, p. 294) suggest the importance of including opportunities for inter-action between and among teachers and students to foster learning in school. In a community of learners (e.g., Wenger, 1999), students learn by listening to each other as well as by listening to their teacher. This kind of teaching and learning requires a teacher to listen to the classroom as a group, to pay attention to how individuals are interacting with and within the group, and to teach students to listen to each other. I call this constellation of activities listening to the rhythm and balance of a classroom. As Lynne responded to the students in her classroom during project time, she listened for the rhythm or the underlying structure, timing, and pattern of the interactions among students and between the students and herself. Lynne noticed the patterns of interaction among the students and timed her entrance into their conversa-tions so that she added new knowledge or prodded their thinking, rather than supplying answers or solutions for them before they had searched for answers on their own. In surveying the whole classroom to note whether and how each child was engaged in working, she listened for balance. She listened for whether the class seemed composed, noting when one child or group of chil-dren was overshadowing the others in either volume or activity. Lynne lis-tened for the rhythm and balance of the class not only during project time but throughout the day. It was a major component of her teaching practice. As a veteran teacher of 31 years, she continued to reinvent how to teach each day, carefully listening to her students.

Lynne's classroom represents a counterpoint to direct instruction, a form of pedagogy gaining in popularity, especially in urban contexts. Increasingly, programs recommended by the federal government, and mandated by local school districts, are based on this pedagogy, which is predicated on the notion that there is a body of knowledge that can be most effectively and efficiently delivered to children through whole-group instruction dominated by teacher talk (e.g., Engelmann & Carnine, 1991). Often programs following direct in-struction methods rely upon scripts that prescribe the exact language teachers use to teach. Student responses are scripted as well. All the teacher listens for, then, is correct answers. Local contexts or the needs and interests of individual students have no bearing on what happens in the classroom. In a classroom where teachers use direct instruction methods, teaching is neat, answers are predictable, and there is little room for invention or improvisation.

In contrast, classrooms like Lynne's have several different participation structures or modes in which students engage with each other and their teacher in learning (Philips, 1992). These various structures reflected Lynne's thoughtful pedagogical decisions about how to teach each subject. For instance, in Lynne's classroom, at times children read individually, either with Lynne or in partnership with a peer, whereas at other times, Lynne worked with small groups of children or read to the whole class. Math followed a similar pattern of individual, small-group, and whole-class work. Often there were whole-class discussions as well as periods of time for children to make individual choices and work at their own paces. As a result, children had many opportunities to learn and practice their new skills and knowledge in a range of settings. Not only did learning transpire between the teacher and her students and between the students and a text, but also among the students themselves as they worked with each other.

In this chapter, I suggest that when classrooms are filled with dialogue and choice, rather than scripted questions and responses, students become more deeply engaged in learning, constructing understanding by building on the knowledge they bring to classrooms, and pursuing knowledge and skills that have meaning to them. In addition to the skills and knowledge they acquire, they learn to participate in a group, that is, to become engaged members of a deliberative democracy. In such classrooms, as in Lynne's, teachers listen as they invite students to contribute their ideas and take an active role in their learning (e.g., Dewey, 1902/1956). To describe how teachers listen to the group as a whole in such classrooms, I use the notion of rhythm to capture listening for the underlying structures and patterns of classroom interaction and balance to indicate listening to the class as an aggregate.

There are many ways for new and experienced teachers to create opportunities for students to talk and learn from each other and their teacher. Teachers hold morning meetings, often called "sharing time" (Cazden, 2001), where students are invited to tell stories from their homes or communities or discuss a topic chosen by either the teacher or the students themselves. These meetings are often used to build community and to bring all voices into the classroom. Teachers also use project or choice time to provide children with opportunities to work in small groups on self-selected activities and to create ways to listen and respond to students' interests through long-term projects. In addition to these routines, Lynne often uses discussions, a form of group conversation with an explicit structure that requires each child in the class to participate. The format of a discussion also provides openings for students to learn to listen to each other and initiate their own learning. In this chapter, I use two of these discussions to illustrate how a teacher listens to the whole group in order to teach academic and social skills critical for their education and for participation in democratic communities. But before describing Lynne's classroom further, I turn to my own experiences as a first-year teacher to highlight the contrast between listening to individuals and listening to the class as a group.

LEARNING TO LISTEN FOR RHYTHM AND BALANCE

I learned a difficult lesson about the fragile and temporary nature of community in my first year of teaching. I had 24 students in my classroom located in an urban, independent school: 10 fourth graders and 14 fifth graders. For the most part, the year began smoothly. I was young and energetic. There was an abundance of resources and I had an endless supply of ideas. The study of ancient Greece united my literacy and social studies teaching for the entire year. As the class became immersed in myths and legends, we read versions of *The Iliad* and *The Odyssey* aloud. For the most part I had strong relationships with even the most difficult students.

When a new student entered our class midway through the year, everything changed. In a matter of days, the tone of the group shifted. This new student was angry and took too much of my attention. I worked hard to win her over and in the process lost my easy relationship with the rest of the class. The most vocal student in the class, a fifth-grade girl who had adored me prior to this time, was particularly furious at losing my attention. She retaliated by acting out and instigating her classmates to rebel. Slowly, I lost my grip on the class. One day I found curses carved into a desk. Another day, students refused to participate in the project I had carefully designed. A few students were loud and disrespectful; they set the tone for the rest of the group. At my wit's end, I called parents and turned to my colleagues for help. Publicly I attributed this behavior to the fact that the fifth graders were on the verge of adolescence; privately I knew there was more to the story. By the late spring I had almost salvaged the year. I engaged the students in a series of culminating activities, and in their excitement about what they were learning, they nearly forgot their fury. Once more, we began to work together, and some of the joy and intimacy returned to our class. Still, something was lost that we never completely regained. I resolved to start the next year differently.

As I look back on my first year of teaching, I realize that one of the many aspects of teaching I did not understand was how to listen to the class as a whole. I had used my youth and sincere interest in the students' lives to form individual relationships with them. I had relied on winning individual students over to involve them in learning. Concentrating my attention on teaching them as individuals, I forgot—or did not know how—to focus on listening to them as a group. While my focus on individual relationships seemed to work when everything was going well, I did not anticipate the power of a single child to disrupt the group. When this happened, my response was to focus on her as an individual rather than to work with the group to draw her into our community. Although listening to individuals is a critical component of education, I needed to learn to listen and to teach the class as a whole so that together we could move past the difficult moments.

I now realize that what I lacked was an understanding of the rhythm and balance of the classroom. Listening for rhythm signals attending to the flow of interactions. There is rhythm in poetry, rhythm in speech, and rhythm in a classroom. Rather than listening for the rhythm of my classroom in order to discern where communication had broken down, I looked beyond the class conversations that were fraught with tension and focused instead on repairing individual relationships. I knew that the class was out of balance, that something was deeply wrong, but I did not know how to listen for how the social fabric of the classroom was pieced together. I did not understand how to pay attention to both individual relationships and the group as a whole at the same time. Most important, I was afraid, or did not know how, to ask the class to listen *with* me.

In subsequent years of teaching, I learned how to step back from a class and think about the dynamics of the class as a group without focusing exclusively on individual relationships. I developed ways to understand and foster the collective learning of the class, in addition to paying attention to the particularities of individuals and my own teaching. I often involved students, especially older students, in discussions about the classroom climate. I established rituals and routines that helped me to listen to the underlying rhythm from which I could rectify the inevitable moments of imbalance in the classroom. These experiences, which are ongoing, have given me the vocabulary to describe how teachers can learn to listen to a class as a whole.

Classrooms as Democratic Communities

Like many others, I believe that a fundamental purpose of education is to prepare students to participate in a democratic community in which individual voices are joined to form a whole whose strength lies in its honoring of diversity (cf. Darling-Hammond, 1998; Darling-Hammond, French, & Garcia-Lopez, 2002; Greene, 1988, 1995; Meier, 2002). Greene (1995) uses the phrase "the common world" to denote democratic community, an always changing state where we discover and affirm commonalities without ignoring differences. She reminds us of the greater purposes for listening for the rhythm and balance in the classroom when she writes:

As teachers, we cannot predict the common world that may be in the making; nor can we finally justify one kind of community more than another. We can bring warmth into places where young persons come together, however; we can bring in the dialogues and laughter that threaten monologues and rigidity. And surely we can affirm and reaffirm the principles that center around belief in justice and freedom and respect for human rights, since without these, we cannot even call for the decency of welcoming and inclusion for everyone, no matter how at risk. (p. 43)

Greene calls on teachers to nurture imagination and a multiplicity of voices though dialogue. I argue that this dialogue involves listening to individuals within the context of a classroom community.

Embedded in a description of creating a democratic community are dimensions of time and space. Classroom communities exist in a physical space and form over time. Here, as throughout the book, I use the term *listening* both literally (teachers pay attention to students' voices and how they are distributed across time and space) and metaphorically (teachers attend to children's verbal and nonverbal interactions; they read their facial gestures and the ways children move through space alone and together). Listening to the rhythm and balance of a classroom takes into account the temporal and spatial dimensions of the formation of community.

Teachers listen for the rhythm of a group's conversation by paying attention to the temporal aspects of talk; they listen for the steady beat and the pace of the interaction. Erickson (1995, 1996) writes about the rhythm of teacher–student interactions, pointing out how students' knowledge of the timing of conversation enables them to either join it or precludes their participation. He describes how students capture the floor or remain silent according to their knowledge or ability to discern the beat of the conversation. If students miss the beat, or the time to jump in and take their turn, they will be shut out of classroom talk. The spaces between words and ideas give students opportunities to enter into and build on conversation. When students lack this knowledge of the rhythm of a conversation, they often do not know when and how to participate in the interaction. Similarly, teachers listen for rhythm by listening for the timing of how and when they and students participate in a conversation and how their participation either impedes or pushes forward the flow of talk.

The spatial dimensions of teachers' listening are captured by the concept of balance. Teachers listen for balance by listening across the geographical space of a classroom. When teachers listen for balance, they pay attention to how interaction is distributed across a classroom group. Teachers listen for balance when they notice who is speaking and how turns are distributed across the individuals in the classroom. In addition, they listen for a balance of ideas, emotions, and engagement. By listening in this manner, teachers create contexts for students to learn from their teachers and from each other. In addition, they teach them essential skills for participating in a democratic community.

Defining Rhythm and Balance

The rhythm of a classroom is the underlying pattern of talk and activity. Teachers listen for rhythm by paying attention to the regularities or patterns of activities with and among students. For instance, teachers pay attention to their turn-taking patterns with students, noting whether or not their talk dominates the interaction. They notice the rhythm of student interactions, attending to the patterns of participation and silence. They attend to the pace of the conversation, taking into account whether silence indicates that students are wrestling with ideas or bored. Lynne listened for the rhythm of her classroom during project time by paying attention to how and whether students were engaged in their various activities. Her work as a teacher involved monitoring or listening to the activity in order to fashion her responses.

Scientists use the term *ecosystem* to indicate how organisms are balanced in relation to each other. When an ecosystem is held in balance, there are sufficient resources (e.g., sunlight, food, air) for each species to survive; plants and animals approach a harmonious relationship. Likewise, when artists speak of balance in the composition of paintings, they refer to a harmonious relationship between the parts. There may be a balance of color or hue or there may be a balance of shape or form. Playwrights and directors seek balance in the characters of a play, making sure that a single character doesn't dominate a scene in a way that detracts from the whole. In classrooms, teachers listen for balance across multiple modalities. They listen for a balance in sound, so that no one voice or set of voices is overpowering, or for a balance in tone or the intensity of activity and interaction. In short, they listen for how talk and activity are distributed across individuals and the physical space of a classroom, noting levels of engagement. Like most teachers, Lynne listened for balance by noticing the times the class seemed to be moving forward together, with students working independently, with their peers, or with their teacher. Though such moments could be fleeting, Lynne's constant listening allowed her to work to retrieve balance once the order was broken. At the same time, she knew that such disruptions could lead to growth (Schultz, Buck, & Niesz, 2000).

Listening to rhythm and balance to gain a sense of the whole group is akin to what Sullivan (2000) calls aesthetic vision.

> Aesthetic vision engages a sensitivity to suggestion, to pattern, to that which is beneath the surface as well as to the surface itself. It requires a fine attention to

detail and form: the perception of relations (tensions and harmonies); the perceptions of nuance (colors of meaning); and the perceptions of change (shifts and subtle motions.) It dares to address the ineffable.

Teachers who function with aesthetic vision perceive the dynamic nature of what is unfolding in front of them at any given moment. (p. 221)

Sullivan suggests a set of criteria that is useful for understanding what is meant by listening to rhythm and balance in the classroom: paying attention to particular moments or detail in classroom interactions; listening for the interrelationships between and among the talk and activity of students and teachers; and noticing variation in attention to the central activity generally initiated by the teacher.

Whereas Sullivan characterizes this pedagogy as "aesthetic vision," my conception of listening includes both the visual modes (reading students) and the aural modes (listening and talking) that accompany a survey of classroom dynamics. This conception includes what a teacher does, as well as what she perceives. Paying attention to individual voices, teachers notice the harmonies and tensions—the ways students build on and contradict each other's and their teachers' ideas. Teachers listen for nuances or meanings below the surface—what is said in word and gesture as well as what is left unarticulated. This notion of teaching suggests that teachers and students also listen for shifts or changes in the conversation and action to notice when to bring an activity to a close or when to let it continue. By introducing rituals—patterned and predictable interactions or routines—into the classroom, teachers provide opportunities for all children to speak and contribute to their learning community. Like aesthetic vision, the conception of listening for rhythm and balance is critical for choreographing learning in a group of students, but at the same time it is ineffable and can be difficult to grasp. Teachers who learn to teach in this manner are constantly engaged in a dance—a give and take—in which they lead at the same time that they respond to the students they teach.

RESEARCH CONTEXT

Every year, Lynne taught her students to participate in what she called class discussions, a form of group conversation that she used both for routine teaching and to address classroom issues. The specialized structure of discussions provided space for each child to speak, as well as room for improvisation. Lynne also used discussions to teach students to listen closely to each other. The two incidents I focus on here both occurred during class discussions: In the first, Lynne was teaching about pattern and attributes through a discussion of fall leaves; in the second, Lynne used a discussion to address a racial incident that had the potential to disrupt the smooth functioning of the classroom community. A close examination of the structures of these two discussions makes apparent the ways in which Lynne listened to the rhythm and balance of the classroom, as well as the ways she created contexts for students to listen to each other. My analysis of Lynne's use of discussions thus illustrates how classroom conversation can teach students critical knowledge and skills at the same time it prepares them to participate in a democracy.

The year I observed in Lynne Strieb's second-grade classroom, 1999–2000, was her last year of teaching before she retired. This gave her—and the class—a heightened sense of the significance of each moment. Lynne would often notice and mention final events in her teaching career. For instance, she constructed a gingerbread house with her class for the last time, and this was her final time teaching students about the life cycle of silk worms by bringing many caterpillars into the classroom. The students adopted her attitude and would often point out examples of final moments on their own. There was a large collection of class books that Lynne had accumulated since 1970. Each year her class wrote a few books, which contained pages contributed by each child in the class on diverse topics such as dreams, students' names, holiday celebrations, and experiences held in common. The books were bound and placed alongside the other books in the class library. The students in every class enjoyed reading and rereading the books from previous years. This particular class seemed to have a strong sense of their responsibility to add to this library as the last contributors to this body of work. They had a sense of participating in a classroom ritual that extended beyond their 2 years in this classroom.

Lynne and I agreed that I should focus my observation on two activities: class discussions that occurred once or twice a week and the daily project time (what many teachers call "choice") described at the beginning of this chapter. In addition, I was often present for the reading and writing periods. Although I acted primarily as an observer and spent much of my time taking detailed field notes, students frequently came to me for assistance and to show or read me their work. These interactions gave me new perspectives to understand the classroom dynamics. My work with Lynne, a founding member of the Philadelphia Teachers' Learning Cooperative (PTLC), was part of an ongoing longitudinal project in which I joined the group to investigate how the PTLC descriptive practices shape classroom practices (Abu El-Haj & Schultz, 1998). For this project, my colleague Thea Abu El-Haj and I, together with members of PTLC, studied the 20-year history of this teacher group through their detailed notes of weekly meetings and the documentation of their current meetings over a 4-year time period. In addition, we documented the practices of several new and experienced teachers. At the same time that I observed in Lynne's classroom, I attended the weekly meetings of the PTLC with Lynne.

The following year, Lynne and I met biweekly for interviews, to analyze my observations in her classroom and her role in the PTLC meetings, and to discuss ongoing questions raised by the research and the writing of this chapter.

In Lynne's Classroom

During this final year of teaching, Lynne's classroom was large and spacious. It was filled with materials accumulated over a lifetime of teaching. There was ample space in the classroom for whole-group instruction, small-group meetings, and individual projects. Desks clustered into three table groups occupied half of the room. Lynne assigned students seats, periodically switching either individuals or the entire table group. A large classroom library surrounded a rug area big enough for the entire class to sit in a tight circle. There was one small chair on the edge of the rug. The class library contained thousands of books that Lynne had collected or purchased and color-coded over her many years as a teacher. A kitchen and art area was located behind the library/meeting area. This area contained many different materials connected to science and social studies themes and used for the innumerable projects that occurred throughout the year. Lynne placed materials for writing, such as paper, pencils, and pens, and for artwork, such as yarn and fabric, so that they were readily accessible to the children. She made math materials and games available for students as well. An alcove provided the block area with a protected space for structures to remain standing for a couple of days. Bulletin boards filled with student work covered each of the walls. There were various science displays placed throughout the room, including a snake, shells, seeds, and other materials for sorting, and various artifacts that Lynne or the students had discovered over the course of the year. A table with three computers stood along one wall next to Lynne's own desk. The design and layout of the classroom, as well as the abundance of materials, illustrate the value Lynne placed on giving students sufficient and varied materials to make choices about how to engage in learning.

Lynne also believed that children learn through a variety of social arrangements. In other words, she did not subscribe to the notion that every child can learn best through a single mode of teaching. This belief was reflected in her daily schedule. Every day the children read, choosing from among the books in the large library. While students read individually or with partners, Lynne read with one child at a time and kept careful notes on that child's progress. The children wrote every day; most often they wrote on their own in notebooks, though later in the year self-selected small groups occasionally worked on collective projects. They usually chose their own topics for writing, and during the year at least one or more of their stories was published or typed and put together into a book that became a part of the class library. There was a period of whole-class formal math instruction, and a time when Lynne read books aloud to the class. These books were often related to the class thematic projects. Most days included a 30- to 40-minute-long project time.

For most of her career, Lynne frequently taught each class for 2 years, beginning with them as first graders and teaching the same group through their second-grade year, a process now called looping. Parents whose older child had been in Lynne's class often requested that the school place younger siblings in her classroom. This allowed her to know families and use that knowledge to build an extended classroom community and to achieve a continuity extending beyond the 2-year time period for each class group. Like the third- and fourth-grade group described in Chapter 2, Lynne's class was unusually diverse in terms of race and social class, and Lynne, like Judy, is White. In contrast to the vast majority of schools in this urban district characterized by student bodies from single racial groups or social background, the racial and social class composition of this school was evenly divided among African American and White students who represented a range of social class backgrounds that cut across race lines.

Whole-Class Discussions

Whole-class discussions have always been central to Lynne's teaching. She used them to simultaneously teach the whole group and listen to the individuals within the group. Their purposeful structure gave her a way to accomplish these goals. Since 1973, when she began her work with Patricia Carini and colleagues at the Prospect Archives and Center for Research and Education in North Bennington, Vermont, Lynne's class discussions have followed the specific format developed there and also used in the weekly PTLC meetings (Himley, 2002; Strieb, 1995).

Lynne generally held one or two classroom discussions a week. At the beginning of the first-grade year, these discussions were centered on concrete topics such as "what are some things you already know how to read" or "describe the shell as it is passed around the circle." For these beginning discussions, Lynne chose topics that she thought would be accessible to all of the students, so that each would have something to add to the discussion. She taught them the rules for participating in a discussion by practicing each component with them, giving them explicit instructions. The discussion format, which might seem awkward to some teachers because of its rigidity, made the rules for participation in a group discussion predictable and understandable to the children.

In a typical discussion—for instance, about a natural object—Lynne initially asked students to give their first impression. After each child had spoken, they were encouraged to add more detailed descriptions. The discussion continued around the circle so that each child would have a chance to speak. There was a clear expectation that everyone would contribute to the discussion. Further, students knew that it was assumed that they would not always agree with their classmates. They were asked to state their agreement or disagreement when it was their turn rather than at the moment someone made a statement they disagreed with. Lynne also assured the students that there was always time for a second turn at the end of the first round. As students spoke, Lynne listened carefully to each contribution. She often waited until the second or third time students spoke to intervene by asking questions or prodding the students to clarify or elaborate their statements. She also taught students to take on this role, so that they were listening not only for when to contribute but also to the content of their classmates' talk and ways to build on what had already been said. Thus these discussions were important tools for teaching students both content and the important skills of listening to and learning from each other. Lynne felt that she could identify the discussions that were important to the students because of the stillness that fell over the group at certain times during and after these discussions (interview, 5/30/01). Lynne explains her role in the class discussions as follows:

> During the discussions, I usually set the topic (though sometimes the topic is something a child has brought to my attention), remind children of the process, and let them know that if they have an opinion different from another child's, it's okay to say it in a kind way. My role during the discussions is to make sure everyone has a turn; to assure children that even if they want to say the same thing someone else said, they should say it in their own words; to remind children to listen. Sometimes I ask a child to clarify what was said or to say a little more. At the end, I summarize themes that have emerged. (Strieb, 1995, p. 5)

Lynne began documentation of the discussions in 1979, when she recorded the discussions by hand. By 1992 she used a laptop computer for this purpose. After most classroom discussions, she proofread them and added an explanatory paragraph as an introduction. The following day she sent the record of the discussion home in students' homework books and asked the students and their parents to read at least the child's individual contributions for homework. This gave the children authentic conversation for reading practice and the parents and guardians a window into the classroom and a way to listen in on their discussions. Later in the same week, she often had the students read the discussions aloud as a class, with each student taking his or her own part to practice reading.

When Lynne began teaching, one of her greatest challenges was to learn how to conduct whole-class lessons. Over time, she learned this process by observing her colleagues, noting the words they used to frame discussions and create opportunities for all children to speak. Building on her experiences with the Prospect Center and PTLC, she brought the processes she used with her colleagues to her classroom, learning to listen and respond in order to lead discussions. Underneath the smooth execution of classroom discussions was her experience and ability to sense the tone of the group.

Discussions in Lynne's classrooms often appeared to proceed on their own, with Lynne as a leader who interacted only sparingly in order to maintain the flow of activity. But beneath this apparently seamless activity lay Lynne's sense of organization and deep knowledge of children and pedagogy. The examples of class discussions that follow reveal the teacher's role in a classroom that focused simultaneously on individual learning and the class as a collectivity. The first discussion occurred during a harmonious time in the class and illustrates the notion of listening for the rhythm of a classroom. Because this first discussion was based more on actions than on words, as will become clear, the structure and routines of a class discussion are more apparent. The second discussion on exclusion emerged out of a period when the class was out of balance and illustrates how a teacher can create openings for students to work together to recreate harmony or balance in a democratic classroom.

LISTENING FOR RHYTHM: A (NEARLY) SILENT DISCUSSION

It was a beautiful and wet morning toward the end of fall. Students shuffled into the classroom from the school yard, talking loudly and leaving wet tracks on the floor. Many had a backpack in one hand and a fist full of glistening leaves in the other. Their homework had been to bring in certain kinds of leaves. The types of leaves were listed in their homework notebooks, which contained spelling lists, and handwritten and xeroxed homework assignments that were stapled into the books each evening. After putting away their bags, students moved into a circle on a rug, with small piles of leaves in their laps or on the floor in front of them. Each sat in his or her assigned spot in the circle. Lynne sat with them in a low chair, a clipboard on her knee.

After talking informally with individual children, Lynne posed the initial question of the formal class meeting—"Who brought in leaves?"—focusing students' attention on the task at hand. Most children raised their hands. A few looked down, avoiding her eyes. She wrote down the names of students whose hands were raised. A stern look crossed her face as she inquired, "Now, who got all their leaves in the school yard? Tell the truth." She had watched as many children scrambled to find their leaves that morning in the school yard before they lined up to enter the building. Lynne wrote down this second set of names. She continued, "I gave you a list of leaves and some of you said you couldn't get them because it was raining or dark." Students murmured excuses and explanations. A student, purposefully seated at Lynne's side, added, "I didn't want to touch them because it was mud on them." During her opening comments and interactions with the students, Lynne surveyed the landscape to notice those participating in the conversation and the nature of their involvement. She used this opening to hold students accountable for their homework and to let them know that she was expecting each of them to participate in the activity. At the same time, her comments and demeanor let students know that she was prepared to listen to each of them during the discussion.

While the students clutched their handfuls of leaves, Lynne began a discussion about seasons, with a particular focus on fall. Although the point of the discussion was to provide students with practice in sorting leaves according to their various attributes—an activity that united mathematics and language—she began the activity by gathering students' knowledge about the season. Adding a personal note and holding out a bunch of brown hanging pods, she informed the class, "As I was walking to school today, I picked up some seed cases. I should have done the homework, but I didn't. I picked up the seed cases instead."

Next Lynne asked a student for his homework book, turned to the page that described the assignment from the previous evening, and asked the students how many leaves they were supposed to bring to school. All at once, students called out various numbers, ranging from 7 to 15. Nearly everyone had an answer, most of them guesses. Lynne quieted the class down by saying in a firm voice, "Let's count." Without instructions, the class enacted a ritual so familiar to them that Lynne did not have to explain the rules.

> *Lynne*: A red leaf
> *Class*: One
> *Lynne*: A brown leaf
> *Class*: Two

They proceeded with this pattern: Lynne read the type of leaf listed in the homework book and the students responded in unison with the next number. When Lynne reached "a leaf with points," a girl interrupted to explain that she could not find one of those. She began to tell a story about looking with her mother until Lynne stopped her, indicating that the task was to *count* the leaves. As a class, they reached 10. Lynne commented, "If you said 10, you were right." A chorus of students claimed to have known the correct answer. Lynne continued, "A good way to make sure you did your homework correctly is to check them off as you find them."

Erickson (1995) suggests that we think of classroom discourse as song and poetry. This familiar routine that the students enacted without an explana-

tion was like a call-and-response ritual. The students understood and participated in the ritual of counting as Lynne called out the characteristics of the
leaves. They knew the rhythm or beat of the interaction and counted together
until they reached 10 with only a single interruption. They responded to Lynne's
cues to keep them focused on the task at hand. To begin, she had simply to
say, "Let's count," and they read the tone of her voice and commenced with
the number one. Erickson (1995) continues his explanation, which characterizes the talk in this classroom ritual:

> As we sing the speech of classroom discourse, temporal and pitch shapes in that
> speaking provide a fundamental structure within which we are able to make lit-
> eral sense of one another's words as they are being uttered. (p. 20)

The structure of counting the leaves in the homework book gave each child a
cue to participate in the collective learning of the class. Erickson (1995) claims
that in order for students to become engaged in learning, they need to understand the beat established by the teacher. In addition to the listening students
must do, I suggest that teachers also listen to the rhythm and beat of the
group as a whole. Lynne's close listening for the beat, her sense of the class
as a whole combined with her deep knowledge of individual learners, helped
her to maintain the flow of the conversation and capture their attention. In
addition to enacting the informative and familiar counting ritual, Lynne used
this ritual to listen to what her students knew in terms of counting. She gave
them advice about how to keep track of their progress and at the same time
listened for who had done homework, holding them accountable. She made
the choice to ignore the comment about leaves with points, letting this girl—
and the class—know that the task was to count, not to report on their success
or failure in finding leaves. By making it clear that her listening focus was
only on the counting, Lynne signaled what she considered appropriate contributions to the conversation. She established the rhythm of conversation that
she both taught and expected the children to join.

Sorting Leaves

After a conversation about various classroom books related to leaves, Lynne
asked the children if they wanted to play a silent game with their leaves. The
class, and especially those children who brought in leaves, indicated their interest and excitement about the game. Lynne explained the procedure. "It is
a silent game. Someone puts a leaf in the center of the circle on the rug. If
you have a leaf that is the same in any way, put it next to that leaf. If not,
begin a new group." One student remembered that the previous year they
had played the same game with apples. Lynne complimented her: "You have

a good memory. We'll also do the game with candy wrappers after Hallow-een." She continued, "Those of you who don't have leaves—maybe someone could give a leaf to someone who doesn't have a leaf." For the most part, the students generously shared their leaves. Before they began, Lynne reminded them that this was a silent game. As was customary, she told them that they would go around the circle and each child would have a chance to place a leaf on the rug when it was his or her turn.

The game began. One by one, students silently put their leaves next to existing groups or began a new group of leaves. After two times around the circle, Lynne engaged the children in a discussion about the groups of leaves. She asked the students to name a category for each group that described how the leaves were sorted. A discussion ensued about the various attributes of the leaves and the many different ways to sort them. Lynne instructed the students to continue around the circle a second time, and this time each student made an observation. The following excerpt from the middle of the discussion is illustrative. Students were in the midst of describing particular groups of leaves. Each speaker pointed to a different group:

> *Sonia*: These are together because they're the same shape.
> *Jim*: These are all together because they all have one point.
> *Jenna*: These are together because they're all long.
> *Zoe*: These are all together because they're all the same shape.
> *Johnny*: They're all big and yellow.

At this point, Lynne (LYS) interrupted the flow of the discussion because the leaves in the group Johnny pointed to were not all yellow and she wanted him to look more closely. The leaves were all relatively large.

> *LYS*: Are they?
> *Johnny*: Some of them.
> *LYS*: I want something they *all* are.
> *Johnny*: They're all big.
> *LYS*: Are they?
> *Johnny*: Yes.

This excerpt from the discussion illustrates how Lynne listened to the group. She timed her interruption carefully. At this point she wanted students to be more precise in their explanations, and Johnny's imprecision provided her with the opportunity to let them know this. Because Johnny knew the interactional requirements of the discussion, he knew that when Lynne asked "Are they?" he needed to look again more closely and clarify his contribution. Lynne's responses followed the beat of the discussion; when Johnny gave this last response, the students knew to continue around the circle on their own. At the same time that Lynne listened closely and insisted that the students give accurate responses, she let student talk dominate the discussion without feeling the need to affirm or comment on each response from her position as teacher, as is typical in classroom discourse (cf. Cazden, 1988, 2001; Mehan, 1979). Thus her questions and talk took up significantly less time than the students' comments. The discussion continued with Lynne asking clarifying questions when the answers were vague or did not seem to match the characteristics of the group of leaves.

As the students continued around the circle, they started to become restless; noticing their movement, Lynne decided to change the form of the discussion. She turned to one of the girls and asked, "Jenna, you wanted to make a change. What was that change?" Lynne had listened to Jenna when she made her initial request and saved her response until the timing was right. When Jenna claimed not to remember her idea, Lynne turned to the entire group and repeated it for her: "If you could make a change, what change would you make?" Various children volunteered to make switches and took turns moving the leaves between groupings. A few minutes later, noticing that the activity was no longer holding the attention of most of the children, Lynne concluded the discussion by saying, "People sorted the leaves by shape, even though they were different sizes. Some people put leaves with one point together. Some people put all the green leaves together. There are four groups of leaves with one point." She paused and continued to describe and explain the different groups. Various children added in details. They quickly finished this discussion and made a transition to a math project they had worked on the previous day.

Monitoring Learning

Lynne used the structured discussion to listen for the rhythm of the classroom. The ritual gave her access to students' knowledge about the attributes of leaves, but also to their understanding of how to participate in a group discussion. For instance, when she asked the students how many leaves they were told to bring in, they gave her a wide range of answers. One response would have been for her to simply say, "The correct answer is 10." Instead, listening to the variety of their responses, she heard that they needed a reminder about how to keep track of homework assignments. Knowing that they could all derive the correct answer together, she drew them into a counting ritual in which they counted as she read the attributes of leaves aloud. Through this ritual she showed them how to find the answer on their own, and they arrived at the correct number together.

At first, as she listened to the rhythm of the discussion, Lynne did not interrupt students who placed their leaves in groups that did not appear to follow the rules she had established. She wanted them to make their initial choices without fear of correction. She waited until the second phase of the discussion when students gave verbal explanations for their decisions about where to place their leaves. That allowed her to listen to their thought processes before making corrections. Rather than immediately correcting Johnny or dismissing his comment when he initially said that all of the leaves in one group were big and yellow, she posed a question that allowed him to clarify the statement himself. As a result, he modified his statement, saying that they were all big (implying that he realized that they weren't all yellow.) She used this moment not only to instruct this one student but to encourage all of the students to pay more attention to their answers in order to make them more precise.

Timing Interaction

Lynne listened for the rhythm of the discussion to time her entrance into it. She used her experience with leading discussions to know when her comments would move the discussion forward rather than bringing it to a halt. She wanted to ensure that she did not shift the course of the discussion, such that the comments would be directed to her rather than to the group. She listened to the rhythm of the discussion, noting the pattern and duration of the individual contributions of each child to determine when she should pose a question or make a comment. She noticed *how* each child was participating and how each individual's participation fit into the larger discussion or activity. In this leaf discussion, the contributions included both actions—the students placed their leaves in groups and moved them around—and words, so that Lynne followed students' gestures as well as their vocal contributions. She also enacted the discussion in a predictable manner, leaving openings so that she could respond to what she learned from the group and so that students could take an active role in both participating in and directing the discussion. The timing of Lynne's comments was critical in maintaining a focus on the students' contributions and helped Lynne support more students to make reflective comments. The structured format of this discussion included pauses that allowed even the most reluctant speakers to talk.

When Johnny finished his dialogue with Lynne about the characteristics of the group of leaves, the child next to him picked up the discussion without missing a beat. The students used the structure of the discussions to understand how to participate in the classroom talk; Lynne used the structure to help her listen to their contributions. It made it difficult for any one person, including the teacher, to dominate the conversation so that as many people as possible were engaged in learning. As Lynne explains:

There are kids who always have something to say and don't realize that the act of speaking all the time keeps others from speaking. If they realized this they might feel badly that they're keeping someone from talking. And for people who are less talkative, it allows them the space to speak.

(interview, 3/19/00)

Lynne's close listening allowed her to maintain the balance of the discussion.

Shifting the Discussion

A critical part of listening to the rhythm of a classroom is knowing when an activity has gone on long enough yet taking care not to move away from it prematurely. There were two ways in which Lynne shifted the focus during this discussion. First, she changed her pedagogical strategy. At a certain point in the activity, Lynne could hear that most of the students had grasped the concept behind the initial set of instructions, that is, they could identify a single attribute of their leaves and place one leaf at a time next to others with that same attribute. In addition, she observed that students were growing tired and restless with the repetition of this activity, probably because they had learned the lesson. Earlier, a student had suggested a new way to do this activity. Picking up on her idea, Lynne asked the students to find leaves they could move from one group to another. The point that Lynne wanted to make with this instruction was that leaves have several attributes and can be placed in more than one group.

The second kind of shift that Lynne made was based on content. Lynne noticed when many students had learned what they needed to learn from this particular activity and made a move to conclude it. When Lynne made this decision, she knew that some students still had extra leaves. But rather than waiting for them all to be placed in groups, she asked the children to put their remaining leaves in the center of the circle before they began the next activity.

In order to help students know how to shift activities, Lynne had taught them rituals that resembled call-and-response routines. She used these rituals to focus students' attention if the room was noisy or to make a transition to another activity. These rituals were also a way of asking students to join her to listen to and pay attention to the rhythm of the discussion. The most common ritual was one that Lynne had learned from a colleague:

> *LYS:* I say eyes (children turn toward Lynne and use a finger to indicate their eyes)
> *LYS continued:* You say—
> *Class:* Shhhh (with a finger on their lips)

By the time the students had finished saying "Shhhh" in unison, they were nearly always quiet and facing Lynne.

Partway through the year, Lynne's granddaughter, who attended a dual-language school in California, visited the class and taught them the following version of the chant in Spanish. Lynne adopted this new call-and-response routine and used it alternatively with the English version.

LYS: Ojas [eyes] (pointing to her eyes)
Class: Orejas [ears] (covering their ears)
LYS: Boca [mouth] (pointing to her mouth)
Class: Cerrada [closed] (quiet)

As before, all of the children would join with the chant as soon as they heard Lynne say "ojas" and were quiet by its conclusion.

Lynne used these familiar chants to break into the rhythm of the classroom talk (interview, 3/6/01). These rituals substituted a new rhythm for the old one in order to focus the students' attention on the teacher. Other teachers use clapping rituals for this same purpose. As in the classroom discussions, everyone could join in immediately because of their clear rules and predictability. During the leaf discussion, Lynne used more subtle means to shift the discussion by listening to the group to determine the timing for taking up a new rhythm or topic. Practice with these rituals helped the class to work together, to listen to each other and their teacher, and also to shift their rhythm as a corporate body.

LISTENING FOR BALANCE: RECREATING HARMONY

Lynne also used discussions to listen to the group in order to build, maintain, and regain balance in the classroom. In my own first year of teaching, when the interactional dynamics of the classroom broke down, students were not as actively engaged in learning. It was only when the interactions between and among students and me were repaired that they became deeply engrossed in their learning once again. Like many teachers, Lynne realized that in order to create a community in which students learned from each other as well as from her, she needed to attend to the social dynamics of the classroom. Discussion thus became an integral element not just of her pedagogy but of her classroom management practices. Although most discussions, like the one about leaves, focused on academic content, Lynne also used discussions to address social issues that were directly tied to children's ability to learn from and with each other. Listening for balance necessarily includes restoring equanimity when a class is in disarray. This discussion illustrates how Lynne used listening to both assess and recreate the balance, as well as to engage the students in maintaining and repairing the social fabric of the classroom.

In spite of her many years of teaching and the depth of her knowledge about children and teaching, this was not an easy year. In Lynne's classroom, as in classrooms across the city, children seemed restless and teachers noticed more meanness than usual. Teachers attributed this behavior to several changes in the school district and the city. For instance, new district mandates meant to increase standardized test scores limited the amount of play teachers of young children could include in their day. At their weekly meetings, teachers in the Philadelphia Teachers' Learning Cooperative frequently talked and worried about the violence and anger they noticed in their classrooms. At a meeting in the spring devoted to classroom stories, Lynne made a general statement about the children in her classroom and went on to describe a particular classroom incident. She declared:

> There are all these angry children and nobody is connecting it to the fact that we're not doing developmentally appropriate practice [because of all of the school district mandates]. Giving kids a chance to play and choose helps the anger go away. I'll believe that until I die.

She continued with a story from that day.

> Two girls came up to me today. A Black girl and a White girl. They said, "We're not going to get Keesha [an African American girl] in trouble but we have something important to say to you. She says that she doesn't like to play with White girls." Others gathered around and said, "She doesn't like *some* White people; she does like other White people." I asked Zoe [who is White] if her feelings were hurt and she said, "Yes." Two days ago someone said that Keesha had stolen something. Another time, Keesha said another child [a recent immigrant to this country] smells. [Keesha] came to this class in December and in some ways it changed the tenor of the class. (There was a pause.) She's an amazing writer.

Lynne concluded with her response to what the girls had told her.

> I will have a discussion in a general way with my kids about this. Otherwise, it will get down to who said what. (She sighed.) These are hard conversations.
>
> (field notes, audiotape, 3/9/00)

Lynne described the shift in the balance of her classroom that occurred when a new and complicated child entered the group. It was reminiscent of my own experience as a first-year teacher. She did not simply describe this child as "bad" or "difficult" but took care to notice her talents as a writer, pointing out that she had strengths to build on. She explained the ways that the presence of this new child created an imbalance in the room. The student had instigated several activities—such as telling secrets and forming cliques—that had not previously been a part of the classroom. Lynne had spoken to her several times about class norms.

In the meeting with her teacher colleagues, Lynne acknowledged both the difficulty and the importance of these kinds of discussions for teaching students to participate in a democratic community. As she later explained:

> It was always a conscious part of my teaching. The idea that you have some responsibility for one another in the classroom. Not only helping with chores, but also helping others learn and behave. I've had discussions where I ask the class, "How can we help x behave better?" I didn't single children out often. Every once in a while—especially when someone wasn't there—I asked what we can do to help. We're all in this together. Even if someone is naughty or bothersome, we can have a role and do something about it.
>
> (interview, 1/10/01)

Over the years, when students came to Lynne to relate a single incident involving a classmate, she often decided to engage the class in a discussion of the situation rather than addressing that child one-on-one. Lynne believes that it is important to use class discussions to work as a group on topics that are of concern to the entire class. These discussions are designed to address the issue behind the incident rather than to confront the particular child who caused offense. The two students who had told Lynne about Keesha had been in her class the prior year. They knew that in going to Lynne they were not simply relaying an upsetting event, they were giving their teacher important information she would use with the entire class. From their past experience, they also knew that Lynne would address the issue without giving away their identities and that they would not be cast as tattletales. The students understood the issue of prejudice and related issues of justice and equity would be of particular importance to Lynne because of numerous discussions they had participated in while in Lynne's class (interview, 3/6/01). She had made it clear to her students in these discussions and others that she was committed to maintaining a just and democratic classroom that addressed issues critical to children and their learning.

Keesha's statement that she did not like to play with White girls had disturbed her classmates and their sense of the class as a community. Keesha's claim had disrupted the balance in the classroom with an assertion that went outside of the accepted norms Lynne had developed with her students. By calling a class discussion to address the particular issue, Lynne emphasized the collective responsibility her students had not only to monitor their own actions but to help their classmates learn to be members of the classroom community. She was teaching them to listen, with her, to the balance of the class. Though at times students tried guessing what the teacher wanted them to say in discussions rather than developing the group ethos themselves, over time, with careful listening and guidance from their teacher, they articulated the nuances and also the boundaries of classroom behavior.

The next day, Lynne opened the class meeting after lunch with these words:

> I'm sad about something. Yesterday two girls, an African American girl and a White girl, came to me because they were upset. I'm going to tell you why. They told me that someone in our class, a Black girl, said that she doesn't like to play with White girls. They weren't trying to get the girl who said that in trouble. They just wanted me to know that they were unhappy. It made me unhappy too. I think I'm unhappy because I thought we were kind of like a family and that we all cared for each other and didn't want to make other people feel bad. I'm really disappointed that it's not true. Well, I want to think about this with all of you. This is what I'd like you to do. Think hard if there was a time when someone didn't let you play. What happened? What did they say? How did you feel? Then I hope you'll tell the story. If it didn't happen to you, tell how you would feel if it happened to you. After that I want you to think about whether you were ever mean to someone else and didn't let them play with you. What did you do? What did you say? We'll all have a turn to tell those stories. Please don't mention people's names. Okay, who will begin?[2]

In this opening statement, Lynne set the ground rules for the discussion and assured the children that they would all have an opportunity to speak. She reminded them not to use names in order to protect all of the participants and provide a measure of safety. Lynne began by speaking about her feelings and asked the students to tell their own stories about times they had had similar experiences. This format resembled the recollection process used in the PTLC meetings and developed in conjunction with colleagues at the Prospect Center (Himley, 2000, 2002). When Lynne invited students to think about this issue with her, she emphasized their collective role in maintaining safety, trust, and a sense of community in the classroom. Rather than imposing her rules or displeasure on the individual or the group (e.g., stating baldly that this sort of talk is not acceptable in school), she set up a discussion that involved the class in reflecting and thinking together about the issue. This enabled her to listen with the students and for the class as a collective to learn from one another.

> An African American boy, Tyrone, raised his hand and made the first statement.

> *Tyrone*: What if someone won't play with you if you don't have hair?
> (In her typed transcript of the discussion, Lynne noted: "Tyrone's mom shaves his head about every two weeks.")
> *LYS*: Just think about it and then you'll have a turn to talk about it.

Lynne knew that in order to listen for balance in the classroom, she needed to pay attention to particular comments and the direction they might take the discussion. She wanted to ensure that Tyrone stayed focused and that the discussion did not stray from the designated topic. Rather than silencing him completely, however, she assured him that she had heard him and that he would have another opportunity to talk and raise questions later on. This was her way of guiding this student and the group to tell stories about exclusion rather than to raise questions. Lynne thus was able to shift the discussion without censoring it. She knew second graders easily went off on tangents, and her clear, yet positive, statement at the beginning was a signal not only for Tyrone but also for the entire class.

The discussion continued around the circle with Lynne calling on students one at a time. As students declared their feelings, Lynne made only a few comments to clarify their statements. They each expressed feelings that echoed those raised by Lynne in her opening remarks. Maya began with a conditional statement and then told what appeared to be a story about a real event. Nearly every student followed her with a hypothetical statement about a feeling. A few students offered actual stories.

> *Maya*: I would be sad if someone said "I won't play with you because you're Black." I asked someone if I could play with you. They said, "No, because you're Black."
> *Naami*: I feel angry at people who don't let me play.
> *Jackie*: I'd feel sad because someone called you a name. You would have hurt feelings. I would play with someone else.
> *Ariel*: I'd be very angry.
> *Shawna*: I would feel sad because if a person said, "You're Black, you can't play," I would just go play with another person.
> *LYS*: Did you ever do it?

Lynne's question to Shawna was the first comment or probe that Lynne interjected into the discussion. Shawna was the African American student who had accompanied her White classmate to inform Lynne about Keesha's comment. Because of the listening she had done over the past 2 years, Lynne knew Shawna well and felt comfortable asking her if she would exclude a child because of her race. She knew, for instance, that Shawna played with both African American and White children. In listening to this moment, Lynne knew that the focus needed to be shifted to the real world of the classroom, and she hoped that her question to Shawna would prompt other students to tell actual rather than hypothetical stories.

However, her attempt was not successful. In response to her question, Shawna shrugged and turned to Ariel, who posed a question. Ariel was trying to remember the word to describe someone who says either "You're Black, you can't play" or "You're White, you can't play." After Lynne supplied the word (prejudice), Ariel nodded to Owen, indicating that he should continue the discussion.

> *Owen*: If someone called me a name I'd get mad.
> *Phillip*: I'd be sad and annoyed if someone didn't like to play with me
> because I'm brown. Someone didn't like my color at [another
> school]. He said, "I only play with White people." I felt sad and
> just stood there and was shocked.
> *Keesha*: I would feel sad if someone said I don't want to play with you
> because you're Black. It doesn't matter if someone is Black or
> White or—I'd play with them anyway.

Lynne took special note of Keesha's comment, because Keesha was the girl who allegedly had said that she did not like to play with White girls. However, she decided that it wasn't the right time to enter the conversation and question Keesha further. She couldn't point out the contradiction between this statement and the one reported to her without putting Keesha on the spot and thus both highlighting Keesha's status as an outsider and undermining the value of a group-centered approach to classroom dynamics. Lynne's past and present listening was essential to this decision and thus, eventually, to the successful outcome of the discussion: She listened to Keesha as an individual, to the balance of comments in the group, and to her own experience and intuition as a teacher who had faced similar situations in the past.

As the discussion continued, several students made direct comments about race.

> *Ross*: I'd be sad because if someone said I don't want to play with you
> because you're White. I'd play with someone else and forget about
> it.

> *Alicia*: I'd feel really sad if someone said, "I won't play with you be-
> cause you're Black." It doesn't really matter which color they are.
> You should play with them. I don't know how it feels because I
> like everyone.
>
> *Elaine*: I would feel sad if someone didn't play with me.
>
> *Andrew*: I'd be very mad if someone said they didn't like my color and
> skin.
>
> *Meg*: I'd feel sad and disappointed if they said "I don't want to play
> with you." Once, at school, at lunch one day, I asked if I could play
> jump rope [and the people I asked] said, "You can't because you're
> White."
>
> *Raymond*: Someone said, "I don't want to play with you." People don't
> like you and call you names.

Lynne interrupted Raymond to try once again to focus the discussion on
stories of actual incidents the children had experienced. Up until this point,
the students had repeated similar statements about feeling sad or mad. They
established a theme with little variation. No students mentioned times when
they were mean to someone else, and Lynne knew that she could pursue this
angle with Raymond. Again, she used her careful listening to the balance of
comments thus far, and her knowledge of the particular child, as well as her
sense of the group. However, she also knew that Raymond often told long,
rambling stories that weren't connected to the theme of the discussion. She
anticipated this situation by asking him to particularize.

> *LYS*: Raymond, did *you* ever say something like that? [Silence.] Tell
> the truth. Did you ever say something like that to someone? Tell
> the truth.
>
> *Raymond*: To my brother. [He began to tell a story that didn't seem to
> connect to the discussion.]
>
> *LYS*: Raymond, I'm going to interrupt you. What are you talking
> about?
>
> *Raymond*: People who don't like you and call you names.

The conversation faltered. Raymond did not seem to have a story to tell about
a time he excluded someone else, despite Lynne's prompting.

  In general, students seemed reluctant to tell the kind of explicit and true
stories Lynne had anticipated. After Raymond gave his response, Maya quickly
offered an answer to Lynne's question, maintaining the flow of the discussion:

> *Maya*: We're talking about if anyone ever said, "I won't play with you
> because you're Black or White."
>
> *Sonia*: If someone said that to me, I would feel angry or sad if they

called me a name and said they wouldn't play with me because I'm White. I would feel sad because it would make me feel like they don't like me because of the color of my skin.

Jim: I would be sad if I couldn't play because I'm White. I'd go play somewhere else.

In this segment of the discussion, two girls jumped in quickly to fill Raymond's silence. In the interest of maintaining the flow of the discussion, Lynne may have let them prevent Raymond from contributing his story. This quick exchange illustrates the difficulty of orchestrating such discussions, protecting silence or gaps so that every voice is heard yet keeping each student focused on the central topic.

After Maya answered the question for Raymond, Sonia quickly returned to the pattern of telling conditional stories that began with "if" and Jim followed suit. Lynne next turned to Zoe, the White girl who had told her about being excluded, to ask her to add to the discussion.

LYS [to Zoe]: What do you have to say?

Zoe: I would say, "I don't think that's nice to say. We're both the same even though we're different colors."

Zoe stayed on safe ground and made a conditional statement like those of her classmates. Not satisfied with her response, and knowing that Zoe had an actual story to tell, Lynne probed further, using her awareness of the rhythm of the discussion and her knowledge about this particular student.

LYS: Did that happen to you? Can you tell us without saying names?

Zoe: When I was in preschool it happened.

LYS: Has anything like that ever happened in *this* school?

Zoe: Shawna told me that in this school a girl said she didn't like White children, just White teachers.

LYS: What did you feel about that?

Zoe: My feelings were hurt. I asked [the girl] if she said it and she said "Yes."

When Lynne began the discussion, she intended for each student to tell a true story. However, she initiated her own comment with the statement, "I feel sad," and the students followed this pattern. They seemed to prefer to talk about their feelings rather than about actual events. Most claimed that they would feel either sad or angry. Inadvertently Lynne may have initiated the discussion in territory where the students felt more comfortable. When it was Zoe's turn, Lynne asked her directly about the initial event that generated the discussion, careful not to implicate her or coerce her to tell the actual story. Although Zoe described the event that had led to this discussion, following Lynne's prompt, she concluded with an expression of her feelings. She did not draw a lesson from the event or restate a class norm.

At this point, each child had been given an opportunity to make a single comment. Many students had additional responses. Lynne varied the format by calling on only those children who had additional comments, rather than going around the circle a second time. Students offered a mix of feelings and specific stories, often expanding their initial statements about how they had felt.

> *Lawrence*: It doesn't matter what color you are, only how you feel. I asked if I could play nine times. They kept teasing me. They said, "You have brown skin. No one can see you because you're Black." I got mad. I felt like punching them. The next day they asked me to play. I said "No." I ignored him. I didn't want to play.
> *LYS*: How did you feel?
> *Lawrence*: I felt mad. I felt like punching him. It's bad because you might get in trouble.
> *LYS*: Was it anyone in this room?
> *Lawrence*: Yes. The next day he kept asking me to play. I said no and kept ignoring him.
> *LYS*: And you didn't want to play with him because—
> *Lawrence*: Because he kept teasing me.

Lawrence introduced a powerful story about race and feeling invisible. He spoke honestly about the rage he felt when he was treated in a hurtful manner. Lynne had carefully followed the discussion up until this point. Rather than leaving this statement unchallenged and turning to the next student, she decided to take a more active role in helping the students to tell stories. In her interactions with Lawrence, she continued to ask him questions until he arrived at a conclusion.

Lynne's goal was not only to give the students a chance to talk about their feelings but also to construct group norms about how children in their class treat each other. As long as students continued to relate hypothetical stories, it was difficult to use the stories to directly address the pressing issues in the classroom. Lynne was listening to the group to gauge how to guide the discussion to move beyond statements about feelings. In addition, she wanted the class to listen to each other's stories to collectively make sense of the events that had occurred in their classroom that year.

Sensing that the discussion had turned to actual stories, after Lawrence finished this exchange, Tyrone raised his hand.

Tyrone: Nothing [like that] ever happened to me.

Elaine: I would feel sad and mad because you're just not supposed to say it. The only reason they do it would be if they didn't [like] me or if I was mean to them.

LYS: Did it ever happen to you?

Elaine: At my other school there was this kid who usually played with me. One day she said, "I don't want to because you're White."

LYS: How did you feel?

Elaine: I was shocked and hurt because I played with the person about every day. Someone heard it and told me, "It's okay. That person does it almost every day because she's a bully."

Johnny: One of my friends, we had skateboards and a kid wanted to play. My friend wouldn't let him play because my friend was White and he was Black. The Black kid walked away.

LYS: What did you say to your friend?

Johnny: I told him if I had a skateboard I'd let him play.

LYS: What could you have done? [Johnny shrugged.]

Lawrence's story, following Lynne's dialogue with Johnny, indicates that her tactic to encourage children to tell real stories had been achieved for the moment. During this round, Lynne continued to ask the students questions in order to prompt these stories. Elaine was the second student to say she was "shocked" by the exclusion of her peers. Listening to the degree of emotion in Elaine's comment, Lynne realized it was time to help Johnny and his peers think about what actions they might take in response to events such as these. It was important to her that the children see their own agency in such situations and share their strategies with one another. The discussion continued.

Katrina: It would be upsetting. I would feel upset. I would try to keep my spirits up because there are other people to play with.

Zoe: I would be sad if someone did that to me. I'd find someone else to play with. Once at ballet there was a girl who didn't say it to me but she said it to someone else. "I'm not going to play with you because you're not the right color."

Marcus: I'd feel sad because if someone said it to me I would play with someone else. Basketball or kickball.

Lynne's plan to bring the discussion to a close by asking the children to offer strategies proved difficult to enact. Before stating their solutions, the children continued to begin their statements with a declaration of how they would feel.

As the children spoke, they were always aware that Lynne was typing their discussion on her laptop computer in order to record it both for them and for herself. In response, they slowed down their pace of speaking to allow her to capture their words. The next few comments in this discussion included a question and then a suggestion that this was a discussion that should not be sent home to be read with family members. The students seemed to sense that this was a private discussion that they wanted to keep within the confines of the classroom.

> *Tyrone*: Is this going to be in our reading homework books?
> *LYS*: Do you want it to be in your homework book? [Tyrone shook his head.] Why not?
> *Tyrone*: Because it's hard to answer all the questions. You might not recognize the periods. You just keep going.

Tyrone could not find the words to describe why he did not want the discussion in their homework books. He may have perceived that conversations about race are sensitive and need to be kept within the context and safety of the classroom (Schultz et al., 2000). Lynne listened closely to Tyrone's comment, and even though he had difficulty expressing his reasons, she followed his request and did not send this discussion home with the students. That move communicated to Tyrone and others that not only were they listened to, but their talk was paid attention to and respected.

Keesha continued the discussion with a story about inclusion and exclusion. As the student who made the initial statement that prompted this discussion, Keesha may have used this final story in tandem with her earlier comment to assure her classmates that at times she *is* willing to play with White children. Her prior school was also an integrated school located in a predominantly White, middle-class neighborhood.

> *Keesha*: At my old school in [a nearby neighborhood], I was at a new school, and I asked someone if I could play with them and someone else asked me to play rope and I said yes.
> *Ross*: One day when I was in first grade a girl in our class was playing outside with the boys. I asked if I could play. She said, "Sorry, you're White." I was sad but I tried to find someone else to play with.
> *Alicia*: Sometimes I see people not playing with other people and I'm imagining if it was me. If it was me I would let the person play because it would be mean to say no.
> *Johnny*: Please don't put this in the reading homework book.

At this point, as an alternative to placing the discussion in their homework book, Marcus suggested that they make a class book from these stories to add to the collection.

Marcus: I'm thinking could we make a book about people who said bad things to you. People who said mean things to you.

LYS: I think that would be a really sad book if it had all those sad stories in it. [pause] I never thought of that. How many people would like to do that? [*Many children raised their hands.*]

Alicia: I don't think it would be a sad book. If we wrote it down, we would be happy because the bad things would be over. We'd just write it down and then we could forget about it.

Students enjoyed reading the large collection of classroom books and could often be seen poring over them in the reading area during silent reading and free times. Marcus sensed that this was a significant discussion that would be important for them to document in a permanent way. Lynne was particularly surprised that this student initiated the idea of making a class book. Marcus was usually quiet and did not often introduce new projects. Through listening to him, Lynne perceived the importance of his comment and encouraged the students to pay attention to the suggestion. The other students were pleased with this idea, and plans were soon under way to make the book. It is notable that although students did not want to take the discussion home, they wanted to make a book to contribute to the class collection.

Although Lynne registered her surprise about the idea, she listened to the students and agreed to help them make the book. Lynne initially was uncomfortable with the idea of a book about sad stories. She did not immediately see the value of focusing on these negative and sometimes painful experiences. The students disagreed. Even though she had been unable to steer the conversation to generate solutions for the class, Lynne listened to the students, paid close attention to their excitement and passion about the idea, and changed her mind. Her listening included shaping the discussion and, in this instance, allowing the students to take the lead in its direction.

By this time, the students had sat for over an hour. They were getting restless and excited about their book. Lynne could hear that it was time to move on to the next activity and concluded the discussion by telling a personal story. Following a routine that is part of the Prospect Center and PTLC processes, she offered a summary. This summary, like the discussion, was more personal than usual. It reflects how Lynne's close listening is not simply passive but rather involves her own reactions and participation in the conversation.

Let me finish up. It made me really sad to think that some of you were excluded because of the color of your skin. Because the way Zoe said it, we are all the same except the color of our skin. Remember all those apples? We had red apples, yellow apples, and green apples. We had them all out on the floor. Even though those apples were different colors, shapes, and sizes, they were all apples and they were all delicious. I said that they were just like you—different on the outside, the same on the inside, and all delicious.

Some people came to me and they were really upset. They said that they didn't want to get the person in trouble.

I'm a White girl. Well, I'm a White lady. When I was a girl, I used to feel badly because I couldn't jump rope. The other day some girls were playing rope and a girl in this class came up and they said she couldn't play because she doesn't know how to jump rope. This isn't the first time this has come up. Children in my class teach people things they don't know. Some girls teach others clapping games.

Lynne's final statement included an explanation of the way things are in their classroom and a personal story. She reminded the children of their historical position as one of her many classes over the years. The description of how students act in this room served to remind students of her expectations for them. Discussions were one way that Lynne listened, responded, and created a cohesive group. The sense of being a group was occasionally broken, and Lynne used discussions such as this one to foster listening and to reestablish the balance of the classroom community.

Lynne trusted the discussion process, which included telling stories and exploring feelings. She had established structures in her classroom that enabled her to listen to students, while she taught the students to listen to each other. The impact of this particular discussion was reflected in the students' interest in continuing the discussion through writing a book for the public to read.

Over the next few days, students wrote stories about exclusion for the class book. When it was difficult for some students to remember or put these moments into words, Lynne helped them to write about the specific incidents. In some cases, she suggested that students write about out-of-school events when they claimed not to remember incidents of exclusion in school. Although the classroom discussion had been largely about incidents when students or peers were excluded because of race or color, in their personal stories students turned to other forms of exclusion and wrote more about times they were excluded because of gender and age. Lynne worked with students individually to write down their stories and describe their feelings. Each story was illustrated (for example, see figure 3.1).

A few weeks later, once the book was bound, Lynne read it aloud to the students and asked them to suggest titles. Children were excited about their book and had numerous ideas for titles. Most were a variation of "The Sad, Sad Story" and "Bad Things That Happened to Us in the Past." The title that

Figure 3.1. *"Shame on Them"*

One day I was at recess and I wanted to play tag with my friends. One of the girls was my friend but she saw her best friend. I asked if I could play but they said no, except my friend. He had a frown on his face. The others just laughed, so I walked away crying.

stood out was one suggested by Ayanna: "The Devastating Day." Lynne was most surprised by this title. Although her focus had been on the telling of events, the students remained interested in articulating their feelings. The children closed their eyes and voted, choosing "The Devastating Day" as their favorite. Lynne clearly did not agree with the choice; however, she went along with it. She asked Ayanna if she knew what *devastating* meant. Ayanna answered, "Almost like confused and angry, but it's not." Lynne went on to explain, "Sometimes if there is a hurricane and the wind blows so hard that houses get knocked down and everything is wrecked, they say there's devastation. Things are destroyed." She concluded rhetorically, "Is that a good title? The day things got destroyed?" The students voiced their agreement on the title and she printed it on the cover of the book, illustrating her willingness to let the children guide the class activity.

Although the students indicated their desire to keep the discussion private by asking Lynne not to send it home to their parents, they decided to create a public record by writing a book that contained a story from each child. There was general agreement for each of these decisions. The students' choice in audiences for their class discussion illustrates the control the children took in determining whom they would speak with and whom they wanted as listeners. It also illustrates their commitment to and role in the creation of a democratic classroom community in which each individual voice is combined in a collective whole.

Creating an Ordered Routine to Listen for Balance

Many of the elements of listening for rhythm and balance in a classroom are present in this discussion. Lynne had taught the students a process for holding and participating in a discussion. This process followed specific procedures, including rules that students were to sit in assigned places during the discussion, that the discussion would proceed around the circle, and that all students were expected to speak at least once. These procedures created a familiar routine for the students. When there was a rupture in the classroom created by the mean words and actions of a child new to the class, the other students and Lynne felt comfortable using this process to regain the balance in the classroom. The order created by the routine allowed the students and teachers to address difficult issues together. The students knew how and when to speak. The exact process is not as important as its familiarity and structure. The structure allowed Lynne to listen—with attention—to each child in order to hear the balance of the group, and it allowed the class as a whole to listen to each other to develop a collective response to this issue.

Balancing Student and Teacher Talk

As in the leaf discussion, there were many moments in this discussion when Lynne took the floor and initiated questions. In most instances, she made these moves by asking clarifying questions or prompting students to tell a different kind of story. Speaking only when she felt it necessary, she paid close attention to the range of students who talked and the length and timing of her statements in relation to theirs. She left openings to listen to students and follow their ideas, while always maintaining control and a vision for the direction of the discussion.

There was an unusual balance of teacher and student talk in this discussion. It was clearly a teacher-directed activity: Lynne sat in a chair, rather than on the floor, and took a prominent position as the leader of the discussion. Yet Lynne clearly recognized the leadership capacities of the students from the very beginning when she asked the two girls how to respond to Keesha's comment and they suggested a class discussion. When the students wanted to turn the discussion into a class book and, later, when they chose the name for the book, she was not only hesitant, she outright disagreed with the students' choices. However, she used these moments to allow students to assert their authority, because the issue was clearly so important to them. Rather than coercing the students to reach her conclusion or, conversely, ceding her authority completely, Lynne carefully listened to the students in order to gain an understanding of how to guide the discussion.

Balancing Academics With Social Learning

This class discussion also illustrates the ways in which the academic and social curricula are intertwined. Lynne initiated the discussion in response to a clear social issue that she felt would affect and potentially undermine the academic learning in the classroom. The discussion generated talk, writing, and reading. After the discussion, the whole class became deeply involved in writing their pages for the book. The opportunity to speak in depth about an issue that mattered to them gave them authentic purposes for their writing. In addition, the writing they worked on was initiated by the students themselves. The book project enabled them to refine and elaborate their ideas. In the end, each child had a story to tell about a time he or she was excluded. During the writing process and when the book was completed, children read and reread their classmates' pages. This authentic writing was powerful for them because of the intimacy and immediacy of the topic. The trust Lynne built with her students through these discussions was fundamental to her abilities to elicit students' attention and participation in conventional school activities. It reflected a sense of trust built over time, which is a critical component of democratic classrooms. Together Lynne and her students began to construct rules to live by rather than rules to follow.

PARTICIPATION IN A DEMOCRATIC COMMUNITY

There are many other moments when Lynne, like other teachers, listens for the rhythm and balance in her classroom. Throughout the day, teachers listen to their students and adjust their teaching to recreate balance and order in the classroom. That balance is not automatically achieved but is dependent on structures and routines established early and reinforced throughout the school year. This example of a classroom discussion illustrates how one teacher established these structures or rituals and then worked to maintain balance, using them as scaffolding.

Although this chapter describes one form of class discussion, a more common way to listen to rhythm and balance in a classroom is through daily rituals such as morning meetings or an activity sometimes called "sharing time," in which students tell stories and events in their lives. These rituals establish routines and opportunities for teachers to listen to and get to know students as both individuals and as a collective. They enable students to learn to trust, respect, and listen to each other. These routines support teachers to listen to the whole group as well as the individuals in the class. Listening to the whole group reflects the value of maintaining a classroom community that is conducive to learning. The recent focus on individual achievement and whole-group learning guided by scripted dialogues make it difficult, if not impossible, for teachers to listen and respond to the rhythm and balance of the whole class. Democratic communities depend on dialogue and the honoring of individual voices that may clash as people work together toward identifying common beliefs (Greene, 1995). Teaching practices like these thus help prepare students to become active members of democratic communities.

Developing classroom rituals like those described in this chapter is not a high priority in the current educational climate, either in school systems or in teacher education programs. Instead, recent educational developments such as the emphasis on testing and scripted teaching reinforce two teaching emphases: individual achievement and whole-group instruction. Many teachers are urged to focus solely on individual test scores. Classrooms are structured to enable students to proceed at their own pace without the benefit of group interaction. Teachers emphasize the acquisition of skills keyed to the current regimen of standardized tests. Some are handed scripted curricula that instruct them to teach the whole group in a lockstep fashion, using direct instruction methods and ignoring the individuality of students. As a result of recent teacher shortages in urban and rural areas, many new teachers have not participated in teacher education programs. In place of such instruction, these teachers are often given scripted lessons to follow. Although scripts might give teachers a temporary sense of order and control, and direct instruction might produce a rise in test scores, it is questionable whether these methods are successful in engaging students in learning past their relatively brief time in school. As well, these methods undermine the intelligence and creativity of teachers, making teaching a rote job. If teaching requires trust and assent (Erickson, 1987), then scripted lessons are unlikely to produce such connections between teachers and students.

In comparison, listening to the whole class involves melding the individual and the group, teaching in a manner that is responsive to the child and the context in which she or he learns. This chapter thus has argued that listening and responding to a whole class on academic, social, and emotional levels is essential to teaching. Children learn when they are deeply engaged in the material, when the material matters to them and builds on what they know, and when they feel respected and listened to by their teachers and peers. Packaged programs cannot possibly account for the variation in students and communities across the country. Routines derived from programs developed outside of local school contexts might prepare students for high-stakes tests; they are poor fare for preparing a diverse and changing citizenry to participate in a pluralistic democracy.

After an extended examination of this discussion about exclusion at a PTLC meeting that spring, a colleague, Betsy Wice, summed up the discussion in Lynne's classroom and in this chapter:

> Having this discussion makes all of these topics sayable. That was
> Lynne's message to the students. That it took an hour. That this is im-
> portant. That experience gave children images and made it possible for
> kids to deal with exclusion differently. I don't think any kid could leave
> the room quite the same. It's become important.
>
> (field notes, 4/6/00)

4

Listening to the Social, Cultural, and Community Contexts of Students' Lives

The vitality of language lies in its ability to limn the actual, imagined and possible lives of its speakers, readers, writers. Although its power is sometimes in displacing experience, it is not a substitute for it. It arcs toward the place where meaning may lie.

(Morrison, 1993, p. 20)

STUDENTS SPEND A RELATIVELY small portion of their day inside the classroom. For many, their lives begin after the school bell rings. Researchers have documented organized programs that provide rich opportunities for youth to develop their talents and extend their knowledge (e.g., Cushman & Emmons, 2002; Gutiérrez, Baquedano-López, Alvarez & Chiu, 1999; Heath, 1994, 1996, 1998a, 1998b; Heath & McLaughlin, 1993; Hull & Schultz, 2001, 2002). In addition to participating in these more formal programs, adolescents gather in informal locations, engaging in sports and a variety of activities that may include reading, writing, and talk (e.g., Mahiri, 1998; Moje, 2000). Typically, teachers include only the knowledge and language students acquire in the classroom in their assessment of what students know and are able to do; tests are calibrated to measure this exchange. What would happen if teachers' assessments included students' accumulated and ongoing experiences both in school and out? How would this knowledge transform notions of teaching and learning and the images and assumptions of schooling?[1]

For instance, teachers most often understand students as readers, writers, speakers, and users of language in relation to opportunities they provide in classrooms. Within this frame, a teacher might regard one student as a competent reader of a particular book and another as a journalist for a class newspaper. On the other hand, if a teacher acknowledges and integrates students' experience with print both in and out of school, then she might know this first student as a reader of particular magazines and a frequent contributor to an on-line zine, and the second as a passionate letter writer and inveterate under-the-covers reader. Rather than knowing students by their school competencies displayed on standardized tests, teachers will understand students through the "actual, imagined and possible" lives they describe (Morrison, 1993, p. 20).

Official school curriculum often has a relatively insignificant influence on adolescents' lives. Popular culture, peers, and the exigencies of daily life hold more of their attention. A typical response to this circumstance in the popular press is to lament the influence of the media and popular culture on adolescents. Commentators decry the pernicious effects of violent lyrics and fast-paced television on students' attention and willingness to participate in mundane school tasks. A corollary response for some teachers is to build walls around classrooms so that they are impervious to outside influences, in order to create a protective space for learning during their brief moments with students.

An alternative possibility is to envision school and the learning that takes place in school as a fraction—albeit an extremely valuable fraction—of the learning a person is engaged in throughout the day and across a lifetime. In other words, teachers might perceive their work with students as representative of a part, but not all, of the students' learning. This suggests the importance of listening broadly to discover more about their students' learning outside of school both during and beyond their time in classrooms. When teachers take their experience with students in the classroom as the sum of their knowledge of students' interests and abilities, they are taking a narrow slice of students' lives and treating it as the whole. This chapter addresses how teachers can extend their understanding of students and teaching by listening to the larger contexts of students' lives. Listening to the social, cultural, and community contexts of students' lives enables teachers to hold larger images of their students as they formulate ways to teach them.

ATTENDING TO THE LARGER CONTEXT

Listening for the larger contexts of students' lives includes inviting students from the margins to bring their stories into the center of classroom life, an approach to teaching and research recently articulated by critical race theorists (e.g., Delgado Bernal, 2002; Ladson-Billings, 2000; Parker, Deyhle, & Villenas, 1999). Known as "counterstorytelling," this practice, as Delgado Bernal (2002) explains,

> serve[s] as a pedagogical tool that allows one to better understand and appreciate the unique experiences and responses of students of color through a deliberate, conscious, and open type of listening. In other words, an important component

of using counterstories includes not only telling nonmajoritarian stories but also learning how to listen and hear the messages in counterstories. (p. 116)

Teachers can find ways to invite students to bring their lives and stories into the classroom so that they are respected, heard, and understood. This does not mean that teachers should give their curriculum over to the students; rather, it implies that teachers take an inquiry stance toward teaching that makes the curriculum and classroom permeable to and reflective of students' lives (e.g., Dyson, 1997, 1999; Fecho, 2000).

I am not simply suggesting that teachers listen to students' stories and interests in order to incorporate those topics into the school curriculum, although that is certainly a vital approach to teaching. Rather, I propose that by holding a larger picture of how students engage in learning outside of school, teachers can enlarge their images, expectations, and interactions with students during their work together in classrooms. In the process, teachers learn students' languages even as they teach students the language of power they need for success in school (Delpit, 1988). Rather than envisioning teaching only as a process of enculturation, we need to view teaching as a reciprocal process in which teachers' decisions and classroom practices are shaped, in part, in response to what they learn from their students. The languages students bring from their outside lives include their passions and aspirations that, if incorporated into the school curriculum, will have an impact on student learning and engagement.

One assignment in our teacher education seminar is to ask students to write a vignette about a time that they were surprised by a student's ability. Often student teachers write about a capacity or interest they did not realize that a student held, or a shift in context that allowed a different side of a student to be revealed. A previously quiet student sang loudly when a particular kind of music was played in the classroom one morning. A student who claimed to hate writing sat down and wrote a children's book in one sitting, when his teacher pointed out that the rhythmic patterns of his language mimicked the Dr. Seuss books his mother had read to him when he was young. The student teachers' examples are generally moments when students were able to bring into the classroom some aspect of their lives and their stories from outside of school. In every case, student teachers' perspectives about the students shifted, and the shift was ultimately reflected in their teaching.

Listening to the wider contexts of students' lives includes learning about students' cultural backgrounds, in order to understand their proclivities, strengths, and stances toward learning. Listening in this manner includes paying attention to students' social networks, which cross school and out-of-school boundaries, and giving students opportunities to talk and write about their involvement in their communities. Teachers who listen broadly to their students attend to the political, social, and cultural histories students carry with them to school (e.g., Delpit, 1995). Close contact with parents and families through letters and other forms of communication (Resnick, 1996; Strieb, 1999) is critical to this work, as are connections with neighborhood and community institutions and resources.

In their work with Latino communities in the Southwest, Moll and his colleagues use the term "funds of knowledge" in order to describe the expertise of parents and community members that can both inform and become a part of school practices (e.g., Moll, 1992; Moll & Diaz, 1987; Moll & Greenberg, 1990). In a related project, Lee (e.g., 1993, 2000) has used cultural funds of knowledge in the African American community to develop culturally relevant teaching methods. These projects and others (e.g., Gutiérrez, Baquedano-López, Alvarez, & Chiu, 1999; Ladson-Billings, 1994; Moll & Greenberg, 1990) illustrate the ways students can be drawn into school practices through the use of cultural forms and tacit knowledge most often associated with out-of-school learning. Each one demonstrates the power of listening to and incorporating students' knowledge and interests into the official school curriculum.

The notion of listening to the wider context of students' lives deepens the meaning of listening that is the underpinning of this book. Listening to know particular students informs teachers about students' individual qualities as learners; listening to the rhythm and balance of a classroom enables teachers to teach to the classroom group; and listening to students' lives beyond school gives teachers broader access to what students bring to their school learning. Taking a listening stance toward learning about students' lives beyond the school day implies adapting classroom interactions and curriculum to both solicit and use this knowledge and epistemology.

Teachers and students are almost always separated from one another by several categories of difference, such as race, class, gender, or generation. If teachers assume they do not know what is behind students' utterances or their performances in school, then learning about who the students are and what they bring from their communities can shift understandings about them, expanding possibilities for learning. Using methods developed primarily from the theoretical frame of ethnography of communication, researchers have documented the different ways students speak and act at home and at school and have used these explanations to account for school failure (cf. Gilmore, 1983; Gilmore & Glatthorn, 1982; Heath, 1983). This notion of difference suggests a static view of culture that has recently been challenged by anthropologists such as Eisenhart (2001), Ortner (1994), and others.

In place of the conception of culture as a bounded set of practices tied to particular groups of people that leads to the study of cultural differences, the postmodern turn in anthropology suggests a conception of culture as variable and shifting according to time and place (e.g., Anzaldua, 1987; Clifford, 1986; Kondo, 1990). Recent theorists have used the notion of cultural production to illustrate how culture is constantly produced in the moment. Using this paradigm, writing researchers, for example, document the ways in which students' writing in classrooms and out-of-school contexts is shaped by larger social forces at the same time that the writing practices contribute to the production of the classroom milieu (Schultz, 2002). As Levinson and Holland (1996) explain:

> Reshaped by the more recent focus on practice and production, the larger question is now one of how historical persons are formed in practice, with and against larger societal forces and structures which instantiate themselves and other institutions. Cultural production is one version of this process. It provides a direction for understanding how human agency operates under powerful structural constraints. Through the production of cultural forms, created within the structural constraints of sites such as schools, subjectivities form and agency develops. [Focusing on cultural production is a way] to show how people creatively occupy the space of education and schooling. This creative practice generates understandings which may in fact move well beyond the school, transforming aspirations, household relations and structures of power. (p. 14)

An understanding of cultural production and a view of culture as contested or a "border zone" (Rosaldo, 1989) suggests reframing cultural differences as a resource for school learning rather than as a barrier to it. This understanding of how students' engagement in learning out of school serves as a link to school, expands a teacher's understandings of the students' capacities, and has the potential to shift classroom practices. Rather than understanding youth narrowly as students whose task is to master the discourses of schooling, teachers perceive and teach them as poets and carpenters, activists and caretakers, expanding the possibilities for teaching and learning. A place to begin is by listening to the larger contexts of students' lives.

The limited and limiting pictures teachers have of students through their classroom interactions and school performances suggest that certain students—those with the most social capital, knowledge, and willingness to participate in school practices—will appear "successful," whereas others—those with less knowledge of school practices or little desire to conform to school norms—will appear to "fail" (e.g., Erickson, 1987). By listening to the stories of students' lives beyond school and by paying attention to students' practices in and outside of the classroom, teachers can work toward teaching students in a more just and equitable manner.

The prescriptive models of teaching that dominate the educational discourse involve enacting a script that is the same regardless of the students' identities, background knowledge, or interests. What is taught—the script—does not change with respect to the context of the learning transaction. In contrast, listening is a stance that actively works against such prescriptive methods, because the underlying assumption is that a teacher cannot possibly know how and what to teach a student until she or he has listened carefully to that student.

In order to illustrate the dilemmas and possibilities of bringing students' out-of-school learning into the classroom, I draw on a longitudinal study of the literacy practices of high school students in a multiracial high school on the West Coast. This study was designed with the goal of learning about adolescents' literacy practices in and out of school during their final year of high school and in their first few years as graduates. The chapter is organized around case studies of three students who each wrote in different genres during after-school hours, and who each constructed a different relationship between this private writing and the academic writing he or she worked on in school. I argue that this understanding of students' lives beyond school is critical for knowing and deeply engaging students in their learning during school so that it endures beyond their time in classrooms. In order to explore how a teacher might listen for the broader contexts of students' lives, in school and out, I focus on writing practices rather than on the actual artifacts of writing. By practices I mean the habits of writing students engage in that embody their beliefs and also the position of the writing in their lives. For instance, I highlight letter writing as a social practice that certain students engage in at particular moments for specific purposes with a designated audience, focusing on this aspect of writing rather than on the content of the letters themselves.

RESEARCH CONTEXT

Situated between African American and Latino neighborhoods, the urban comprehensive high school where I conducted this research project housed a multiracial group of students who were approximately one-third African American, one-third Mexican American or Latino/a, and one-third Asian American. A high fence surrounded the school with a single gate monitored by a security guard. Those students who arrived late to school were held outside the gate until a bell signaled the next class period. The two-story school building was built in a U-shape around a central courtyard. Students crossed the courtyard between classes, which alleviated pressure in the crowded and noisy halls. Toward the end of my year at the school, a local artist completed a large outdoor mural near the school's entrance that reflected the multicultural and multiracial heritage of the students. This was one of many outward symbols of the teachers' and administrators' work to achieve unity and respect in the school. Still, many days were marked by racial tension, and it was not uncommon to see a police car circling the school.

The school was divided into houses where students took most of their courses. The classes I observed were in the health house. Most students in this house had indicated an interest in pursuing a health career such as nursing or pharmacology. Others chose careers such as cosmetology. In the social studies classroom where I spent most of my time, students crowded into desks at the beginning of the year. After a few months, fewer students came to school and there were enough seats for each student. Decorating the walls were posters celebrating famous African Americans and Mexican Americans. Later in the year, student work covered the walls.

Marta, an experienced and highly respected White teacher, taught the senior government and economics classes in this house. Initiating many of the reforms and innovative programs in the high school, including an internship program, she had taught in the school for many years and lived in the neighborhood. Fluent in Spanish and knowledgeable about a range of issues that had an impact on students' lives, Marta had an easy relationship with even the most difficult and least engaged students. At the same time that she listened to their countless stories about the challenges they encountered at home and in the community, she held the students to high standards.

There were frequent writing assignments in Marta's social studies classes that enabled her to listen to who the students were and to what they cared about. For instance, students kept a daily log of their responses to class activities. Toward the end of class, Marta often asked them to write their reactions to class discussions. She took these responses seriously, using them to plan the next classes and as a way to gauge the students' learning and involvement. In addition, students were frequently asked to write at the beginning of class to prompt their participation in class discussions. Again, this allowed the students to voice their ideas, bringing their knowledge and experience into the classroom through a modality other than speaking aloud.

For instance, in order to introduce students to how the U.S. Constitution was written in multiple drafts, Marta began class with the prompt: "Write about a time you made a mistake but you feel you learned from it and won't make the mistake again." After a broad-ranging discussion, she connected the students' stories to the process of writing the Constitution, explaining that the U.S. Constitution was a second attempt. When she asked students to write about controversial issues such as "Should welfare be cut off for teenagers?" or "Should abortion be legalized?" Marta often collected the logs, typed up a range of responses without the students' names, and then used those responses to foster discussion during the following class. Her teaching included simulations that required students to work together in groups, including de-bates of Supreme Court cases and a mock hearing about the Bill of Rights. In addition, there was a senior project involving several written and oral components that the students worked on in their English and social studies classes toward the end of the year.

I spent 3 to 5 days a week in two senior government classes and, once a week, attended an advisory period and English class with the same students. I ate lunch with students and attended activities and meetings after school; occasionally I met with students at their homes and in community centers. As my original questions centered on the literacy practices of adolescent women, the initial 12 focal students of the study were all female students whose participation in the school reflected the range of engagement in school exhibited by their female classmates. Six of these students identified as African American, three as Mexican American or Latina, and three as Asian American or Pacific Islander. All were low-income and eligible for free and reduced lunch from their school.[2] During the second year, the focus was on a group of 12 students out of the original sample, ten female and two male, who had graduated from high school and were working or looking for a job, attending community college, or vocational school. I observed them regularly at community colleges, in vocational and job-training programs such as a beauty school, and in their jobs at youth centers, data-processing centers, and grocery stores (cf. Schultz, 1996, 1999, 2002).

In this chapter, I draw on findings from across the data set to focus how listening to students' lives in social, cultural, and community contexts can inform the pedagogy and content of classroom teaching. Whereas Chapters 2 and 3 focus on teachers' practices and the ways in which teachers developed a pedagogy based on listening to students, this chapter and the next focus on the students themselves and what might be learned about the relationship between listening and teaching through an examination of students' talk. To highlight the complexity of listening to the larger contexts of students' lives through their writing, I posit two dilemmas: How can teachers invite students to write about their lives when their texts might contain content that is inappropriate for school, and how can teachers account for students' private writing in the public space of the classroom? I assert that in spite of these challenges, if we are to envision learning as extending beyond students' hours in school, then listening that responds to students' practices and identities from out-of-school contexts is critical.

THE FIRST DILEMMA: CENSORSHIP AND SCHOOL TOPICS

When teachers invite students to bring stories of their own lives into school, they may hear about events and topics that are difficult or inappropriate, depending on the age of the student. How does a teacher listen to the broader contexts of students' lives by asking them to write about their home lives, while at the same time maintaining a classroom atmosphere that is safe for all students? This question raises several related ones: What if students write about topics that the teacher deems inappropriate for school? Who decides on appropriateness? Should a teacher limit or control the topics and language students use in their writing? How can teachers recognize and acknowledge writing about controversial topics as a promising practice without necessarily incorporating it into the official discourse of school? Finally, if we agree that most people do their best writing when it is honest and close to the bone, how can we bring that authenticity into the classroom?

One risk of inviting students to bring their home and community experiences into school, in order that we may listen more broadly to their lives, is that it puts teachers in the position of deciding what topics and language are appropriate for school and what to do with information that might put them in difficult or compromising positions. This dilemma is particularly salient for young or inexperienced student teachers. If teachers open up their curriculum to students' out-of-school experiences, then they are ceding a measure of control to students. Parents, colleagues, and administrators, as well as other students, might be uncomfortable with the discussion of particular topics, such as drugs or sexuality, whether in writing or through class discussion. On the other hand, by failing to listen to these dimensions of students' lives, teachers may have a limited understanding of students' capacities. In this section, a focus on Luis, a high school student who considered himself Latino or Mexican, and wrote poetry outside of school, illustrates this dilemma.

Luis

Luis was essentially born into a Mexican gang. His father, brothers, and extended family members all belonged to the same gang. The chief task of the gang was to protect his neighborhood block. As he explained, "I didn't gangbang because people told me to do it. I did it because I care for my neighborhood. I'm down for my street. I'll love it until the day I die" (interview, 12/13/94). At an early age, Luis learned to make drug deals and keep up with the gang activity on his block, reporting that he earned hundreds of dollars a day. Later, as a teenager, during countless evenings, he sat alone in his car waiting to make a sale and writing poetry. He explained that he wrote to stay alive. His poetry was about the deep conflicts and emotions he experienced growing up. It helped him to express himself and keep a perspective on his life. His poetry also described illegal activities, such as the drug dealing and gangbanging, and was often sexually explicit.

One day Luis was at a party with a close friend and fellow gang member. Members from a rival gang showed up at the party and shot his friend. At that moment Luis decided to leave the gang. In his negotiations with the gang leader, the leader readily agreed to let him sever his connections—a rare decision. The leader explained his actions by declaring that Luis was someone who would be able to turn himself around and make it on the outside. Although Luis continued to wear the colors of his gang, he changed his lifestyle and began to work at a gang prevention center with younger children and adolescents from his neighborhood. Luis also began to work harder in school. Suddenly high school graduation was a possibility. He continued to write poetry.

Although Luis only wrote poetry outside of school, he explained that his writing had its origins in one of his classes. In 10th grade a teacher had introduced the students to poetry through the study of the musical genre of the blues. Even though most students had dismissed the teacher as young and hopelessly naive, her ideas and the study of music as poetry struck a chord for Luis. This writing gave him a way to express what he saw in the world. After 10th grade, he continued to write poetry and occasionally showed it to his mother and girlfriend. Although Luis carried a couple of poems around school under the clear cover of his notebook, it did not occur to him to show the poetry to his teachers. He kept most of his poems in his bedroom, tucked between CDs and tapes on his bookshelf in a manila folder. His mother submitted one of his poems to a church newsletter, where it was published in English and Spanish. This same poem, about the meaning of love, was published in the newsletter of a youth center where he worked during his senior year in high school.

LOVE, A WORD I NEVER UNDERSTOOD

I thought it meant money, from the words of my father. I found out later it was the misery of my father.
I wanted to ask my brothers and sister for an answer; as I entered the room of cries, I found sadness running down their eyes.
I turned to my friends for love, only to find out it was a joke to them all.
I cried to the Lord for love, and heard nothing from above.
I roamed the streets looking for my answer, just to enter darkness with all the gangsters.

This poem captures the dark side of Luis's life. It describes the hopelessness he often experienced. His use of vivid images to display emotions is markedly different from his school writing. His writing for school was generally short, straightforward, and with minimum detail. His teachers knew Luis to hold strong opinions, yet because they did not see his poetry, they did not have access to the more reflective and artistic renditions of these opinions.

Despite his professed determination to graduate, Luis continued to miss school and assignments. It may have been Luis's need to start a new life and reengage in school after leaving his gang that kept him from writing poems during school and from showing these poems composed at home to his teachers. He chose to maintain and respect the divide between home and school. When I asked him about this, he shrugged and indicated he was primarily interested in getting by in school.

Later I asked Luis what inspired him to write poetry. He replied:

> But I really just wrote what I seen in the streets. What happened, how I felt, and what I seen in the streets. How I really, how I felt in seeing the streets, I seen. I really never knew how to spell real good, but I still, to this day, I don't know how to spell real good or what really, what big words means to this day, again. I learned a lot in 12th grade, but I don't know, back in those days, there was, just like I said, if the teachers ain't fun, they just boring, they don't have, they disrespect you, how you going to learn?
>
> (interview, 12/13/94)

Like his peers, Luis frequently made negative comments about his teachers, tying these observations to his sense of himself as a writer. He gave a brief explanation of where he found inspiration for his poems, which immediately led to the contrast between his street world and his experiences in school.

I talked with Luis about his passion for writing and his difficulty in school. I wanted to know more about his understandings of the possible connections between school and home writing, and his perceptions of himself as a writer. I sought to comprehend how he explained his struggles at school and his confidence as a poet outside of school.

> KS: So how do you explain [the fact] that you clearly are such a good writer and that you couldn't pass English?
>
> Luis: I don't know. It's just so much things, so many things that I see in life, my family, every, other people's family, everybody, other people's hurt and my family's hurt that I just put everything together. My way to express how I felt was to write. I really started like this. I was just so mad or I was just sad and all that and I just started thinking in my head, real, real good sentences. I said, "God damn, man. Maybe I'll write this down." I started just writing it down.
>
> (interview, 6/13/94)

Luis described the role of writing in his life, explaining that he used it as a means to express his intense feelings. He remembered the genesis of some of his writing and the thoughts and feelings he had as he wrote. He did not, however, account for the apparent disjuncture between his writing outside of school, which was fluent and powerful, and his school writing and participation in class, which were often more reluctant and faltering.

Luis informed me that the first poem he wrote was for his brother, who never had the chance to read it because he went to jail for 11 years. The poem follows:

IN THE RAIN

1. Can't you see I'm in the rain
Can't you hear me calling your name.
You look at me
With so much pain
I'm out here with the rain

2. Look at me I'm not afraid.
I'm out here getting paid.

This simple poem describes Luis's life before he left his gang and quit selling drugs. In it, Luis uses writing to reflect on his own life and that of his family, which included illegal activities such as dealing drugs. This poem reflects his sadness. He uses the poem to step outside of himself to take a critical stance toward his position in society. In the first stanza, he reaches out to his brother, asking him to notice him; in the second, he claims to be unafraid. His statement that he is unafraid seems to be written with a false bravado; with his brother in prison, the consequences of these choices are clear. This knowledge engenders irony or a critical stance. Evidence for this interpretation is Luis's decision, shortly after writing the poem, to extricate himself from the gang.

The critical stance in these poems is similar to the approach Luis's teachers wanted their students to assume in reading and writing school texts. However, one of the many questions his teachers faced in school was how and whether to allow this discussion of an illegal activity. In addition, the teachers were challenged to help Luis think about his multiple identities, including that of writer. Although this poem, set in the past, is not explicit about how he sold drugs, it raises questions about what a teacher might do with writing set in the present that describes or mentions illicit activities.

Luis also wrote powerful and explicit poems about his girlfriend and their sexual relations. His writing is urgent, displaying intense feelings. The poems convey an intimacy that may not be appropriate for school. How can a teacher encourage this writing without necessarily inviting the author to make it public? Some poems Luis wrote were filled with curses. These words weren't gratuitous, yet they would make some teachers uncomfortable. Taken together, these writings illustrate one aspect of his learning during the time he was in school. Without access to Luis's writing and life, teachers missed opportunities for conversations, their understandings of his capacities eclipsed.

One day, after reading about the Aztecs and the colonization and destruction of the culture by the Spaniards, Luis wrote a poem titled "God Bless America." A program on a Mexican radio station sparked his interest in learning about the Aztec Indians. He convinced his father to tell him stories he had learned growing up in Mexico, stories his father had avoided in the past. After learning as much as possible from his father, Luis searched for books on the topic. He read every book he could find and became angry in reaction to what he read. His poem, written in response to these events, was filled with irony. The poem combines social critique with his developing cultural awareness.

God Bless America

God bless America for all she did for us . . .
Robbed us like the thief of the night,
Killed and took the land of Aztlan

God bless America for what she did for us?
The White man has raped our beautiful women, killed our warriors,
and burned our land. And now you say "Thank you?"

To whom you say thank you, is it the White man who killed our great grand-
fathers and grandmothers—who once were kings and queens who ruled our
land?

Indios, so beautiful and strong. I once was a king covered with gold, eating the
fruits of my land—all so sweet and tasteful.

As I walked the streets of gold, I vanished forever.

Now I walk the ghettos!

In this poem Luis wrote about a topic he had never studied in school. He often mentioned his frustration that this aspect of his culture and identity was omitted from the school curriculum. In this poem he positions himself as a social critic and writes with confidence rarely displayed in his school writing.

Luis explained the genesis and context of the poem. One day during the same time period that he was reading about the destruction of the Aztec and

Mayan civilizations, Luis was stopped by a police officer because his car had no lights. He felt obligated to say "thank you" to the police officer because he was scared the officials might open his trunk and send him to jail for its contents. He connected this acquiescent stance to the oppression he had experienced as a Mexican American and recent immigrant in the United States. As he explained:

> So when I was writing this poem I had a million things going through my mind. But I got the most important one. So this is why I got this. The White man has raped our beautiful women and killed our warriors and burnt our land. And now you say "thank you." So when I got that ticket, it was like I'm telling him "thank you" and all. So that's when I said, I'm never going to say "thank you" to no cops and I haven't.
>
> (interview, 1/19/95)

Listening to Luis as a Social Critic and a Poet

In this poem, Luis used knowledge gained from reading widely on his own to author a critical piece about the inequities he had experienced. It reflects social and political insights and critique. It was a piece of writing that he shared with his family and friends, but rarely his teachers. Neither he nor his teachers made the connection between the critical stance in this poem and the ways of reading and writing he was learning in school.

Writing enabled Luis to develop a critical lens that he occasionally applied to school discussions, though rarely to school writing. At the same time Luis wrote poetry that analyzed power and institutions and reflected on his own difficult life choices, he struggled to pass each class and graduate. Although he occasionally contributed to class discussions with a clear and critical voice and wrote short papers that got to the heart of issues, his most passionate and personally meaningful writing was done at home beyond the purview of his teacher. For example, in response to his social studies teacher's question about a mistake students had made and learned from, described in the introduction to this chapter, Luis wrote the following paragraph during class.

> One mistake that I learned from was for me not to trust [those] who talk to talkers?
>
> I learned from this mistake because I trusted someone that talk with out wisdom. That person would just talk and not listen. I thought I could trust that person. Because I knew that person all my life. But I found out later I was [w]rong!
>
> [10/12/93]

The prior week, in a more controversial response, Luis commented on a class discussion.

> What was most interesting to me today was that 30 years ago Black people took a lot of jobs. But now that other races are taking jobs. The Black people are getting mad of this? Why should they act like this if they were in the same place at a time?
>
> [10/7/93]

In these journal entries Luis raises authentic questions and addresses issues that concern him. However, the school writing is strikingly different from his poetry for a number of reasons. The length of the writing is shorter than in his poems and does not contain the detail and elaborated images of his poetry. Whereas school assignments were often written under time constraints, his writing out of school reflected a longer time frame and perhaps a stronger commitment to write for his own purposes and chosen audience. Luis wrote these school essays in response to teacher assignments; the poems were born out of his own desire to express his beliefs and articulate his experiences. He did not seem to translate his ability to use language to craft critical arguments, which is so apparent in his poetry, to his expository writing in school.

At times Luis identified as a poet and made that part of his identity public. When Luis Rodriguez, the poet and social activist, visited the school, Luis talked to this older, former gang leader about his poetry. Rodriguez listened with interest. Later, Luis read Rodriguez's books. However, his temporary identity as a poet did not carry over to his sense of himself as a student. He always felt on the brink of failing and did not believe that he had actually graduated until he saw the piece of paper. It was only then that he breathed a sigh of relief and celebrated.

How could his teacher, Marta, have listened to Luis in such a way that he might have identified as a poet at school? Delpit (1986, 1988) makes a convincing argument that low-income students of color don't need to practice writing forms like rap that are familiar to them. Instead, they need to learn the culture of power, which includes the use of formal language. I agree with Delpit and add that although teachers have the obligation to teach students the knowledge and skills they need for their future lives, teachers must also listen for, recognize, and build on the students' serious talents and passions outside of school. I suggest that it is not enough to bring interests into the school curriculum. Rather, teachers need to learn about and engage with students' learning and practices that take place outside of the school day.

For instance, even if his teachers did not read his poetry or chose not to acknowledge poems with violent or sexually explicit content, or those referring to illegal activities, just the knowledge that Luis wrote poetry and considered himself a poet would change how his teachers taught him—their pedagogy and curriculum. They could listen to him as a poet, acknowledging his writing practices (that as a poet, he composed poetry outside of school), without always reading the texts themselves. The teachers did not have to teach a poetry unit to count this writing in their larger assessment of Luis as a writer and learner. Instead, they could use it to broaden their notions of school writing and their understandings of students as writers to include their work outside of the classroom. In response to the question of what teachers should do with poems written out of school that may be inappropriate for the classroom, I encourage teachers to listen to learn about students' identities in relation to learning in and out of school. Knowing how they perceive themselves as learners—whether working on cars, designing websites, coaching young children, or writing poetry—gives teachers a broader understanding of their students as a basis for teaching them. Listening to Luis's poetry—how he perceived the world as a poet, and the role poetry played in his life—could have shifted his teachers' conception and assessment of him as a student and learner.

THE SECOND DILEMMA: MAKING THE PRIVATE PUBLIC

KS (interviewer): Do you do any kind of reading and writing at home?
Ellen (high school senior and mother): Um yeah, I—this is embarrassing, but um I have a book. It's like a little, let's say it might be a diary.

(interview, 10/6/93)

Students I spoke with were often reluctant to talk about their writing outside of school. This writing was often private; they worried that their peers would learn of this practice and accuse them of taking school seriously. These notions of privacy and the reluctance to identify as a writer led me to the second dilemma: How does a teacher listen for a student's private writing practices in order to construct a fuller, more nuanced picture of that student, yet respect the student's desire for the practice to remain hidden? Teachers may not want to co-opt students' writing by asking them to bring it into school. How can they listen for and acknowledge the existence of this private writing without necessarily reading it, using it as a basis for their own knowledge and understanding of their students? What does it mean to listen to students' writing out of school without learning about the details? What are the possibilities and limitations of this teaching decision?

Ellen

As illustrated in the short exchange with Ellen, students were often hesitant to take on the identity of a writer. It was rarely considered "cool" to publicly engage in school practices. Despite their reluctance to engage in school writing, however, nearly half the students I spoke with turned to writing after school hours, often to make sense of the conflicting and complicated events of their lives. Most, like Ellen, hid this practice and rarely mentioned it, especially to peers. An African American student who was alternatively engaged and disengaged in school, Ellen kept two kinds of diaries: one public and one private. Neither was directly associated with school, although at times Ellen brought each into the classroom.

When Ellen was pregnant with her first child in 11th grade, her mother encouraged her to begin writing in a diary. Afraid that her daughter might follow her own pattern of turning to alcohol and drugs in times of extreme stress, Ellen's mother counseled her to write down her feelings and secrets in a diary. She had witnessed the importance of writing in her own life and passed along this knowledge to her daughter.

On her own, Ellen began two diaries. Labeled "writing for myself," the first contained her most private reflections on her life. When Ellen was pregnant, her boyfriend—or, as she more often referred to him, her baby's father—was in and out of prison and their relationship was tumultuous. Ellen confided that she wrote in her private diary every night so that her son would have a record of their life together. Like her mother, she used this diary to cope with the daily stress of her life. Her second diary was her public diary, which, on occasion, she showed to her family and close friends. Once or twice she brought this diary to school. She used it to write about her daily life, her dreams and plans for the future. She also used it to collect artifacts from home and school. She called this her "writing for society" (interview, 7/8/94).

In my initial interview with Ellen, quoted briefly at the start of this section, she told me about her public diary. We spoke about her plans for the year following her graduation from high school. Our conversation continued as I asked Ellen about her reading and writing practices.

> A lot of things happened in my life once I got pregnant. A lot of things changed, a lot of people changed, and I just wrote down everything that happened to me. Everything I did. You know what I'm saying? All my innermost thoughts. When my father got sick with cancer, everything, what he was going through, things like that. And uh, I write it, and everything, and after I write it I go back and I read it and stuff. My mom told me I could make a book. "Just keep it, Ellen, you know, get over it and you can write a book about it. You know, get over on it." And that's

the only really writing I do. Everything that happens to me. Like, today, I write in my little book, "I had a interview." Like that, uh, how I feel and stuff, that's, mostly um, what I write.

(interview, 10/6/93)

I was interested to learn about Ellen's writing and also the reasons for her embarrassment about keeping a diary. In my interviews with other female students in this school, many confessed to me that they wrote in diaries, quickly adding that they told few people about this private practice. I asked Ellen to explain her feelings about her diary writing.

> *KS*: So, back to the writing. Why are you embarrassed to tell me that you have this diary?
>
> *Ellen*: Because, I don't . . . well . . . it's sorta like stuff, 'cause like people try to stereotype people. You know what I'm saying? And they always like, "Oh, she's bad for writing this." "Oh, she's such a good person for writing it." All I know, ain't nobody seen my book. 'Cause there's things that go through a person's mind that trips me out.

(interview, 10/6/93)

I'm not sure I fully understand why Ellen and her peers were ashamed of their writing. This out-of-school writing often did not figure into students' conceptions of themselves as writers at school, even though they occasionally brought the journals or diaries to school and shared them with peers. They thought of themselves as people who hated to write, ignoring the writing they did outside of the school walls. Ellen and her peers may have been hiding their interest in writing for fear of "perpetrating"—their term for acting better than everyone else—or they may simply have thought of writing as a private rather than a public act.

Later in the interview, Ellen explained what writing in a diary meant to her. She connected her writing to a discussion she had had with her father on his deathbed. Her father fought in the Vietnam War and, as she explained to me, had kept things "bottled in." She speculated that this had made his time after the war more difficult and may have been related to his prolonged illness. In keeping a diary, she seemed to be choosing between her mother's decision to write and her father's silence. Ellen talked about the importance of writing about feelings and events so they were off her mind. She explained that she began one diary the day she discovered that she was pregnant. The only person she showed this diary to was her best friend, whom she sometimes referred to as her "cousin." Her narrative of how she started to write in a diary began this way:

I just sat down and I was writing a letter. I started out writing a letter. Wasn't addressed to nowhere, I just started writing a letter. And I said, "You know, I ought put this in a book." And then I, um, after I had went to summer school, um um, because I, you usually just take a piece a paper, take a piece of paper. And I went to summer school and I just jotted it all down in a book.

(interview, 10/8/93)

Ellen described her initiation as a diary writer without making a connection to school, which was an event in her writing rather than the motivation behind it.

I was curious to understand why Ellen kept two diaries and pressed her on that issue.

Ellen: 'Cause in one of them you have to keep, in one of them you have to keep all of your um letters in, and, poetry that you write at school and your little print outs on the computer.

KS: So what gave you the idea to have two different journals, two different diaries?

Ellen: My mama got three.

KS: Really?

Ellen: Yeah, and she gave me a book, that she used to write one of hers in and uh. . . . She said here you can have this one. Because my mom (whispers) used to be a drug addict. [*KS*: Uh-huh.] And she wrote down everything that happened. All the bad stuff from I got to go get a hit to I'm gonna, I'm gonna, straighten up. That's what she said, I really want some crack, I'm going to smoke a cigarette. And she let me read the whole thing. 'Cause I wasn't around her. I was where my daddy at. Do you remember? [*KS*: Uh-hmm.] So, um, I read it and I was like, that's a good thing to do. But you know, if you ever, this is the best way to keep up with your thoughts. Because you forget things. If you ever want to go back, you can, I know you did this to me or I know what I been through and don't tell me. You go and get your book and whip it out and people be like whoa. You don't know what you're thinking at that time. Anything ever gets heavy in my mind, I whip it out in a minute. Just get to writing.

(interview, 10/3/93)

Like her mother, Ellen used one diary to reflect on and cope with the stresses in her life; she used the other as a record. I remained interested in how she chose when to write in each diary. Although one seemed more private and the other more public, their uses and audiences were somewhat blurred. For instance, her private diary was a record for her son and included tales of the men in her life, as Ellen explained:

KS: But how do you decide whether to write in this one or in that other one?

Ellen: This one [with a lock] is intimate. Right. This is a Neville [the baby's father] book. (laughs) This is the men in my life book. This is, has to do with my love life. The other one has to do with society, has to do with job[s], has to do with school, has to do with money, you know. Because you shouldn't mix those two together, you know? When my son gets older, I'm going to let him know, whatever you feel, you can either talk to me, or write it out. It feels good when you write it out. You noticed when I was reading to you. I was reading, you could tell how, I was really thinking, what I was writing. Yeah. And it's good when people do that. And they, my mom could write a book on her. She could really write about a 30-page book on her experiences with drugs and alcohol and could sell that book. Just by, from what she was thinking. And how society treat her. Society can mess you up. It can. And it's good to be able to, that's my quiet time. Just to be able to sit down and write it up.

(interview, 7/8/94)

Ellen pointed out the many benefits of her diaries. She made sure that I noticed the quality of her voice and her engagement with the text while she read to me from one of them. She used the diaries to separate her life into private and public spaces. It was interesting that as someone who joined her friends in resisting writing at school, she had constructed an unusual system of journal writing at home. She never saw a reason to mention this writing to her teachers.

The Private/Public Divide Between Home and School Writing

Throughout the year that I worked with Ellen and her peers, I learned of the various ways in which students had developed writing lives at home. Many did not publicly admit to this writing, nor did they see it as related to their identities as students in school. Unlike the writing described by other researchers (e.g., Camitta, 1993; Fiering, 1981; Finders, 1997; Moje, 2000; Shuman, 1986, 1993), this was not oppositional writing or writing performed in groups; it was simply separate from school. Other researchers have observed various forms of out-of-school literacies, including Heath's (e.g., 1994,

1998a, 1998b) recent studies of youth involvement in arts-related after-school programs (cf. Hull & Schultz, 2002). In some cases, teachers make efforts to incorporate students' out-of-school writing or literacy practices into the school curriculum (e.g., Dyson, 1997, 1999), and in other instances, the writing remains in the private domain.

This public/private split mirrors the separation of writing in and out of school. Although she did not give this explanation, the split between school and home worlds may have helped Ellen to make the distinctions between her two diaries, at the same time that the diaries themselves bridged both worlds. Her public diary contained writing from school and also letters she had received from friends and relatives. Although her private diary contained her secrets and the details of her relationships outside of school, she also used it to record the intrigues that occurred during the school day. Together they were a composite record of her life.

Ellen's teachers, including Marta and an English teacher, Diane, attempted to make these connections and gave students opportunities to write about issues that mattered to them. Ellen chose alcoholism as the topic for her senior project. It was a topic that held personal interest to her because of her own family history. She also wrote about friendship in an essay that hung on her English classroom wall for much of the year. It was the longest piece she composed at school other than her senior project.

FRIENDS! FRIENDS! FRIENDS!
    To all of those best friends out there. I have something very special to say. NEVER, NEVER, let "nothing" break up your friendship. Friends are supposed to love one another and be there for one another. Never get jealous, or be rude, or get foul towards one another. Let me tell you something if you have a friend like that. Let me tell you that backstabbing B!@#* is not the friend you were looking for. Don't get me wrong, it could be a boy or a girl. You need someone who is just as crazy as you, or just as even minded as you. People, what you don't need is,

    #1   JEALOUSY
    #2   PUT DOWNS
    #3   LAST BUT NOT LEAST—IMMATURITY

    People these things are the most important things that two friends sometimes go through. If you can't get through the easy things, then you damn sure couldn't get through the hard things. If you find yourself in something like this, GET OUT OF IT! YOU DON'T NEED IT! YOU DESERVE BETTER!!!!!!!

This essay grew out of Ellen's personal and social experiences and addressed a topic that was both important and consuming for her as a high school student. The writing is conversational in tone, yet it is missing an emotional dimension. Ellen's voice and perspective are clear in this piece; the drama in her actual friendships is absent. Although teachers made topical connections between home and school, they did not often listen closely enough to build on students' writing practices outside of school, such as Ellen's habit of writing daily in her diaries. In school she wrote about topics that had meaning to her; however, she did not carry the practice of using writing to make sense of her life from home to school.

The challenge for teachers is not necessarily whether or how to listen to learn about particular pieces of writing or texts. Rather, teachers can listen for instances of learning reflected in these practices and persuade Ellen and her peers that they are learners and writers in school and at home. Unlike Luis and some other students, over the course of the year Ellen never considered herself a writer. She saw her diaries as connected neither to school nor to her identity or abilities as a writer. Although we know that school writing should not be the only kind of writing that "counts," we also know that most students assume that it is. Teachers can listen closely enough to their students' practices, even if they are private practices, to help them see connections to school and reframe their identities as learners in school and beyond.

Toward the end of the school year, most seniors purchased a copy of the school yearbook. They carried these books to each of their classes, surreptitiously passing them to each other to get signatures. Although students wrote long and often thoughtful notes in each other's yearbooks, many refused to write essays about the books they read in class. Others claimed to hate writing. I do not suggest that these genres or formats for writing are the same or even similar. Instead, I wonder how a teacher can listen to students to draw on the passion for reflecting and interacting through writing that students often display outside of school assignments.

The hybrid nature of Ellen's public and private diaries suggests that students might not neatly divide up their learning and literacy between home and school. By listening to students' lives, and engaging their peers in this conversation, teachers might devise ways to convince them to take on identities as writers as they move back and forth across the boundaries of the different worlds they inhabit. For instance, teachers might listen for the writing and learning students do out of school to find connections with school projects. Either teachers can believe that students like Ellen hate to write, or they can reframe writing or literate identities in school to acknowledge that students can claim to hate writing at the same time they gravitate toward this activity. Listening for students' learning outside of school will help teachers to construct a larger and more nuanced picture of their students. Even more important, this type of listening will help teachers articulate these practices to their students, enabling the students to take on new identities as learners.

One response to the dilemma of how to keep practices private while acknowledging them in school lies in focusing on the practice of writing or learning rather than on the actual product of these activities. Thus, if teachers listen to learn all of the ways that students are engaged in learning outside of the context of school—be it writing in private diaries or writing to care for their child—they can focus on the students' identities as learners—as writers and caregivers—rather than on the details of their learning. The assessment methods most commonly used in schools—including more authentic forms such as portfolios—limit visions of students to the work accomplished under the teacher's purview in school. This limitation puts many students at disadvantage. If the conception of students' capacities is broadened to include their learning outside of school, assessment procedures will change and teachers will listen more broadly to the stories of their students' lives.

BRINGING OUTSIDE WRITING INTO THE SCHOOL CURRICULUM

Like Luis and Ellen, many students kept school and out-of-school writing practices separate. Denise's case illustrates a contrasting instance, in which a student used her writing out of school to form a bridge to a school assignment and, in the process, claim the identity of a writer. This case suggests how teachers can listen for the possibilities for incorporating out-of-school writing into school, even for reluctant participants in classroom life.

Denise

Denise, an African American student in this high school, enacted a resistant stance toward school. If she did not like or agree with an assignment or project, she simply refused to engage in the activity. She was particularly insistent that she would not participate in public performances. In fact, she felt strongly enough about this position that she led a large protest that culminated in a sit-down strike against newly instituted senior projects that included a performance component to assess the students.

In the course of our work together, Denise reluctantly showed me her writing. First, she showed me poems and, later, a long play written for a favorite middle-school teacher who worked in an after-school program that her brother attended. The play, entitled "Gangsta Lean" after a rap that was popular at the time, was based on an actual event in Denise's own life: the shooting death of her cousin in a drug-related incident at a dice game. The script also included a poem Denise wrote at the time of her grandmother's death. Denise cast her brother in her cousin's role, and she named and modeled the sister after herself. With my encouragement, Denise showed the play to her drama teacher, who produced it with the only drama class in the school. Local actors worked with the teacher and students on the performance. Denise kept her distance during the play practices and only stepped forward at the final evening performance to receive flowers.

During the fall of her senior year, Denise's teachers had introduced a senior project that included research in the community and the library, work with outside mentors, and a public presentation. Denise and some of her peers were angry when they learned of this project, feeling that this new requirement was imposed on them at the last minute during their final year of high school. They saw it as yet another barrier to graduation rather than as the authentic learning experience their teachers envisioned. Denise was shy and resisted performing in public. She claimed that she would make the choice not to graduate if forced to comply with the public performance requirement of the project. A group of student leaders met with the principal and a team of teachers to work out a compromise. Most students were satisfied with the new form of the project, which became an in-class assignment for their English and social studies classes. Denise alone remained dissatisfied because of the requirement for a public performance. For weeks, Denise held her ground and sat apart from the rest of the class during work periods, refusing to participate in the project.

Although her initial plan was to boycott the senior project, after the performance of her play, Denise seemed to link her work as a writer of poetry and plays at home to her identity as a writer at school. When her teachers pointed out that she could use this play as her senior project, she began work on this step toward graduation. However, when it came time to present her project, once again she refused to participate in a public performance. She calculated that she could graduate without completing that portion of the project. The teachers listened to her hesitancy and, knowing her well as a student, crafted an alternative. She, in turn, listened to and responded to the solution they devised. Rather than present her senior project to a panel of teachers, community members, and students, Denise was allowed to make an audiotape for her teachers that described her experience writing the play. On the tape she spoke these words that describe the role of writing in her life:

> Growing up in [our city.] Me, my mother, and my brothers. It wasn't easy. It's not easy. And it ain't going to be easy. Every time I walk home from school, I don't feel safe. Not at all. I start to think of my family and all the friends I have seen killed, that have been killed. And I also think about the one that might be killed. When a car goes past me, my neck shrugs as if I am going to be shot. It's a terrible, terrible

feeling. People ask me what I think about what's going on in the world today. Sometimes I don't answer, but others, I cry and I say, the world is just hell on earth. But every day I leave my house telling my mother I love her because I don't know whether I'll see her again. This world is a world of fear and hate. That is what led me to be a writer.

While writing I don't feel nothing. I don't think about nothing, I don't hear nothing. All I think about is writing. If I don't write, all I think about is the deaths in the world today. So to keep my mind off of that, I write. It's not easy to be a writer. You have to have your mind set on being a writer. You have to know how to write. It's a lot of have to's in the world today.

Writing my play was not quite easy. When I was writing my play, all I thought about was my play and how it was going to come out. I made the mistake of letting people help me. And when I did that I had to go back and rewrite it. But that's all right. Writers have to go through things like that. Some writers have to go over their formats a million times. When writing a play popped into my mind, all I thought about was the painful things that I see in the world today. So I started to write about one. Which was of my cousin [Billy]. So, I started to write. And I couldn't stop. It felt like I was being trapped. I was being held captive. And believe me, I know what that feels like.

(senior project tape, June 1994)

Denise used writing to both describe and escape the present. After Denise refused to stand up in front of others to speak about the process of writing her play, she made this tape about her life, her writing process, and herself as a writer. This intensely personal writing and her discussion of writing about her play allowed her to bridge her home and school worlds. She chose the format—a tape made on her own at home—to convey these feelings and knowledge to an outside and public audience. Although she claimed not to care whether she graduated, the tape about her experience as a writer and the role of writing in her life reflects a serious and thoughtful tone that indicates her willingness to embrace this opportunity.

Most often Denise claimed not to be a writer; she said that she had no interest in pursuing writing in her future. She resisted efforts that others made to help her pursue these talents. However, toward the end of the year, in an essay on American dramatists, the required companion piece to her play for her senior project, she took on the identity of a writer. Denise wrote:

As a young American writer I am not known to write a lot but if I sat down for a whole day with nothing else to do, I would write until my hands fall off. I admire Langston Hughes mostly because of his abilities and efforts to sit down and try to make young Americans write more often. The world would be a better place if we had a lot more dramatists than we do because Drama is based on reality. The meaning of drama to me is to show your feelings, to make people see what the world is today. I think more people would write if they knew what it could get them and what results would come out of writing.

Among the many activities that Denise resisted in school was a display of her feelings. Yet her tape, her play, her poems, and this essay are packed with emotion. Even though Denise was a reluctant speaker, her teachers were able to listen to her interests and capacities through her writing out of school. They allowed her to use this writing to graduate from high school. Denise attended school in a troubled and troubling world, and through her infrequent writing she shared her fears. Unlike the out-of-school writing documented by other researchers (e.g., Camitta, 1993; Finders, 1997; Heath, 1998a; Moje, 2000; Shuman, 1986), her writing was solitary and reflected her own struggles to address her current predicament.

Despite the distance Denise attempted to maintain from her teachers and school, Marta, Diane, and Denise's other teachers found ways to listen closely and respond to Denise's worlds outside of school. The school's drama teacher took her play seriously enough to stage a performance. She was patient with Denise and let her stand apart from the performance until the final moments. She was able to read how Denise wanted to be involved in this event. This careful listening was respectful and affirming at the same time. Denise was a talented individual, but she rarely displayed those talents in public settings. Her teachers devised ways to make her work public, while allowing her to retain her privacy.

Initially, when Denise refused to complete her senior project, Marta and her English teacher, Diane, acknowledged her stance but continued to press her to participate. Behind her protests to the contrary, they heard that she was interested in graduating on her own terms. Without compromising their own standards and integrity, they worked with Denise to find a way for her to complete the project to everyone's satisfaction. Denise felt heard, and she complied, exceeding their expectations in the emotional involvement she brought to the project. They listened to Denise, posed an alternative, and gave her the time and space to come to her own decision. Listening requires action and also, at times, inaction or waiting, so that the person being heard can respond on her own terms.

By bridging her world with the world of school and bringing her work into the school curriculum, Denise's teachers were able to hear Denise in new ways and support her growing sense of a writer's identity. For this moment at least, Denise took on the mantle of a writer. Buoyed by the surprising success of her play, she wrote about herself as a dramatist and began to value her writing anew. Ironically, it was a public performance of Denise's work that affirmed this identity.

AFTER GRADUATION

Although the story of Denise's play and last minute engagement in school might be considered a success, it was not enough. After graduation from high school, like Luis and Ellen, Denise reported to me that she no longer wrote. All three of these students claimed that their lives were filled with work and, in some cases, children. They confided that they were no longer engaged in writing poetry, keeping diaries, or producing plays. This finding caused me to question what it was about being in school that supported students to write at home and in the community, even if that writing was not counted or brought into school. One possible explanation is that while in high school, these adolescents might have been particularly self-reflective and that writing could have seemed more necessary or accessible to them.

If one goal of schooling is to develop "habits of mind" (e.g., Dewey, 1902/ 1956; Meier, 1996) or an intellectual aliveness (Lyne, personal communication, 1/20/00) such that people pursue interests and learning beyond their years in school, then as educators, we might listen for new forms of engagement beyond writing. After their high school graduation, when I asked the students if they were still writing, they all replied that they hadn't recently found time for that activity. Now I wonder if I asked the right question. More significant, I wonder if I listened carefully enough to their responses for a broader conception of literate activities. In my framing of the question in terms of writing, what literacies did I fail to learn about that therefore remained outside my field of vision?

It seems critical for teachers to listen not only for the writing a student is doing outside of school but also for ways students continue to learn past their experience with formal education. In order for teachers to accomplish this form of listening, it is critical that they construct an image of a student as a learner outside of school categories. For instance, when I talked with students about their out-of-school literacy practices, they mostly talked about school-like literacy activities. What other evidence of learning could I have discovered if I had broadened my scope of what counts as literacy? How might a teacher incorporate this same vision of literacy in her knowledge of students? How could this knowledge of literacy learning spill over to a broader picture of the student as a learner? Finally, how can a teacher listen to students long and hard enough in order to know how to reach them past their time in school?

It is understandable that students will often invest more of themselves in their learning and writing outside of school. If teachers acknowledge the importance of taking a critical stance toward texts and events, personal writing may become a resource for their teaching. In addition to building curriculum from students' interests in particular topics, a focus on listening to students' practices might help teachers to transform curriculum to incorporate and reflect home and community learning. For instance, a teacher might use Ellen's notion of public and private diaries to reimagine the genres of writing in a classroom. Luis's habit of writing poetry to understand his life could be used as a tool or a bridge to understanding difficult school texts through a critical lens. Denise's performance pieces might provide a means for students like her to participate in the group projects that were central to the social studies curriculum. The information for each of these teaching decisions is linked to close listening beyond the school walls.

OUT-OF-SCHOOL LEARNING AND LITERACIES

The examples of students' writing practices performed in out-of-school contexts lead to several new questions: How do we listen to all of the ways students are engaged in learning? What counts as school? What counts as learning? What counts as growth and progress? Do we count only work accomplished during school hours as an indication of students' performance, or are there ways to listen to students' lives outside of and beyond school walls to broaden our understandings of students as learners?

In our current educational climate, high-stakes testing drives many curriculum decisions. There are numerous proposals to increase assessment, which, if implemented, will further limit the role teachers play in decisions about their curriculum. As tests proliferate and as the stakes increase, teachers are forced to limit their curriculum to teach exactly what is evaluated by the tests. Space in the curriculum to include knowledge and practices students bring to their learning from outside of school is rapidly disappearing. On the other hand, learning theory suggests that people learn new information, skills, and, I would add, practices on the basis of their expertise (e.g., Bransford, Brown, & Cocking, 1999). How might a new understanding about how and where learning takes place in students' lives change how we assess students and design curriculum?

Students merge their lives from various contexts, including home, school, neighborhood, and work, when they arrive at school. Given the various constraints on their time and choice of curriculum, teachers frequently have little or no time to learn about students' lives outside of school. As a result, they teach to only a small part of who students are and the knowledge they bring to school. For their part, students might want to keep what happens at home and in their communities separate from school. They might think of school as a place that is distinct and removed from the other worlds they inhabit. How can schools build on students' capacities, interests, and knowledge while protecting their privacy? How might teachers construct larger and more inclusive portraits of students within the confines of school mandates? What are the mechanisms that might allow students to be assessed on their learning outside of school, without necessarily bringing the products of this learning into school? Morrison (1993) writes about the ways in which language approaches but does not replace experience. How can teachers hold on to their curricular goals and still create opportunities for learning about students' experience and language in the community to shape learning in school? Teachers of younger students as well as those who work with older ones can listen to learn about students' strengths by finding out more about their engagement in learning outside of the school walls.

My own son hated to write as a young child. His handwriting was labored—he formed letters with great difficulty—and his stories were always as short as possible. When his third-grade teacher introduced him and his classmates to writers' notebooks (Calkins, 1994; Fletcher, 1996), he filled the pages with scores of baseball games or the latest trades. His writing was repetitive and contained little more than lists. However, buried in this writing were phrases that were descriptive and vibrant. Every once in a while, out of sheer boredom with his own writing, he described a sound or a nuance in short, pointed phrases. He continued to think of himself as a poor writer.

At the time, his father was experimenting with writing short stories and screen plays in his spare time. One day when my son tried to lure his father away from his computer to play, they decided to write a short story together. With his father at the keyboard, my son narrated a long and complicated story about dragons. The story reflected their shared sense of humor and was filled with clever wordplay. This project continued for some time. Years later, when my son was given an assignment to write a creative piece, he resurrected the story, added to it, and turned it into school writing, earning praise from his teacher and classmates. I often wondered if he might have felt differently about writing early on, had his teacher found a way to gain access to this home writing during third grade. Although it was a collaboration with a parent, the writing displayed my son's interest in and capacity for using words and humor to convey character and plot.

The examples I give in this chapter address more difficult questions. When teachers listen for stories that students bring from outside of school, students might introduce topics and material that some consider out of bounds or private. The examples suggest that teachers must go beyond the scripts they are handed to learn about who students are and what they care about.

They infer that teachers can respond best to students when they base their response on knowledge of who the students are outside of school as well as inside the school walls. The listening this requires might be complicated and painful. It is undoubtedly courageous. I am not implying that teachers should give up their roles as instructors to become people who pry into the inner lives of their students. Many teachers simply believe it is inappropriate to ask for these details. Some feel that it is a violation of privacy and respect. Rather, I suggest that teachers provide multiple opportunities for students to bring their identities as learners into the classroom. This will entail listening for *how* students go about learning in their lives outside of school without always seeing tangible evidence of this learning. A focus on practices suggests that teachers listen for students' cultural and social identities as learners in and out of school. It suggests that students are given opportunities to talk, to write, to act, to represent their interests and activities in ways that protect their privacy yet convey their passions.

Listening as Surveillance

Thus far, I have written about listening to students across multiple dimensions as an affirming act, implying that listening and close attention are benign. There is also a negative side to listening. Listening can be thought of as prying or surveillance. Listening closely to students can be interpreted as coercive.[3] Close listening is not necessarily innocent. Drawing on Foucault (e.g., 1977), Hogan (1990) distinguishes between "sovereign power," which functions through terror and repression, and "disciplinary power," which is based on systematic knowledge of individuals. (See also Walkerdine, 1991.) Teachers always hold institutional power and authority over students in the form of "disciplinary power"; their listening is always laced with power and control. Close listening increases this power, and this control. Acknowledgment of this dynamic suggests that teachers pay close attention to what they listen for and how they respond to what they hear. It implies that teachers disclose themselves as listeners to their students.

I suggest that, rather than listening *in* on students, teachers listen *for* understanding, sharing their knowledge of students gained through this listening with the students themselves. Although I advocate that Marta and her colleagues listen closely to the broader contexts of their students' lives to learn who they are as poets, diary writers, playwrights, and the like, I suggest that it is probably more important that students such as Luis, Ellen, and Denise take on these identities themselves. It is important to listen to *who* students are in contexts outside of school, and to share the learning from this listening with the students so they take on a more expanded vision of themselves as learners and actors in the world.

In a discussion of writing, Lensmire (1994, 2000) warns teachers not to abandon children in writing workshops, suggesting that, mindful of the power they hold, teachers take an active role in questioning, confronting, and critiquing students' work. Likewise, a listening stance suggests that teachers actively participate in dialogues with students rather than passively observe them. Listening to students does not imply passivity, particularly when students bring stories and practices from outside of school. As teachers listen closely to students, they need to act to ensure that students remain authors and authorities over their own stories and lives.

By acknowledging and learning more about the students' writing that I describe in this chapter, the teachers did not become overinvolved in the young people's lives. Rather, listening for their writing practices provided a new kind of window into the students' identities and abilities in a range of contexts. Style (1988) suggests the metaphor of windows and mirrors for curriculum design. Curriculum should lead students into new knowledge at the same time that it reflects students' interests and identities back to them. Curriculum constructed in this manner allows students to recognize themselves at the same time they are invited to pursue new ideas more deeply. The image of a window with panes of glass implies that a teacher can listen to students without necessarily stepping into their lives.

Listening to teach also implies that teachers create openings in their classrooms so that students can bring their lives, cultures, passions, and wonderings into the classroom. Teaching then becomes an extension of life rather than a place separate from where real living occurs. Style's (1988) image of mirrors suggests that teachers develop curriculum that mirrors students' experiences. This involves the acknowledgment and incorporation of students' multiple cultures and ways of knowing into classroom life. It builds on the notion that students and teachers work together to construct their own classroom ethos or culture.

My conception of listening builds on and complicates Style's (1988) description of curriculum in two ways. First, it suggests that there are some aspects of students' lives that may be important for teachers to recognize and affirm but not necessarily incorporate into the curriculum. It may be enough for teachers to learn about the existence of aspects of students' learning to construct deeper and more complex understandings of them. Second, it suggests a more difficult task: that teachers strive to teach students tools not only for the time they are in school but also for a lifetime of learning and engaging in inquiry after their graduation.

The cases in this chapter address different aspects of this first task of listening to and recognizing students' lives. Luis's story raises questions of censorship and how teachers make decisions about what to include in the curriculum. Ellen's story suggests that teachers confront issues of privacy and create conditions for students to go public with their writing while saving face with their peers. Finally, Denise's story illustrates a compromise of sorts. This student took a risk to bring her writing into school, and her teachers adapted the assignments to accommodate her. In the end, both the student and the curriculum were strengthened. The cases suggest that as teachers we need to find new ways to listen so that students continue to learn past their days in school. I can only speculate that close attention to students' identities as learners in and out of school will make this kind of difference.

Listening Beyond the School Walls

Many fine teachers make decisions to listen to and bring aspects of students' lives into the classroom. Numerous examples illustrate how teachers have adapted curriculum and created classroom spaces that reflect students' lives (e.g., Levy, 1996; Meier, 1996; Skilton-Sylvester, 1994). This chapter adds to this understanding of listening to teach by articulating the challenges and possibilities of listening closely to students' practices and lives outside of school. By focusing on practices rather than content, I offer teachers a way out of the dilemmas they might face in terms of censorship or privacy. I emphasize the limiting views teachers hold of children when they fail to listen to their lives outside of school.

Although students are in school for numerous hours, many spend much of their day simply biding time, waiting for their real life to begin. How can schools merge these worlds without pretending that there is no difference between the two contexts for learning and living? Denise was often a difficult student to teach. In response to her refusal to participate in the senior project, her teachers could easily have let her fail. Many would have seen that as just punishment for her rigidity and lack of cooperation. Instead, by paying attention to Denise, they learned about her writing outside of school and together they imagined a solution. They listened beyond her protests and scowls so that they could hear about her passions. In the process, they helped her to acknowledge and begin to create her identity as a playwright, an identity she had not previously held in school. Unfortunately, this story does not have a happy ending.

Although Denise successfully completed her senior project, walking at graduation alongside her classmates, and even earning an award for her effort at the senior awards assembly, she has not been able to hold onto this identity as a writer since her graduation. Perhaps her identity shifted and she has continued to learn and pursue her interests in ways I did not hear as a researcher when we spoke. More likely, she reinscribed the separation between school and home, a writing identity and a street identity, and chose the latter to match her new status. I am not suggesting that simply listening more to

Denise would have made all the difference to her and other students like her or that listening in this manner is simple. Rather, I believe that we need larger understandings of students and that they, in turn, need bigger pictures of themselves to hold on to when they leave school. Those pictures won't come from teaching with scripts and covering textbook materials. They will come from inventing a way of teaching as listening that builds on and goes beyond students' lives in and out of school.

In Morrison's (1993) acceptance speech for the Nobel Prize, which opened this chapter, she uses a parable to argue for the role of language in our lives:

> Word-work is sublime, the old woman thinks, because it is generative; it makes meaning that secures our difference, our human difference—the way in which we are like no other life.
>
> We die—that may be the meaning of life. But we *do* language. That may be the measure of our lives. (p. 22)

The adolescents I describe in this chapter used writing and language to make sense of their lives while in high school. They all stopped writing regularly after their graduation. By listening to the social, cultural, and community contexts of students' lives, teachers assist students to bring their most intimate experiences into the classroom; by listening more broadly to how students actively engage in ideas and meaning beyond school, teachers can find ways to encourage students to hold on to their intellectual aliveness and habits of mind past their hours and years in school. The students described in this chapter had many teachers who cared deeply about them and went far to ensure that they succeeded while in school. Often their actions were restricted by external limits imposed by the school and their own time. I suggest that a listening stance that includes attention to students' practices beyond the classroom, informing students of the insights gained from this listening, and shifting pedagogy, curriculum, and assessment, will go far in reaching students while they are in school and beyond. In other words, teachers can learn to listen for and acknowledge multiple ways to "do language," and they can support students to continue their exploration and use of language in their lives.

5

Listening for Silence and Acts of Silencing

What would happen if one woman told the truth about her life?
The world would split open.

(Rukeyser, 1962/1973)

THE POETRY OF MURIEL RUKEYSER opens this chapter. Rukeyser was a political activist and feminist who wrote poetry about a range of social issues, often breaking silences to raise questions no one else dared to ask. This chapter raises questions about how teachers might structure their classrooms and teaching to allow students to break the silences that pervade most schools. Listening for silence and acts of silencing is a critical and often overlooked aspect of teaching. Listening for silence includes listening for missing conversations and overlooked perspectives, and also listening for the moments when students are actively silenced by individuals and institutions. Listening for acts of silencing compels educators to notice and respond when students' talk and participation are eclipsed so that schools and classrooms, indeed all teaching interactions, can be fully representative of all students. As Fine (1991) explains, "Silencing is about who can speak, what can and cannot be spoken, and whose discourse must be controlled" (p. 33).

In addition to listening for moments when conversation is cut off, listening for acts of silencing suggests that teachers examine all of the interactions in their classrooms to notice when and where openings occur for students' voices to permeate the curriculum. This conception of listening suggests that teachers notice and create the opportunities for students—both individually and collectively—to reveal their understandings and themselves as they learn.

Listening for silencing includes listening for divergent perspectives and the moments when individuals have been shut out of the conversation. The acts of silencing I describe in this chapter include the institutional silencing of students as well as the moments when students and teachers silence themselves and each other. As Fine (1991) explains, "Silencing signifies a terror of words, a fear of talk" (p. 32). Drawing on conversations about race and race relations in a postdesegregated middle school, this chapter explores listening for silence and silencing during times when this "fear of talk" was temporarily forgotten.

AT SUMMIT SCHOOL

A scene from Summit Middle School will introduce a normative event at this suburban school, against which acts of silencing can be understood.

> The induction of the National Junior Honor Society took place on one of the final days of school. The large cafeteria was packed with proud parents and family members, each holding a program listing the names of the inductees. Although nearly 25% of the students in the school were African American, there were only four African Americans in the audience: the vice principal, the two African American teachers in the school, and a visiting high school student. There was not a single African American student in either the old or the new group of students entering this nationally recognized society. New inductees walked casually into the room, picking up their candles, and stood in a group to listen to the speeches. After the pledge of allegiance and several speeches by students and faculty members, the student officers lit the candles of new members. Students recited the Honor Society pledge. Jill, a popular White student and secretary of the Honor Society, presented the new members to the vice principal, reading from the script she was given. "Mr. Wheelan, these students are qualified as new members of the National Junior Honor Society according to our criteria of scholarship, leadership, citizenship, service and character."
>
> (field notes, 6/3/99)

There was irony in Jill, a White student, informing Mr. Wheelan, the African American vice principal, that certain students, most of whom were White and middle class, were qualified for this honor. The overwhelming presence of the White, middle-class students at this event raised questions about the students absent from this ritual, particularly African American students. Jill was representative of the students inducted in the Honor Society in many ways. She occupied a prominent leadership position in the middle school. Her mother was a key member of the parent association. As the lead in the school play that she and her best friends had written, Jill was generally one of the most vocal students in the school. Teachers and administrators all agreed that the school was run by Jill and the group of White, middle-class students, who, backed by their parents, set its tone. Although teachers criticized this popular group of students for "thinking they are special," they consistently selected them for leadership positions.

Caroline, an eighth grader and member of the Honor Society who considered herself half-American and half-Japanese, stood both inside and outside the mainstream of the school. She observed that the White students in the popular group held the key positions in the school. Caroline's theory about the Korean American girl who was president of the class was that she "acts so American that people can get over it," implying that White students are willing to ignore her ethnicity because she acts like them. She added that, although the class president wasn't White, she acted as if she were White, earning a position as a member of the popular group of students. When asked to elaborate, Caroline concluded that in this school "everyone wants to be standard White." Students who weren't "standard White" and those who articulated different perspectives were mostly absent from the stage that day when Honor Society members were inducted. Portraits of the missing students provide another lens for listening for silence (Schultz, Niesz, & Buck, 1999).

The induction of the mainstream students into the Honor Society, which opens this chapter, is but one of many events that highlight those students whose voices are dominant in the school. In contrast, this chapter points to the silenced students and the events that silence them. This chapter addresses the various ways that silencing occurs between and among students, teachers, and schools as institutions, and suggests the importance of paying attention to and addressing these moments in teaching. Listening for acts of silencing is described across the three domains that are explored in the previous three chapters: listening to the silencing of individual students, listening to the silencing within groups, and listening to the silencing that occurs in the broader contexts of students' lives.

RESEARCH CONTEXT

During the summer of 1995, following a pattern that is sweeping the country, the court in the metropolitan school district where Summit Middle School is located rescinded a desegregation ruling that had mandated the racial balance of the district's schools. After testimony from a wide variety of stakeholders, the court found that the district's schools had reached "unitary status"—in other words, a segregated dual system was no longer in operation. In response to this ruling, mandatory busing—which had maintained a racial balance of the schools at about 70% White students and 30% students of color (mostly African American students)—was replaced with a district-wide school choice program. As my colleague James Davis and I listened to the testimony by various community leaders and advocacy groups, we noticed that student perspectives were missing from the conversations about the future of their schools. In response, James and I designed a 3-year research study to document students' and teachers' talk about their experiences of race and interracial relations and to track demographic and interactional changes during this transitional period in a postdesegregated middle school, which we call Summit.[1] Our goal was to gather the missing student perspectives on their racialized experiences in school during the desegregation time period (Schultz & Davis, 1996; Schultz et al., 2000). Although students had been sorted for years by race, when we entered the schools to talk about this issue, we found silence.

From a distance, Summit School resembles a typical upper-middle-class suburban public school. Sitting on the crest of a hill in a predominantly middle-class, White neighborhood, Summit is surrounded by parking lots, green playing fields, and ranch-style houses with well-kept lawns. Its hallways are gleaming and surprisingly orderly. A poster composed of hands cut from multicolored construction paper, with the words "Summit welcomes you with open hands," is visible in the front hall. Plaques in the hallways indicate strong academic, athletic, and music programs. The school is predominantly White and middle-class, with most students choosing conventional or "preppy" clothing reflecting the latest styles tempered by rules established by parents and the school. There are scattered students of color—some blending into the White background, others proclaiming their presence with a style often bolder and louder than that of their more subdued White peers (Schultz et al., 2000).[2]

As an African American male and a White female, James Davis and I consciously formed a multiracial partnership to talk about race and interracial relationships with students within and across racial categories (Schultz & Davis, 1996). From the beginning, our goal was to address issues of race as directly as possible. Our data collection methods included focus groups; extensive participant observation in classrooms, hallways, and during a range of after-school activities; informal and formal interviews; and student writing groups that met weekly over the course of a semester (Bates et al., 2001).

Because of our interest in studying interaction, including students' understandings of race and their racialized experiences in schools, we chose focus groups as our primary site for data collection. We met with 30 focus groups over 3 years to provide the middle school students opportunities to talk together in single- and mixed-race groups. All of the group meetings were both video- and audiotaped. In the focus groups we encouraged students to talk about their particular experiences in the school. We invited students to have honest conversations by asking open-ended questions, prompting them to pursue topics of interest, and encouraging them to question or disagree with each other's assertions (Schultz et al., 2000).

In order to illustrate the silencing of the voices of particular students and to suggest ways of teaching that include listening to silence, this chapter opens with portraits of three students. Their stories illustrate silencing at the institutional level, silencing by peers, and silencing by teachers. The silencing that took place in the focus groups reflects the patterns of silencing we observed in classrooms and in informal spaces throughout the school, especially in the rare moments we witnessed discussions about racial issues. There were two dominant forms of silencing in the focus groups: the shutting down of conversations by both students and leaders, and the enactment of a color-blind discourse. The topic of the focus groups—race and racialized experiences in schools—was itself silenced in school. Discussion of this difficult and controversial issue therefore brought acts of silencing into relief. The moves that students and teachers made to silence these conversations in the focus groups were reflective of the less obvious forms of silencing that occurred across the school day. At an institutional level, the dominant patterns of silencing occurred through the exclusion and selection of both speakers and topics. (See Table 5.1 for a summary of these forms of silencing.)

PORTRAITS OF SILENCE

Listening for silence implies listening for the words that are not spoken and for the missing voices of those who are silent. The following portraits of three marginalized students suggest that silence was located in the moment-to-

Table 5.1. *Patterns of Silencing*

Types of Listening	Unit of Analysis	Patterns of Silencing
Listening to know particular students	Portraits of individual students	• Institution silencing • Silencing by peers • Silencing by teachers
Listening to the rhythm and balance of a group of students	Mixed-race and single-race focus groups	• Individuals—students and leaders—shutting down conversations • Groups silencing themselves through enacting a color-blind discourse
Listening to the social, cultural, and community contexts of students' lives	School-wide practices and policies	• Silencing through exclusion processes • Silencing through selection processes

moment experiences of students as well as within curriculum, actions, and speech.[3] Margaret was an academically successful African American student whose voice was silenced in part by the tracking policies of the school. Caroline was silenced by her peers who insisted on conformity. Zakiya was silenced by teachers who consistently misunderstood the contribution she might make to their classes; her experiences and understandings of urban life were missing from the curriculum, leaving her with few opportunities to engage in school.

Margaret: Going It Alone

Margaret lived in a well-maintained row home in the city with her mother and two sisters. At Summit, Margaret was the highest achieving African American student in her grade and one of the highest achieving students in the middle school as a whole. She was frequently the sole or one of a very few African American students in her honors classes. As a result, her teachers claimed that there was a lost opportunity for her to serve as a role model for other African American students. As her math teacher explained: "Unfortunately—and I have her for algebra—and she is the only Black girl in there. And, so then, that is a shame because it would be nice to get her with some kids to be able to be that positive role model for them." Her teachers complained that she shirked her responsibility, as a highly successful student, to motivate less advanced students. Another of Margaret's teachers declared, "I wish she would be less quiet and more sharing of her knowledge—take more of a leadership role." Margaret decided against joining the Honor Society. She claimed that it was a group primarily for White students (interview, 2/11/99). Leaving Summit early to catch her bus back to the city that day, she was missing from the cafeteria for the Honor Society inductions.

Despite her academic accomplishments, Margaret was not well known by many students. Working diligently and silently at her desk, Margaret seemed withdrawn and out of her element in the classroom in terms of her ability to develop relationships with teachers and her White peers. She was cut off from her White peers, who did not understand her silence or empathize with her isolation as one of the few Black students in each of her classes. Margaret was also isolated and disconnected from the majority of her Black peers. She claimed that she needed to turn away from them in exchange for academic success. In a school where most of her African American peers opted out of academic pursuits, Margaret was willing to face alienation, loneliness, and invisibility. She had to struggle daily to disassociate herself from the negative images of the urban Black students in the school. She described the choices that her academically talented African American peers made that were different from her own.

> They are kind of locked in a stereotype that Blacks not supposed to be smart not supposed to talk a certain way or dress a certain way or anything or else they will be White or anything. Even when I told one of my friends, Selene, that I got straight A's she called me a nerd and White and things like that. But I didn't care.
>
> (interview, 2/11/99)

Margaret could not explain where she found the courage to go against the stereotype of Blacks who underachieve or do relatively poorly in this school. And although she worked hard to achieve high grades, she did not go as far as joining the Honor Society, which she considered "too White." In contrast to the highly visible White, middle-class girls and her more vocal Black peers, Margaret was practically invisible. Her academic success, which required her to step outside of the practices enacted by her African American peers, was barely recognized. Isolation from her peers acted to silence her; in essence she was consigned to "go it alone."

Listening for silence requires not only that teachers notice the academic success of students like Margaret, but also that they find ways to create a classroom and school culture in which their talents and contributions are recognized and valued rather than blaming them for a perceived failure to be leaders or role models for their peers. The narrator in Ellison's (1952) novel *The Invisible Man* asks:

> To whom can I be responsible, and why should I be when you refuse to see me? Responsibility rests upon recognition, and recognition is a form of agreement. (p. 16)

Listening for silence suggests the importance of recognizing students and their talents, in order to construct classroom communities that honor and build on their contributions. As Greene (1988) explains, the narrator in *The Invisible Man* makes sense of his life by looking back on it, "telling a story about it, imposing form, and attaining visibility for himself" (p. 99). Listening to silence includes providing students with the opportunities to reflect on their positions in the classroom and school with forums to make their stories public.

Caroline: Silencing Critique

Caroline, who identified alternatively as "American" and "half-Japanese and half-American," was a successful student at Summit by traditional standards. She was a high-achieving student in her honors classes and participated in a number of extracurricular activities, including athletics, the school newspaper, and the Honor Society. She took a different stance from most of her peers at Summit, who were reluctant to deviate in any way from the norm, conforming to the standards set by the popular group. She spoke out against school practices in class discussions and in a column she wrote for the school newspaper. Although she could take strong positions on unpopular but relatively safe issues, such as her support of Amnesty International, her writing in this public forum was limited. As she explained: "I'm on the newspaper, but you can't print anything controversial. I do a point and counterpoint, and I wanted to do it on abortion, but they wouldn't let me" (interview, 5/3/99).

Confident in her voice, Caroline was outspoken about her beliefs, which often placed her outside the norm at Summit. She condemned the racism, sexism, and elitism of her peers. She considered herself a feminist and spoke frequently about her need to defend these views to her classmates, including her closest friends (Niesz, 2000). In our interviews, she consistently returned to her conclusion that her peers held narrow views and were afraid to speak up if they disagreed:

> And most of the people [at Summit] were brought up thinking [racism] was okay. And a few people who were brought up thinking it wasn't okay don't say anything because everybody else thinks it's okay.
>
> (interview, 5/3/99)

This statement, as well as her earlier comment about how everyone at Summit wants to be "standard White," illustrates Caroline's ability to name silences in the school and critique her peers for their conformity.

In another interview, she described the strategy she devised in response to her frustration with her seventh-grade social studies teacher, who she thought displayed racism in teaching about China and Japan. According to Caroline, the teacher presented stereotypical and inaccurate information about this area of the world. Her response:

> Instead of yelling at her I brought in everything I had from Japan. I practically got up and taught the class myself because I wanted the class to see what Japanese people really were like and that they're not like that.
>
> (interview, 5/3/99)

Although her peers ignored or limited their response to what Caroline considered to be poor teaching, she took action to rectify the situation. She felt personally affronted by the presentation of the material and wanted to correct or broaden the understandings of her peers who might not have recognized the inaccuracy of the teacher's material.

Although Caroline prided herself on acting as a leader in class discussions, she struggled to balance her desire to be popular with her refusal to be silenced. At a school where most students, teachers, and parents professed to get along with one another, neither her teachers nor her peers felt comfortable with Caroline's strong and articulate positions that raised questions and critique. Caroline explained that although she was successful in her classes, "[My teachers] don't like me because I'm too controversial. And I speak my mind. And I tell them when I think they're wrong, which they don't appreciate" (interview, 5/3/99). Even more difficult for her to deal with was the response of her peers.

> I'm Unitarian Universalist. My mother and dad were complete hippies. They brought me up exactly the same. I'm like totally anti-war, totally anti-guns, totally anti-segregation, all this stuff. And I get a lot of crap for it from everybody, especially in social studies where I'm always getting up and saying what I think. Everybody's always, "Shut up. Sit down."
>
> (interview, 5/3/99)

Caroline's lack of social status in the school bothered her on several levels, not the least of which was her inability to be elected to traditional leadership roles, such as officer positions in the Honor Society. She likened the officer elections to a popularity contest. Caroline recognized that social status combined with popularity among peers translated into institutionally sanctioned leadership roles in the school. She expressed a strong desire to be a leader and noted with irony that it was her own leadership qualities in the classroom that kept her from winning these school-wide positions. She was silenced, cast on the sidelines as the critic; her willingness to question, critique, and articulate her positions effectively shut her out of the contest.

In our work at this middle school we saw few instances of critique, either initiated by students or supported by the school curriculum. Caroline's statements stood out for their critical edge; she was one of the few students willing to publicly articulate a position that raised questions about the practices and beliefs of her peers. At the same time, Caroline yearned to be accepted by her more popular peers. Unlike Margaret, Caroline joined the Honor Society and actively sought a leadership position in that organization. In Caroline's view, she ultimately failed to reach her goal to become a leader because she could not pass as White.

For a period of time in eighth grade when she dated a popular boy, Caroline became less outspoken. She consciously traded her outspoken stance for popularity. A few months before she graduated from the middle school, their relationship ended and she reclaimed her critical voice. She became outspoken in her classes and in her interactions with peers. However, as Caroline prepared to graduate, she reconsidered this stance. She made the decision to enter high school with a different reputation in order to be accepted by more students. In this prospective decision to mute her critique and downplay her interest in academic subjects, she was effectively silenced by her peers.

Listening for silence includes noticing when students take critical or risky stands and supporting them to articulate these positions. Although teachers cannot affect how peers treat each other outside of their classroom, they can teach students how to recognize and honor multiple perspectives. They can listen for the internal dynamics of a classroom that might silence students from articulating alternative views that challenge or fall outside of the mainstream. Students of color, and girls, in particular, are frequently discouraged from displaying their intelligence in school (e.g., Fine, 1991; Fordham, 1991, 1993, 1996; Fordham & Ogbu, 1986). They are often high-achieving students at the expense of their popularity. Teachers can listen for how students silence their own success or strong opinions in exchange for popularity. Listening for silence includes paying attention to how teachers and students structure talk, to both silence and promote conversation. As Greene (1993) explains, "There are ways of speaking and telling that construct silences, create 'others,' invent gradations of social difference necessary for identification of norms" (p. 216).

In many schools, students—and particularly adolescents—work hard to create conformity and set a norm. Teachers can listen for the silences or silencing moves that prevent students from stating their own perspectives and contributing to a diverse and challenging classroom community. Teachers can learn to recognize not only when they silence students but also when, as teachers, they allow, or even encourage, students to silence each other. Caroline vowed to mute her opinions during high school in exchange for popularity. Teachers can listen for this kind of self-silencing, but also for opportunities to structure different kinds of conversations so that students like Caroline can offer critical perspectives without fear of dismissal by either students or teachers.

Zakiya: Using Talk to Mask Silence

A large African American girl, Zakiya was a commanding presence in her classes. In the middle school, nearly everyone knew her, and many of her peers from a variety of racial and class backgrounds liked her. Unlike Margaret, she was not willing to act in an accommodating manner. Although Zakiya and Caroline held many of the same critical views, Zakiya was sometimes more openly resistant and combative, and other times more silent and not invested enough to offer a critique. When she did not agree with a teacher or a group of students, Zakiya was likely to "tell it like it is," which often led teachers to consider her adversarial, demanding, and difficult to teach. As one teacher described her:

> I think that she thinks that the rules don't apply to her. I think that she has tremendous potential. She is very verbal, vocal, uh, really good mind, inquisitive. Really can think things out. Think things on a really deep level. Has great questions. But boy is she difficult.
>
> (interview, 5/19/99)

During the afternoon when the Honor Society students inducted their peers into their group, Zakiya sat in the office. Earlier that afternoon, she had confronted a group of teachers in the hallway when she overhead them talking about her (field notes, 6/3/99). Zakiya frequently stated that she had little time for poor teaching in the school. Although she had close relationships with several White teachers at Summit, calling them "mom" and "aunt," if she did not agree with a teacher or felt that the teacher was wasting her time, she did not hesitate to state her views.

In seventh grade, Zakiya was an unwitting leader of the African American girls from the city who referred to themselves as the "ghetto girls." Although she claimed to prefer to sit by herself, her peers seemed to find her and cluster around her in the lunchroom and classrooms. She did not seem to know how to reconcile her popularity with her desire to be by herself. In an interview she described the change in her role at school after she returned from a year away from school. She had gone to stay with relatives in Louisiana because she was failing in school and facing difficulties in her own family. As Zakiya explained,

> My attitude is shifty sometimes. Either I want to be completely by myself or I want to be around people. Last year when I left here I was really really popular. I was going to be the one keeping all the Black girls together and keeping us from fighting with each other. We were all tight. And then when I left everyone started fighting. When I go in class I go in the back of the room but everyone comes and sits around me. I don't know if they consciously know what they're doing or if they do it subconsciously. People gather around me. And people crowd around me and I move and people follow me. Mr. Wheelan [the vice principal] says, "Zakiya why don't you keep this from happening." I say, "I didn't have anything to do with it." He say, "Zakiya you're the leader in the group." I say, "I'm not trying to be." He was like, "They made you the leader so you have to take that responsibility." I try to be by myself but it just don't work.
>
> (interview, 6/3/99)

Zakiya was talented and had clear goals for herself. She described herself as eager to learn, which was exemplified by her extensive reading and studying about topics that captured her imagination. Zakiya appeared to have natural leadership abilities, yet she was unsure whether, in the context of this school that was removed from her daily experiences, she wanted to take on this role or the responsibility suggested by the vice principal.

Like many of her African American peers who lived in the city, Zakiya took on sometimes demanding responsibilities once she returned home from school. In addition to her mother, who she claimed was more of a peer, there were friends and neighbors, children and older people alike, who depended on her care. Yet these roles and responsibilities were not well understood by many of her teachers. One day a teacher demanded to know why she was in class without a pencil and notebook. Zakiya replied that she did not have money that week for a pencil. Her teacher replied, "Well go and baby sit then to earn enough money to buy one." Zakiya had responsibility for childcare nearly every afternoon; like many of her low-income peers, she was not paid for this work. She answered the teacher with silence and a scowl (field notes, 10/28/98). Zakiya was failing her eighth-grade year. Her mostly White and middle-class teachers and peers knew little about her life at home, her goals, or her aspirations.

In the focus groups connected to our research project, Zakiya added her strong and intelligent voice to the conversation and listened respectfully to others. The issues discussed in this group seemed important to her; each student's voice was solicited and valued. She was never resistant or difficult with the adults in this group. Perhaps this was because we attempted to run the group in a democratic manner, and her ideas were listened to and clearly respected by her peers and the leaders. In addition, the group gave her a venue for using the common-sense knowledge she developed in her family and community (Luttrell, 1997). In general, opportunities did not exist for her to use this knowledge based on her experiences of urban life or to take on positive roles in the school.

Listening for silence and silenced students includes listening beyond the loud talk that might mask students' true talents and contributions. It encompasses listening for openings in conversations—or in the curriculum—for students who hold alternative perspectives to participate and feel respected in such a way that their voices and identities are recognized. Listening for silence includes creating opportunities for students to go beyond their resistance and alienation to care about learning and to contribute to the collective knowledge of the class. Zakiya was silenced by some, although not all, of the teachers in this school; they saw only her resistance, not her deeply felt interests and talents. Her loud, aggressive manner masked her potential contributions to her classes and enabled the teachers to give up on her as difficult to teach. In spite of her loud voice, she was as silenced as Margaret was, because her true talents and interests went unheard and unseen. At the school, she was worlds apart from her home and community, her lived experience, and ultimately her education (Fine, 1991).

Each of these portraits describes, in broad strokes, a student who was silenced at this middle school. None of these girls was part of the mainstream; none was recognized as a leader in the school. Most notable, their voices were missing from the mainstream discourse heard in classrooms. This is not to say that as a group they were silent. In fact, Caroline and Zakiya were known as vocal students with strong opinions. However, both were excluded from traditional leadership positions in the school and their particular perspectives and understandings were not present in the mainstream discourse of the school or its curriculum. The institutional structures of the school, the administrators, teachers, and students all worked together to silence these students. As a result, they and their peers missed opportunities for learning.

THE SHUTTING DOWN OF CONVERSATIONS BY INDIVIDUALS

We conducted focus groups twice a year for 3 years, each time including any student who indicated an interest in joining the group (cf. Schultz & Davis, 1996; Schultz et al., 2000). The purpose of the groups was to break the silence about race and racism in this desegregated school and to promote conversation among members in both single-race groups and across racial lines. At times the focus groups represented a border zone (Anzaldua, 1987; Rosaldo, 1989), where silence was broken, and public and private conversations mixed. Perhaps because the conversations were begun in single-race groups and were conducted by outside researchers rather than teachers, they often were what Fine, Weis, and others (e.g., Fine, Weis, & Powell, 1997; Weis & Fine, 2000) characterize as "safe spaces." They were also opportunities for students to explore topics often silenced in the regular discourse of the school. As leaders of the groups, James and I did not have an official role in the school and could not affect students' grades. As a result, students were often more willing to discuss topics that were not encouraged in the regular course of their school day. However, in spite of these conditions, there was often more silencing— with students silencing or censoring themselves, and both leaders and students silencing risky conversations—than talk.

Silencing by Students

In our conversations about race and students' racialized experiences in their middle school, there were numerous examples of times when the students themselves shut down conversations. In the following exchange, a South Asian (or Indian) student, who was very much a "minority" in the school, chose several times to change the topic in order to shut down a heated conversation about race. This particular mixed-race group, which included both Zakiya and Caroline, had agreed to continue to talk about racial issues across race lines beyond our initial focus-group meetings, and we met with them three more times. The students were interested and willing to talk about their racialized experiences in school and, although different from one another, they seemed to feel particularly comfortable in these discussions. Over the course of our meetings, there were moments when students engaged in honest conversation across race lines. These moments were rare and generally short-lived.

Zakiya often took a lead role in the group's discussions. Perhaps because students from a variety of race and class backgrounds respected Zakiya, and because she distanced herself from the interpersonal politics of the school, she frequently articulated bold positions and asked incisive questions. Unlike Caroline, she was not invested in popularity. On this day, she broke the silence around racism and asked a direct question to a White student.[4] Although as the leader of the group I supported her questioning, as did many of her peers, ultimately the conversation was silenced before real learning occurred.

The following conversation illustrates the ways students both opened up possibilities for talk and shut down discussion. As the leader, I initiated the conversation by asking students to talk about their experiences in school. Typically, the students talked more easily about teachers or parents than about their own experiences with race. It was easier for them to claim that a particular teacher was racist than to confront and discuss their own racism. In addition, they were more likely to talk about difference in terms of music and clothing than in terms of their own relationships. Together, Zakiya and Kyanna broke this tacit agreement.[5]

> *Kyanna* (B): I have no problem with the other race. It's like a couple racists, like people in this school that you don't really get along with. And, I don't, I don't have no problem with the other race. It is just that some people, they don't like me because you don't like something . . .
>
> *Zakiya* (B) (to Mark as if getting to the point that Kyanna is hesitant to make): It is rumored that you're a racist.
>
> *Kyanna* (B) (emphatically): Yes.
>
> *Zakiya* (B): It is rumored that you don't like Black people.
>
> *Mark* (W): It's not true. My aunt is Black.
>
> *Kyanna* (B) (definitively): No. We're not asking you about your aunt. We are asking you about how *you* feel.
>
> *Zakiya* (B): Why is that, I mean, why is that going around?

Mark (W): I don't know.

Doris (I): I mean rumors start because of little, little (indicates something small with her hands).

In response to the direct question to Mark about whether he is racist, Doris, a student whose family is from India and who considers herself "brown," swiftly deflected the question. A friend of Caroline's, Doris was one of the few other members of the Honor Society who was not White and middle class and, like Caroline, spent much of her time vying for leadership positions and popularity with her peers. Ignoring Doris, Kyanna and Zakiya continued their line of questioning.

Kyanna (B): Yeah, remember in language arts [class] you were like, "a nigger is a Black person."

Mark (W): No.

Kyanna (B): Yes, you did say that.

Mark (W): I said not all Black people are niggers but some, okay. But, and I said . . .

Kyanna added an emphatic statement that is inaudible. She and Mark spoke at the same time. In the end, Mark claimed the floor.

Mark (W): And, I said—

Danny (B) (speaks over Mark): But White people can be niggers.

(Doris laughs.)

Mark (W): And that's what I said. I said that too.

Ricky (W): Yeah, I'm not prejudice and, like, I've called like White people niggers. (Several students laugh.) And, I got a lot of friends that are Black.

Kyanna (B) (in a friendly tone): Yeah, we know *you* [emphasis added] Ricky.

Ricky (W): And, I've, like, called White people niggers just cause, like, they're ignorant and that's not, like, because, like, Black people are that, like, that's just—

Kyanna (B): Yeah, that's not like—

Ricky (W): A name that came up to mind.

Caroline (A): It's just a bad thing to call somebody. It's not that it is connected to the—

Kyanna (B) (interrupting, to Mark): Well, now you're saying that Black people are just niggers. That's what you said in language arts.

Mark (W): No, I didn't, I—

Caroline (A): You want to start a fight with a whole bunch of them, though. I know 'cause I was talking to Michael Carr and, it's not right, like, you were, you've got this whole group that were like ready to kill everybody. They were originally ready to go around. They were gonna go and just beat everybody up, but there were like six of you and twenty of them and that just doesn't work.

Mark (W): That's him, not me.

Caroline (A): He said he got the idea from you and you were going around and saying it.

Mark (W) [sarcastically]: Yeah, right.

Doris (I): Okay, Okay, let's ( )

KS (W): No, but it is interesting. Say more. (to Zakiya) I think that was very bold of you to say that to Mark, so say more about how you feel like he's prejudiced. So say more and maybe we can settle it. I mean one of the things is, is the "n" word, right? Why don't you talk about what it means?

(Many students speak at once.)

The conversation continued as the students tried to unpack the rumor about what Mark said in their language arts class and potential threats he and his peers had made. Kyanna reassured Ricky, the other White male in the group, who was popular with both African American and White students, that they were not talking about him. Caroline joined the two African American girls to interrogate Mark about both his language and his actions. Still uncomfortable with the topic and the direct and personal interrogation, Doris attempted to quiet the conversation again. In my role as leader, I directed a question to Zakiya to keep the conversation going. Tanisha, Kyanna, and Zakiya all attempted to explain the significance of using the word *nigger*.

KS (W): Why don't you explain to him what it means to you because, I think maybe he doesn't understand.

Tanisha (B) (at the same time as Kyanna): You don't think about a White person. You think about a Black person.

Kyanna (B): Automatically. Automatically. It is like (laughs and stops because she has trouble pronouncing automatically)

Zakiya (B): It takes you back. It takes you back to like American history and what your mom and dad talk about or your grandparents talk about.

Doris (I): I'm in the middle sort of 'cause I'm like brown and not White and not Black and I've never grown up, like my mom, like no one's prejudice in my family—

Caroline (A): Everyone is prejudiced about something.

Doris (I): Yeah, but they are, like, not prejudice about, like, race. They are prejudice about other things (waves her hand as if dismissing that as another topic) but they, um, I remember, like, growing up and, like, even in school, 'cause I went to, like, St. Mary's [a private school] and all you saw was White people. There was nothing but White people.

Kyanna (B): St. Mary's is. It's like for rich, White kids.

Doris (I): But, um, I went there when there was still guys in the school before third grade. And I mean, how do you. Like, when they talked about Black history, it was like a week, no more (many students respond at once) and I, like, I'd stand up for, like, Black people cause I was, like, a brown person and nobody, I mean, I had friends that were White, but they were just like. I mean it was really funny because I'm not Black and I'd just stand up for them because I'd feel bad because they don't even talk about—

In this final turn, Doris succeeded in diverting the conversation away from Mark and from this school. At the same time that she shifted the topic and focus of the conversation, she described her own role in promoting fair treatment of African Americans. It was as if she felt a need to justify her move to silence the conversation by describing a moment where she had initiated talk about race on a safe topic—a conversation about history. Her turn continued for an extended period of time. When she finished speaking, Danny made a joke about Black History month as the shortest month of the year, and all of the students joined him to talk about curriculum and history. Despite my attempts to return to a discussion of their own experiences in school, the group continued to talk about abstract topics such as the importance of Black History month.

This conversation about race and racism continued longer than usual. Students of color were in the majority in this particular group and spoke in support of Zakiya and Kyanna's questions. In the end, however, the conversation was silenced by one student, without any opportunity for real learning to occur. This focus group illustrates that despite strong interest in pursuing Zakiya's question, the students colluded with one another to silence the conversation about race. I was unsuccessful in overriding this move toward silence.

Silencing by Leaders

In the following examples of silencing, the leaders played a more explicit role in silencing the discussion of race. The silencing we enacted is similar to the ways students and conversations are silenced every day in classrooms by teachers. An examination of our moves in silencing conversation is suggestive of how these processes occur in classroom settings.

Collaboration to silence conflict. The first example of silencing by leaders occurred during the meeting of another mixed-race focus group.[6] On the surface, this group presented a picture of racial harmony similar to the image the school hoped to convey. In their conversations, there was often more agreement than disagreement. At the beginning of their meeting, the group was discussing low-income Mexicans; Maria, a multiracial student who identified as White and Puerto Rican, had claimed that this group of people were "dirty." There were no Mexican students in the school and the students, although claiming racial tolerance, seemed to feel safe in generalizing about outsiders. At first there seemed to be agreement about this statement.

Emerson, an African American male, offered an alternative perspective to the group's position that Mexicans were dirty, explaining that there were not enough jobs for Mexicans and that they faced the same difficulties African Americans once confronted. He placed the blame and responsibility for their situation squarely on the government. His close friend, Belinda, who was also African American, immediately disagreed with him and initiated a heated exchange.

> *Belinda* (B): I would like to comment on what she said. (She motions toward Maria.) And I understand, I see eye to eye with you (looks toward Maria), but I don't see eye to eye with you (nods to Emerson). Okay, because the government, they ain't givin' me nothing, but you still see I'm clean. Okay?

Belinda made the point that unlike the Mexicans, she was low-income and *not* dirty. Further, she asserted that she did not receive any support from the government. In her statements, she questioned stereotypes (i.e., all poor people are dirty) at the same time that she reinforced them (i.e., that it is the fault of the Mexicans, not the government, that their living conditions are poor). Students responded to her point all at once, so that their individual statements were inaudible. Reclaiming the floor and insistently restating her position, Belinda continued.

> *Belinda* (B): I'm talkin'.
> There continued to be inaudible overlapping talk by students.
> *KS* (W): Wait, wait, wait. Let Belinda finish.
> *Belinda* (B): I'm talkin'. I'm talkin'.
> *Emerson* (B): You don't gotta talk that way.

The students in the group laughed nervously. Emerson's tone suggested that he was chiding, although not silencing, Belinda. He was asking her—in a teasing manner—to soften her aggressive tone. Emerson and Belinda were speaking as intimates and also from adversarial positions. Their discussion took on a more emotional quality as they continued to address each other personally.

> *Belinda* (B): I'll talk the way I wanna talk.
> *Maria* (L/W): Okay you guys. Chill. Chill.
> *Emerson* (B): I don't understand what you was—
> *Maria* (L/W): Chiiiiill.
> *Students*: Shhhh (more inaudible talking).

As the discussion grew heated, Maria and her peers attempted to quiet the conversation. They were uncomfortable with its emotional tenor. The two African American students continued to exchange comments.

> *Belinda* (B): Anyway, like I—
> KS (W): You guys can have different opinions, okay? You can have different opinions.
> (Maria made a comment that was mostly inaudible.)
> *Emerson* (B): Everybody's mad because I have my own opinion. Why?
> *Belinda* (B): Like I—like I said—

First, I quieted students down to encourage Belinda to speak. Next, I joined the group of apprehensive White students and jumped in to calm the heated exchange. I picked up on the nervousness in the room and made an attempt to restore peace. The two ignored me and continued. Belinda repeated her assertion. The group responded with more laughter.

Prefacing her comment with an explanation of her close relationship with Emerson, perhaps to calm *us* down, Belinda loudly declared her position that she was able to manage without help from the government, wondering why others shouldn't be expected to do the same.

> *Belinda* (B): Emerson know I love him, that's why I'm messin' with him. But like I said, it's not, you can't, you can't sit there and be like, "Oh, the government." The government ain't giving me nothin'.
> KS (W): Wait, wait, but that's not actually what his point is. Listen to what he has to say.
> *Belinda* (B): But yes that is.
> *Emerson* (B): I'll tell you, all right. Black people. We've been goin' through it for a long time so we've begun to work our way, to get

our education, and go to school and all this. But now they're going through that so they have to learn to get an education and better themselves.

Kevin (W): Yes, but, where they are there is no—

Mandy (W): [way] to get good jobs.

Emerson (B): They have to, they have to learn to better themselves.

Julian (W): Can I speak?

At this point, Emerson switched his position to agree with Belinda. Interestingly, the two White students picked up his original point about the lack of jobs. In the meantime, Emerson's strong statement in tandem with my comment seemed to silence Belinda, who chose not to speak again until the topic changed.

This excerpt illustrates an instance where the leader collaborated with the students to successfully silence conversation, because of our shared discomfort with conflict. Acting as a teacher and a facilitator of the discussion, I tried to help students clarify their statements and positions so that as a group we could critically examine the issues and learn from each other's experiences and perspectives. Although the conversation proceeded for several turns, ultimately we concluded without a deeper understanding of the two viewpoints. In my attempt to clarify the students' positions and encourage the students to listen to each other, I effectively silenced the conversation.

By way of contrast, the two African American students felt comfortable disagreeing with each other. There are numerous other examples in the focus-group conversations of students disagreeing with each other within racial groups. Sometimes we allowed these conversations to proceed, other times they were shut down by leaders or students. This silencing of conflicting and controversial positions was common in this school and fed into the image the school promoted as a place where "everyone gets along."

A More Definitive Act of Silencing. A second form of silencing by an adult had more serious consequences. From the beginning, the conversation in this mixed-race group was heated, as students expressed divergent viewpoints across race lines. There was a turning point in the conversation when a loud and confident White student turned to his African American classmates and asked, "What does honkey mean?" (Schultz et al., 2000).

Michele (B): It's *honk*ey, not honkey. (student laughter)

Conner (W): What's, yea, what's that mean? (student laughter) Honkey . . . *honk*ey.

Phillip (B): What does say, what does nigger mean?

Michele (B): I know!

Conner (W): I was told that nigger means a lazy Black person. That's what I was told.

Shadee (B): Oh!

Michele (B): Oh! Ah—I'm not even gonna start with that.

Phillip (B): Who said that?

Conner (W): Ashley Jones. No Ashley said it was a lazy person.

Shadee (B): A lazy *Black* person.

Conner (W): And someone . . .

Michele (B): It's not a lazy Bl– a nigger could be a White person, a
  Puerto Rican—

George (L): Yo, that's ignorant.

Shadee (B): Can you shut up cuz I'm talking! Why don't you let me
  talk? You said a Black person; you could have said anything. You
  didn't have to just say specifically "a Black person." You could've
  said a White person, or Puerto Rican or any um race.

(focus group, 5/23/97)

The group leader (JED) was listening intently to the conversation, but as
tension increased in the room, a White camera assistant, Brad Thomas (BT),
stepped out from behind the camera in an attempt to cool things down.

BT (W): Listen up. Everyone needs to be quiet. This isn't easy, but
  what he's asking is—he knows there are derogatory terms for, for
  Blacks and he's, he's not really sure what the derogatory term for
  Whites means. So he's curious, and uh, and he's familiar with what
  it is for Blacks. Now it's a stereotype and it's a derogatory term,
  but he fe– he's curious as to what the term is for him, and he just
  wants an explanation.

George (L): He just wanted to know . . . what it was.

BT (W): So there's no reason for you guys to be upset at each other.
  He's just trying to clarify and ask that question. So maybe somebody could answer him that was in the Black group or somebody
  that was in the mixed group today that knows.

Tim (B): Honkey's a White person. Let it go. That's it.

Shadee (B): And I don't understand why people be asking, keep sayin'
  somethin' every time after they—when they say something. I don't
  understand. N'huh?

Roberto (L): I got, I got a question—

Throughout this discussion, the White student, Conner, mocked a characteris-
tically Black way of speaking and had a smile and a nervous laugh that the
Black girls later described as "acting smart." His behavior upset the two black
girls, who became angry and raised their voices. Shadee's statements in particular were filled with emotion. As the conversation continued, she became

more and more agitated. She stood up and waved her arms and her comments became impatient, direct, intense, and filled with exasperation. Although Conner matched the loudness of her voice, he was careful to maintain a rational façade. He leaned back, sat with his arms crossed, and offered comments in a dispassionate tone.

Nervous at the language and especially the feeling tone of the conversation, Brad, the White research assistant, attempted to calm the students down by interpreting Conner's statements for him. Observing the dynamics of the conversation and the interruption, Shadee pointed out that each time Brad stepped into the conversation it was to side with the White student. She indicated the ways in which she was silenced by the leaders and by her peers. The students chose not to recognize her critique; they ignored her and redirected the conversation.

When the bell signaled the end of the school day and the meeting, the disagreement that had built over the course of the focus group, and was only temporarily silenced, spilled out of the room into the hallway. Rather than accepting these silencing moves, Shadee chose to take the conversation outside of its officially sanctioned forum and into public space—the hallway and the phone lines. Students were called names and racial conflict, which the school had worked so hard to suppress, flared. That weekend, the school administrators called James Davis and me to reconvene the group in order to repair the situation.

Our strategy during the second meeting was to reintroduce the misunderstanding and conflict and then let the conversation go unfettered so that we all could listen to each other. We chose to allow the conflict to play itself out so that students could find the words to articulate their understandings of the events. This approach was very different from the process used during the first meeting of the group, where conflict was quickly cut off or silenced. Students rose to the occasion, speaking openly and honestly and, eventually, finding the words to both describe and learn from their differences.

For instance, after a heated interaction between Shadee and Conner, James asked the dumbfounded group to reflect upon what had "just happened." The group fell into a long, tense silence. This question proved to be a turning point in the focus group. Students hesitantly offered reflections. Timothy, a White boy, couched his own insight about difference in a plea for tolerance:

> I don't think anyone should get mad at anybody, because I think his
> way of explaining things is just [to Conner] when you laugh that's [to
> the whole group] that's just his way of explaining something and making
> it easier to understand, [to Shadee] I think and your way is just to ex-
> plain it.
>
> (focus group, 5/27/98)

I responded to Timothy's remark by encouraging others to provide similar critiques. This prompted a flurry of reactions from a range of members who began to build upon each other's ideas. One student explained, "Conner was just trying to bring some humor to the subject." Another added, "[Shadee] is just loud. She can't help it that she is loud." A third interjected, "It's like he says one thing when he means another and she says something and does another." More than one student surmised that they "both misunderstand each other."

Before the group concluded, they identified specific ways in which Conner and Shadee misunderstood and offended one another. Students defined Conner's habit of laughing at inopportune moments, his tendency to smirk and shrug, as "acting smart." Across racial lines, students suggested that Shadee appeared disrespectful when she raised her voice and countered each of Conner's comments. Shadee seemed to listen closely to her peers' observations and suggestions. From that point on, though maintaining her resolve to challenge group members' assertions—especially those made by Conner—she never raised her voice. Although Conner did begin to play a less vocal role in the group's discussion, transformations in his behavior were less immediately apparent (focus group, 5/27/98).

Students concluded that they learned valuable, although not easy, lessons from each other. Among their many comments, two capture the group's general sentiment best. Michael, an African American boy who offered Shadee quiet comments of support throughout the sessions, said, "I learned that some people have different ways of expressing themselves." George, a close friend of Conner's, said, "I think at the time we all might get mad at each other. But, once we resolve it, it can all get better because everybody knows more about the other person and what makes them upset so they won't do it again." Close listening by both leaders and students coupled with careful analysis that we worked on as a group led to critical learning and possibly deeper relationships across racial lines (Schultz et al., 2000). Although difficult and sometimes painful, the listening was generative and led to new understandings. The silencing that had occurred in the first conversation was recognized, acknowledged, and at least partly repaired in this follow-up focus group.

SILENCING THROUGH THE ENACTMENT
OF A COLOR-BLIND DISCOURSE

In many of the focus groups, students worked together to produce silence about race. White students in their single-race groups enacted this silence by avoiding talk about difficult topics and by reaching agreement quickly, masking dissenting opinions. In several of the all-White and mixed-race focus groups, students claimed to be color-blind and participated in talk that erased their differences, working toward common ground. However, students speaking candidly in the single-race groups of African American students did not claim to be color-blind.

Although we attempted to create a context for students to discuss their questions and understandings in the mixed-race focus groups, White students, in particular, often silenced these pointed questions before they were asked. In a more subtle form of silencing, students and discussion leaders often enacted a color-blind discourse of race. Rather than relying on one person to silence conflict between individuals, as Doris and the leaders did in the focus groups previously described, in many focus groups students worked together across race lines to produce a conversation where they could easily agree with each other and reinforce their similarities rather than focus on their differences.

In a Single-Race Group

The silencing of difference and the construction of a color-blind discourse began in single-race groups. In one conversation that mirrored many others, the White students struggled with a way to articulate their notions of difference. The students unpacked their understanding of difference as they attempted to explain how they communicated and interacted with their White and African American peers. The group concluded by agreeing they would try not to understand or even acknowledge difference.

> *Mandy*: Like, you really have to watch what you say and how you act [around Black students].
> *Jeff*: Yeah, and interact.
> *Christa*: You are kind of afraid to say the wrong thing.
> *Mandy*: Sometimes things are taken the wrong way. You say one thing one way, and they take it the other way.
> *Maria*: And then they tell their friends—
> *KS*: So does that change the way you interact with all Black students or is it Black students who aren't really your close friends? How does that affect your relationships?
> *Mandy*: It doesn't affect your relationship with all of them; there are just some you have to be careful around and others you can say things around and it's fine.
> *Maria*: Because some know you are kidding and others don't.
> *Julian*: Like if, you don't know them, they might think the wrong way. Like if you don't know them.
> *Christa*: Well, how do you find out?
> *Mandy*: Like if some are your close friends.

KS: So how do you cross that boundary and become friends with people without having to worry about what you are saying?

Mandy: Well, they are your friends. Like your White friends, the ones that you can tell anything to. Like I call my friends names and we joke around, but they know I don't mean it and I know they don't mean it. But other people, on the other hand, aren't like that.

Julian: Yeah, but some people joke around too much.

Mandy: I am not talking about Black people. There are White people I can't say stuff around. There is no difference really.

Christa: It depends upon how they act.

KS: How who acts?

Christa: Everybody.

Mandy: Like some people think Whites and Blacks are totally different and if some White people hang around Blacks more than they do Whites some people think they change. So like their reactions are different and what they think, so some people think that some Whites are just like Blacks and some Blacks are just like Whites. Or really, everybody is the same but nobody is going to say it. So I mean, it is just weird.

In this excerpt, White students struggled with whether or not the differences they felt between themselves and their peers from other racial backgrounds were similar to or different from the differences they perceived among peers from their same racial background. They expressed their fears of misspeaking with their Black peers. Later they couched these as fears not necessarily based on race. They concluded that although people perceive differences, the differences don't really exist. Because there was general agreement, it does not appear that there was silencing in this conversation. Instead, the comments seemed to build on each other. On the other hand, when there is so much agreement, it is likely that students refrained from expressing divergent views. Listening for silence and silencing is often more challenging when there is apparent agreement. It requires carefully timed and worded questions. In addition, it requires the leader or teacher to notice who is not speaking and what is not being said, in order to push a conversation further.

In Mixed-Race Groups

In comparison to the easy agreement of the all-White focus group, students in a mixed-race focus group collectively constructed a different kind of color-blind discourse. This mixed-race group—the same group that discussed Mexicans in an earlier excerpt—was remarkably upbeat and positive from the beginning. While I set up the videotape recorder and arranged the chairs, they chatted amicably across racial lines. Belinda, the confident African American student who was vocal in the first excerpt, leaned across the table and asked a group of White students, "What did you talk about [yesterday]?" referring to their single-race focus-group meeting in which there was so much agreement. Around a square table in a fairly racially mixed seating pattern, the students sat close to one another as they talked excitedly about the apparent similarities in their single-race conversations. Overall, the 11 students in this group appeared eager to talk with one another about race.

Throughout the meeting, the students engaged in an animated conversation with overlapping speech. Frequently breaking into laughter suggesting solidarity, they were careful to avoid disagreement across racial lines. Like that of the prior mixed-race group, their conversation opened with a question across race lines. However, the question and the response of the individuals and the group were markedly different.

The previous day, both the White students and the students of color had collected questions to ask across groups. The students in the White group wondered: Why do Black students treat different White students differently? In other words, they noticed that some Black students were "cool" with some White students but ignored others. In her halting explanation of this question, Mandy referred to a comment Belinda had made earlier in the focus-group conversation that she liked all White people.

> *Mandy* (W): There is one thing I've been dying to say and I wanted to say a long time ago but I forgot what I was going to say, and it was about like Belinda was saying something like, she was explaining why like Black people treat some White people differently, you know. Well, see, some Black people. I don't understand how they could like every White person because White people don't even like all White people. Like I don't get along with half of the White people in this school. How could she get along with—
>
> *Maria* (L/W): I like more Black than White.
>
> *Cynthia* (W): It's the way you act.
>
> *Christa* (W): It's who you're friends with, and you can make that choice yourself. And you have to look at the person, is that a good person to hang out with? If that will lead you towards where you want to go in life. You have to make that choice yourself.

In this segment, Mandy directed her initial question to Belinda. Her White peers answered for Belinda, who is African American, without giving her a chance to speak. The White students were quick to point out that they were friends equally with Black and White students, claiming that they were not racist and saw the world through color-blind eyes. They agreed with Belinda and quieted Mandy's direct question to her. In their discussion of this familiar

topic in a mixed-race group, they smoothed out their questions and presen
a less complex view of their feelings about race and interracial relationship
In this excerpt, White students worked to silence the question and prevent
"hard" feelings on the part of Belinda, rather than working together to deepen
their understandings. They enacted silence with a color-blind claim: Choose
a person to be your friend on the basis of whether she or he can help you,
rather than on the basis of race.

Buoyed by the general good feeling in this group, the students continued
their conversation, constructing themselves as friends who had much in com-
mon. In addition, they enacted multiple and overlapping ethnicities for them-
selves. Once again, Mandy initiated this conversation by quietly disclosing that
she was part Latina. This seemed to generate respect from her peers, who
joined her in elaborating their ethnic identities.

> KS (W): So, what's—so, um, go ahead, Mandy.
>
> *Mandy* (W): Like my, like nobody knows really what I am. I'm not
>   ashamed of it but like—shut up Jeff. Ah, um, like, it's like, yea um
>   everybody sees me as a White girl. You don't really know what I
>   am. You couldn't guess what I am.
>
> *Maria* (L/W): What are you?
>
> *Jeff* (W): Spanish.
>
> *Maria* (L/W): Are you a Latina?
>
> *Mandy* (W): Yea.
>
> *Maria* (L/W): Cool.
>
> *Mandy* (W): I'm Spanish, Italian, and German and Irish.
>
> *Jeremy* (W): I got a little bit of Irish in me.
>
> *Leila* (L/B): My mom got Irish in her.
>
> *Jeremy* (W): I got a little bit of Irish in me.
>
> *Belinda* (B) (to Leila): *You* got Irish in you?

By the end of this conversation, nearly everyone in the group had claimed to
have multiple ethnicities. Simplistic constructs of race were unsuitable for
these students' identities at least at the moment. Maria playfully called herself
"Hawai-rican" to signify her complex identity as Puerto Rican, Irish, and
Hawaiian. At the same time, nearly everyone claimed to be part Irish. Mandy
softly and hesitantly disclosed her own mixed-heritage background as she explained that "nobody knows really what I am." Although she had previously
identified as White[7]—and had always "passed" as White—her Latina heritage
was a valuable asset in this particular conversation. She was able to claim
commonality with other students in the room by denying her whiteness,[8] la-
menting that "Everybody sees me as a White girl." In this instance the group's
listening included building on each other's statements. Those who had single
ethnicities in their background were suddenly silenced in this conversation.

Students literally made themselves similar, erasing difference, by claiming similar and overlapping ethnicities and identities. This conversation began with a discussion of race and difference. In their move from a discussion of race to one of ethnicity, students successfully avoided talk about difference. In this topical shift, students silenced themselves and chose to move away from what they saw as a potentially difficult conversation. Their move away from race to the safer ground of ethnicity did not occur in any of the single-race focus groups of the previous day.

As the group leader, I could have pushed students to talk about race and ethnicity more explicitly and asked them directly about the meaning of their color-blind talk. If listening to silence includes listening for openings for talk and learning, this was a missed opportunity. This is not to say that teachers should be responsible to follow every thread of every conversation. As teachers we can learn to become aware of those conversations we pursue and those we fail to follow up. In this instance, my omission can be interpreted as silencing.

These conversations illustrate how students and leaders or teachers silence each other in focus groups and in classrooms. Listening for silence suggests the importance of noticing these moments and working to repair them. I am not claiming that enacting a conversation about race is easy, or even possible, for all teachers within the context of a classroom. However, I do suggest that teachers notice what conversations are carried on in their classrooms, and also the conversations and students that are silenced. In listening for silence and the moments when students, conversations, and topics are silenced, teachers can acknowledge the omissions in their curriculum and find ways to make changes. Listening for silence also includes action. It requires taking steps to bring voices, individuals, topics, and structural changes into a classroom and school.

SILENCING THROUGH THE ENACTMENT OF SCHOOL-WIDE PRACTICES AND POLICIES

In this school, silencing also occurred through structural decisions made by administrators, teachers, and parents. An analysis of these decisions suggests two patterns of silencing at a structural level: silencing through exclusion and silencing through selection processes.

Silencing Through Exclusion

During the first year of our research, we often heard about fights that occurred after school. Sometimes these fights were between students of the same racial background, but other times, we were told, the fights mirrored the rarely discussed racial tension of the school. Over the subsequent 2 years, we noticed that fights were mentioned less frequently in our conversations and interviews. The school atmosphere seemed calmer, reflecting the state White students, teachers, and administrators constantly claimed—everyone seemed to get along. Informally, teachers and students disclosed that the difficult—or, in their words, the "bad"—students had been sent to different schools. Everyone seemed to agree that the disappearance of these students from Summit had resulted in a semblance of more agreement and less discord in the school. The school appeared more settled, and also more White.

When we asked for statistics about the students who were told to leave the school, the administrators were not forthcoming and claimed that the school's racial balance remained the same as it had been when we began the project. Students, particularly African American students, were insistent that there was another story. As one student, Tanisha, explained, "They just put 'em out, one by one" (interview, 4/26/99). She explained that not only were the "disruptive" students consigned to an alternative school, Perkins, but that placement was a step in the process of dropping out. Perkins was an alternative middle school in the district designed to house the disruptive students who were not welcome in the mainstream schools.

The suburban location of Summit, Tanisha claimed, meant that most teachers, students, and administrators forgot about the students from the city who were sent to this alternative school. However, Tanisha noted, African American students who lived in their neighborhoods remembered and noticed their absence from the school. As she explained:

And, like, all the boys, like, my cousin and all his friends that was here—none of them go to school anymore. None of them. And I know all [of them]. It's about, it was like a whole clique of boys. It was probably about 15 of them. And then no (inaudible) school anymore. And I know all of them. They all quit school.

Once you're at Perkins, that's just the end of it. And then, sometimes they say if you get a certain amount of credits from Perkins, you go to high school. But I don't even know anybody that ever went from Perkins to high school. 'Cause most high schools don't want you after you were there.

(interview, 4/26/99)

More often than not, as a consequence of being sent away from Summit, students dropped out or were dismissed from school soon after their arrival. According to the students who remained at Summit, they were sent to Perkins because of minor infractions; their dismissal was due more to their attitude than to specific incidents. Institutional silencing meant that the school became more segregated, with fewer interactions between students from different racial and class backgrounds. In this school, the goals of desegregation—translated into bringing together students from a range of backgrounds to learn together—were replaced by a focus on order and academic excellence for the few students who met the norms established by the school. The other students were sent away.

Exclusion Through Selection Processes

The second form of institutional silencing occurred in the selection of students for honors. Institutional decisions kept honors classes and honor societies mostly segregated. Tracking and honors classes were contentious issues at Summit and ones we spoke about frequently with the administrators. During the first year of the research project, there were no honors classes because the principal wanted the classes more integrated and also wanted to provide a high-quality education for all students. White, middle-class parents rebelled at this decision, organized, and brought the issue to the superintendent in a year when an important bond issue was on the ballot. The principal who had eliminated honors classes was transferred to another school. Classes that once were more integrated in terms of race and class became more segregated, with honors classes filled by mostly White and middle-class students. This served to further isolate the students of color and also to deny opportunities to many students, including those students in the honors classes who no longer were in classes with students from a range of racial and class backgrounds.

During the second year of the project, the new principal disclosed that admission into the honors classes was based on teachers' recommendations and tests constructed for this purpose. He admitted that teachers also looked for certain kinds of students and attitudes toward learning that favored White, middle-class students, who the principal felt were overrepresented in the classes, explaining, "The vast majority of students in the honors classes are nice, quiet, compliant, White females" (interview, 11/24/98).

In addition, we were told that students were selected for the Honor Society on the basis of their grade point average, community service, and recommendations from teachers. The vice principal confirmed our conjecture that "minority" students did not want to be in the Honor Society because it was perceived to be a White group. He said, "The ideals of the Honor Society don't coincide with the ideals of the minority students. White kids, Honor Society kids do their community service in suburbia. They never go into the heart of the city to do community service." Reflecting on this group, he informed us, "The Honor Society kids feel attached to the school. They feel as though 'this is my school.'" In the hallways, classrooms, cafeteria, and after school, this court-designated desegregated school did feel White and middle class. The vice principal concluded with a tinge of bitterness, "This community doesn't want a multicultural wall of fame" (interview, 11/24/98).

Nearly all of the teachers and administrators spoke of the racial breakdown of the honors classes and the Honor Society. They were less aware that most of the high-status after-school groups were predominantly White, giving White, middle-class students more opportunities than their Black peers to gain leadership skills. School administrators and teachers ignored the disparity in the opportunities for students from different racial, ethnic, and social class backgrounds[9] and the pattern of "racial nepotism" that was reflected in the process of creating and administering the honors program (West, 1993). Silence on these issues kept some students from participating in all aspects of school including the Honor Society and undermined the goal of equal educational opportunity, which was an important aspect of the original desegregation order in the district.

NOTICING AND ADDRESSING SILENCE

Listening for silence suggests a close examination of conversation, curriculum, and school structures for openings that invite all voices and perspectives into the classroom. It also places responsibility on teachers to look beyond their classrooms for instances of institutional silencing and to imagine ways to work with others to address these inequities.

Every day in schools, as in focus groups, teachers (and here we include ourselves) silence some conversations while allowing others to occur. Most often contentious discussions centered on risky topics are the ones silenced. Not surprisingly, it is often the students of color who find themselves in the position of disagreeing with the dominant assumptions and ways of being in the school. As a result, they experience a disproportionate share of silencing by their teachers and peers (Fine, 1987, 1991).

In contrast to acts of silencing that shut down conversations, teachers can add silence to their classrooms to promote participation and talk. Teachers can create silence or spaces in their classrooms in order to invite voices from students who are too easily overlooked or unheard. In addition to wait time (Rowe, 1986), teachers add silence to their classrooms by asking open-ended questions; ensuring that there are pauses and spaces between talk; constructing curriculum based on students' questions and interests; and taking an inquiry approach to teaching. Through these openings, teachers and students bring their passions into the classroom, deepening the processes of learning. Greene (1988) describes her conception of openings as both physical and metaphorical:

Such efforts unleash imagination in unexpected ways. They draw the mind to what lies beyond the accustomed boundaries and often to what is not yet. They do so as persons become more and more aware of the unanswered questions, the unexplored corners, the nameless faces behind forgotten windows. These are the obstacles to be transcended if understanding is to be gained. And it is in the transcending, as we have seen, that freedom is often achieved. (p. 128)

Greene describes these spaces or silences as both metaphorical and real. They may be actual pauses in talk, but more importantly they are a stance or a disposition that a teacher takes which includes not knowing, curiosity, and possibility. Listening for silence is taking this stance to create openings for new learning to transpire and all voices to be included. The poet Eva Figes (1986) expresses the idea of creating openings or listening to silence in this way:

I can hear the silence, and through it individual sounds.

And the dark silence that surrounds me is full of possibilities.

(pp. 1, 14)

In my own experience as a teacher, I invented ways to notice silenced students and acts of silencing. For instance, I would often go through a list of students at the end of the day to recall my interactions with each one and to record what they did during that day. If I could not recall a specific interaction with each student, whether it was words we exchanged or an interaction around learning, I would make a note to purposefully interact with that child the next day. This daily record keeping helped me to notice the students who were silent or less active in my classroom and the ones with whom I had a stronger or weaker relationship. A systematic examination of students I knew about and those who were more opaque to me led me to reexamine my pedagogy, my interactions with students, and my curriculum.

It was always more difficult to listen for silencing in group conversations and silence that was woven into the fabric of classroom life. Although I was sometimes able to bring out voices of silenced students through varying the contexts for displaying knowledge, countless moments slipped by that I did not notice or pursue. Students' ideas were dismissed; I did not push past the surface harmony to uncover dissension.

Addressing silencing on an institutional level is more difficult still. In our research, we found that the most powerful instances of silencing were at this level. Tracking and subtle policies of exclusion kept students of color from fully participating in the life of the school. As a White, middle-class teacher, I attempted to pay close attention to the taken-for-granted privileges and assumptions, and to question policies that silenced students. I am sure that I did not see or interrogate them all. Such questioning is never comfortable. Yet, if schools are democratizing institutions, it is incumbent on teachers and administrators to ensure that they are places where all students participate.

Noticing, however, is not enough. In addition to listening for acts of silencing and creating openings for talk, as educators we need to change our practices to reflect what we have heard. Lorde (1984) articulates this challenge for Black women that I believe parallels a critical goal for all teachers:

> Certainly for Black women our struggle has not been to emerge from silence to speech but to change the nature and direction of our speech. To make a speech that compels listeners, one that is heard. (p. 124)

Thus listening includes finding a way to respond, to speak, and to be heard.

A focus on listening to acts of silencing and adding silence to a classroom builds on the framework for listening to teach described in this book. When students are silenced, they suffer as individuals and the school suffers as a community. I suggest that teachers listen for the particular voices of students in their classrooms and devise methods for listening to the voices of students who are silenced—or who silence themselves—in classrooms. Processes, such as the descriptive review process elaborated in Chapter 2 (see also Himley, 2000, 2002), allow teachers to listen closely, in concert with others, to students in their classrooms who may be hidden from them or difficult to teach. Although classrooms might favor the most vocal students who are comfortable with the format of class discussions or assignments, teachers can work to create structures and activities for all students to display their knowledge and contribute their perspectives to classroom discussions.

Poets, novelists, feminists, and scholars from a range of disciplines have explored the meanings of silence and acts of silencing in women's lives (e.g., Daley, 1973; Lorde, 1984; Olsen, 1978; Rich, 1979). This same silence exists in classrooms. Responding to silences—creating openings to listen, by listening, and by responding—provides the opportunity for fundamentally changing our conceptions of teaching.

6

Listening to Learn to Teach

> For democracy to survive and flourish, those who have been
> silenced need to find their voices. Those who have been marginal-
> ized need to seek, create, and find a myriad of possible places
> for themselves in society. They must be able to find their dreams
> in the American landscape if our nation is to enact the demo-
> cratic dream.
>
> (Darling-Hammond, 1998, p. 91)

IN MY FIRST YEAR AS codirector of the elementary teacher education program at the University of Pennsylvania, an African American student, Tammy,
wrote the following question on an evaluation form: Why are you teaching us
urban theory and suburban methods? Interested, I asked her what she meant.
What ensued was a conversation that has continued over the past several
years, beyond Tammy's graduation from the program and into her first few
years as a teacher in a public elementary school in an urban district. By her
question, Tammy meant that our program emphasized what she considered
to be urban issues; we had heated discussions about pedagogy and curriculum
for students from diverse backgrounds, often specifically focused on African
American students who were in the majority in most of the urban public
schools where the prospective teachers did their student teaching. And although we directly, and sometimes insistently, addressed issues we felt relevant to urban teaching, we also introduced students to ways of teaching that
student teachers labeled "progressive" and that Tammy labeled "suburban."

Tammy was raised in Los Angeles and attended a small, progressive,
independent school on a scholarship. She often felt a clash between what she
learned at home and the practices of her school. Dedicated to teaching in an
urban public school, Tammy saw the methods we introduced to students in
our teacher education program as suited for "suburban" or privileged, inde-
pendent-school environments. She did not observe many of these practices,
such as writing workshops and reading taught through literature, in the school
where she did her student teaching. She could not imagine that they would
work in her public school context. My goal, since that time, has been to find

142

ways to teach prospective—and experienced—teachers to think about pedagogy not as progressive or traditional, urban or suburban, suited for public or independent schools. Rather, I have been seeking a way to introduce conceptions of teaching that are respectful of students and reflect the values of their local communities and those that undergird the notion of a pluralistic democracy (Darling-Hammond, 1998). I began to see listening as a critical response to this challenge. Along with my colleagues, I encouraged student teachers to envision teaching as listening, to learn who their students are, and to understand their local contexts in order to develop ways to teach all students, especially in contexts where, as teachers, they crossed boundaries of race, class, or culture.

Over the course of her year in the teacher education program, Tammy came to envision the possibilities of actively engaging students in meaningful learning. She began to understand the ways in which the educational practices she learned could be respectfully adapted to urban settings. The following year, when Tammy entered an urban public school as a new teacher, she began by listening to the administrators, teachers, parents, and children in her school community. During her first year, Tammy was required to use a structured phonics program to teach reading. She was told to follow a script in order to drill her first, then second, graders in sounds each day. Beginning each morning with scripted lessons, she took the mandate seriously and displayed the progress charts for her principal to monitor. In the afternoon, she brought out books and engaged students in elaborate writing projects connected to thematic units. Over time, her colleagues and, later, her principal, became interested in the reading and writing that went on in her classroom. She was asked to assume a leadership role in her school to introduce some of these methods to her colleagues. Parents heard the excitement in their children's voices when they described their classroom activities and were curious to find out more about how their children were learning to read and write.

Tammy constantly searched for a balance between following the school mandates and trying on the approaches she had learned in graduate school. She did not simply replace one orthodoxy for another but studied her local context, listened carefully to everyone around her, and fashioned a way to teach that was based on relationships and a belief in the humanity of her students (e.g., Bartolomé, 1994; Freire, 1970; Macedo, 1994). Tammy continued to have challenging moments. However, students flourished in her classroom, benefiting from pedagogy and curriculum she had once thought were reserved for more privileged students with the luxury of time. Rather than adopting a particular set of methods, she taught in ways that were at once respectful and challenging, that built on students' strengths and interests. She established trust in her classroom, while introducing students to skills, knowledge, and dispositions essential to their education.

GOING BEYOND THE DICHOTOMY OF TRADITIONAL AND PROGRESSIVE PEDAGOGY

This book describes teaching as listening through an exploration of teachers' and students' experiences across multiple contexts. Taken together, the four components of listening comprise a stance. This stance invites teachers to engage students as active participants in their education. Listening in this manner supports teachers to create openings that enable them to look, with students, "toward untapped possibility" (Greene, 1995, p. 42). Rather than adopt a set of methods that can be labeled progressive or traditional, I suggest teachers create a context for learning based on relationship and respect. Macedo (1994) describes this as an "antimethod pedagogy." He writes:

> An antimethod pedagogy points to the impossibility of disarticulating methods from the theoretical principles that inform and shape them. An antimethod pedagogy makes it clear to educators that a method of teaching reflects a particular view of the world and is articulated in the interest of unequal power relations. . . . [and] education is involved in a complex nexus of social, cultural, and economic and political relationships that involve students, teachers, and theorists in different positions of power. (p. 181)

In the current climate, the focus on testing and delivering content has made it difficult for teachers to remember and act on their knowledge that students have to assent before learning can take place (Erickson, 1987; Kohl, 1994). In this book, I have suggested that teachers begin by listening to students as individuals, to the class as a group, and to the students' communities in and out of school. As teachers come to know their students, it becomes incumbent on them to provide students with skills and habits of mind (Dewey, 1902/1956; Meier, 1996) for their futures. A listening stance is fundamental to educating students to participate in democratic society.

PLACING THE CURRENT EDUCATIONAL CLIMATE IN PERSPECTIVE

The current climate of educational reform and the attendant focus on high-stakes testing and curricular standards do not mark this moment as either a crossroads or a unique time period. Since the turn of the century when John Dewey introduced the set of principles that became known as progressive education,[1] there have been waves of reform nearly every 30 years that have countered this education movement. In the 1920s, the efficiency movement introduced factorylike practices to public schools. In the 1950s, teacher-proof curricular reforms were introduced, and more recently, the "back-to-basics" movement of the 1980s replaced practices more commonly associated with progressive education (Darling-Hammond, 1998). Each of these reforms was fashioned in response to an educational crisis; the solution was to seek uniformity and control. Rather than offering a single solution to the current educational crisis, the stance of listening cuts across the various approaches to teaching. This stance toward teaching gives new and experienced teachers guideposts for learning how to cross boundaries of difference to create contexts in which students can learn, at the same time that teachers acquire deeper understandings of their students.

In her landmark set of articles, Delpit (e.g., 1986, 1988, 1995) raised questions about whether methods commonly associated with progressive education, such as writing workshops and whole-language teaching, meet the needs of African American children. Delpit's critique of progressive education was based, in part, on her findings that many White, middle-class teachers enacting these methods were unfamiliar with the cultures of their students and made assumptions about their needs based on this limited experience. More recently, Reyes (1992) has argued that whole-language advocates may ignore the cultural and linguistic competencies of their students, especially those who are not native English speakers, in their advocacy of a single method. In particular, she faults the "one size fits all" approach that does not take into account students' cultural resources. Rather than offering a critique of particular methods, Bartolomé (1994) urges teachers to take a sociohistorical view of "minority" students in order to understand their failure in school. In lieu of "fixing" students with new methods, she suggests that teachers adopt an educational philosophy that acknowledges power differentials in society and classrooms, in a manner that respects students' cultural knowledge. As she explains,

> Unless educational methods are situated in the students' cultural experiences, students will continue to show difficulty in mastering content area that is not only alien to their reality, but is often antagonistic toward their culture and lived experiences. Further, not only will these methods continue to fail students, particularly those from subordinated groups, but they will never lead to the creation of schools as true cultural democratic sites. (p. 14)

Each of these critiques suggests the importance of listening as a way to interpret and adapt any set of methods to local situations. By listening closely to students across multiple dimensions, teachers can go beyond a focus on methods to base their pedagogy and curriculum on a deep understanding of students' lives. As Roosevelt (1998) explains:

> We can and must understand the institution of public education as both an expression of faith in the possibility of democracy and an effort to further democ-

racy: thus, an institution dedicated to the premise that all children, as citizens, can have worthwhile ideas, ideas that can enter powerfully into the experiences and imaginations of others. (p. 64fn)

Through listening, educators can have access to these ideas, integrating them into the classroom and curriculum. Dewey's (1916/1944) conception of critical democracy suggests that people enhance each other's experiences by listening, raising questions that interrupt habitual ways of thinking, and opening doors to new possibilities.

The underpinning of each of the four components of listening to teach articulated in the preceding chapters is a belief that a central purpose of education is to prepare individuals to participate in a pluralistic democratic society. In order for students to learn the knowledge, skills, and dispositions essential for participation in democracy, schools and classrooms must embody and enact that democracy. As Darling-Hammond (1998) explains,

> Schools must provide an education that enables critical thinking *and* communal experiences so that citizens can intelligently debate competing ideas, weigh the individual and the common good, and make judgments that sustain democratic institutions and ideals. (p. 80)

Listening to teach enables teachers to learn from students how to cross cultural boundaries so that they can join together to establish classroom communities that teach and reflect democratic values.

RESEARCH CONTEXT

A central aim of our elementary teacher education program at the University of Pennsylvania is to introduce student teachers to pedagogy and curriculum that is based on listening closely to students and their communities, hearing what they say, and acting on that knowledge. Our goal is to prepare teachers to adapt their teaching to the children and the contexts in which they teach, by listening carefully to individual children—in and out of school—and to the rhythms and silences of their classrooms as a whole. This is a complex process, one we have time only to introduce in our short teacher education program. We try to cultivate dispositions or habits of mind (Dewey, 1902/1956; Meier, 1996) that student teachers will carry with them, adapt, and transform, as they become full-time classroom teachers.

To illustrate how we teach the processes of listening, in this chapter I draw primarily from data collected during the fall of 2000, when a colleague and graduate student, Sarah Jewett, and I led the field seminar for the entire group of 40 student teachers in the program. In addition to my own weekly field notes, weekly plans, student papers, and e-mail correspondence, a graduate student, Patti Buck, assisted me in data collection by keeping a second set of field notes and audiotaping each class. I held monthly focus groups with 12 student teachers who agreed to participate in the research project. These same student teachers wrote in separate journals for the project, noting the connections between the seminar and their teaching, and their responses to the seminar itself. The patterns reported in this chapter reflect a careful analysis of the transcripts and artifacts of my own teaching from this class over a 3-year time period (1998–2000) as well as the seminar I taught with Sarah.

FRAMING LISTENING FOR STUDENT TEACHERS

In order to structure the seminar, Sarah and I used the framework for listening described in this book. The first type of listening we introduced to student teachers was listening to the details or particularities that a student brings to the classroom in order to make the student visible to teachers. One way that we explored this form of listening was with the descriptive review of the child, a process developed by Patricia Carini and her colleagues at the Prospect Center in Bennington, Vermont (Carini, 1982, 1986; Himley, 2000, 2002; Kanevsky, 1993), and described in Chapter 2. After student teachers became familiar with this process, we introduced the child study project, which gives student teachers the opportunity to examine their pedagogy and curriculum through the close study of a single child. Student teachers spent nearly 6 weeks observing a single student, documenting his or her learning. The descriptive review and our assignment of a child study are collaborative inquiry processes that enabled student teachers to focus on the strengths or capacities of individual children through a set of categories and a structured process. This format supports teachers to construct new knowledge about children in order to listen to and understand the students beyond surface categories that might interfere with knowing the students.

A second type of listening involves listening for the rhythm and balance of the classroom (see Chapter 3). Listening for rhythm and balance allows teachers to both take leadership and simultaneously follow the direction set by each group of students. In the seminar, student teachers were introduced to rituals in classrooms and the process of forming classrooms into pluralistic democratic communities. We taught student teachers to assess each day's activity and plan curriculum on that basis, rather than planning by the week. New student teachers are often most worried about classroom management or discipline. The concept of listening for rhythm and balance provides a way to address issues of management and classroom control. In the seminar, we used the notion of the rhythm and balance of a classroom as a way to develop an understanding of how to maintain a classroom community that allows for and honors multiple perspectives. We used this discussion to explore classroom rituals and routines.

For instance, we introduced students to a ritual that an elementary teacher in Baltimore, Stephanie Terry, uses to begin each day (see Rose, 1995, for a detailed description of this ritual). In tune with her students, Stephanie starts each day with a Morning Unity Circle (also called an Umoja Circle by many teachers). Students recite a poem beginning with "I am a special person. My teacher knows I'm special" (Rose, 1995, p. 105). At the end of this time together, children shake each other's hands. In the seminar, we talked with the student teachers about how to adapt this ritual to their own classes as a way to gather the students together at the beginning of the day. We suggested that this ritual provides a way to listen to the concerns students bring into the classroom, preparing them to focus and engage in academic learning.

The third form of listening includes learning about the bigger picture of who students are and the social, cultural, and community contexts of their lives (see Chapter 4). We asked student teachers to find out about and attempt to understand their students' lives outside of school, including the resources they brought to school from their homes and communities. In order to explore this form of listening, student teachers began our elementary teacher education program by conducting neighborhood studies. They constructed curriculum resource guides from the content they gathered through oral histories and neighborhood research during the first month of our program. In addition, in the fall seminar, student teachers carefully examined a set of classroom letters between a teacher and her students' parents. They also interviewed children in their classrooms about their literacy and learning outside of school. They learned about an aspect of popular culture that captured the attention of children in their classrooms. In these ways, student teachers developed deeper understandings of their students, listening closely to the larger contexts of their lives.

Finally, listening to the silences and the ways in which students are silenced helps student teachers learn how to notice who speaks in the classroom and who remains silent, which topics are addressed and which are ignored (see Chapter 5). We introduced student teachers to issues in schools, such as tracking, that structure students' experiences in the classroom, in order to alert them to this form of listening. We asked them to document forms of silencing in their classrooms and schools and discuss them in relation to teaching decisions they make in their classrooms. We showed videotapes of conversations about race and students' racialized experiences in school to prompt conversations about race and schooling. These issues were particularly germane to the predominantly White and middle-class group of student teachers in the program, many of whom student taught in urban, public schools. Student teachers analyzed how power works in their classrooms. They discussed how to recognize and draw out students' voices that may have been silenced or extinguished. We talked about whether and how to discuss topics, such as race, that are often assumed out of bounds in schools. We worked together to construct ways to ensure that multiple perspectives were represented in these discussions. These aspects of listening provided a frame for the syllabus and the central themes of the seminar.

Listening to teach is woven throughout the seminar and each of the courses in our teacher education program. Three processes characterized how we introduced the various ways of listening to student teachers. First, we taught student teachers particular tools for listening. Next, we used analytic frames with them to critique teaching. Finally, we provided them with ways to imagine how they might transform their teaching conditions as activist teachers.

Developing Tools for Listening to Children

Student teachers in our teacher education program were introduced to the processes of conducting teacher research or inquiry into their own practice from the beginning of the program. In addition to teaching student teachers to take an inquiry stance in their teaching, we explicitly taught them tools for listening to students, observing and collecting information about students to inform the myriad decisions they made as teachers. The teacher education program was structured to begin in the first term with a focus on community and the relationships between neighborhoods and school. In the second term, the course work focused on the theme of learners and learning, emphasizing the way that teaching grows from deep and specific knowledge of students, families, and communities. We gave student teachers tools or methods for collecting information about students and classroom practices through three major assignments: a neighborhood study, a child study, and an inquiry-into-teaching portfolio. For each of these assignments, student teachers formulated inquiry questions that helped to focus their listening. In the next section, I describe an assignment and a process integral to a second assignment—the child study and the formulation of an inquiry question—to provide examples of the tools we teach to students.

Composing a Child Study. During the second term, when the programmatic emphasis was on learners and learning, student teachers chose a single student in their class for their practitioner inquiry project. They composed a child study, which included a descriptive review or exploration of the child's stance in the world, the child's strengths and vulnerabilities, a portrait of the child as a literacy learner in and out of school, and a description of his or her mathematical understandings. It is our belief that the close study of an individual child will allow student teachers to learn to listen for, notice, and gather information about each child in their classroom across multiple dimensions. The goal was for student teachers to make recommendations for how to teach the child. Rather than selecting a child whose stance as a learner stood out because he is difficult or perplexing, we asked student teachers to build their child study around a central question about teaching. After deciding on a question, student teachers identified a student to study closely in order to explore these questions, which in turn gave them insight into the other students in their classroom.

One student teacher, Shana Duffine, wrote about the challenge of using knowledge gained from close study of an individual child to inform her teaching of the whole group. When she was initially presented with the idea of a child study which included a Descriptive Review of a single child, she balked, quickly deciding that it was inherently unfair to focus her attention on just one student. She worried that the knowledge would be gained at the expense of failing to notice and attend to the other children. However, her understanding of this process and its value changed after she presented her child to a group of peers and teachers. She realized that she could use the feedback and her growing knowledge of a single child, not only in teaching this particular child but also in working with all of the children in her class. In writing about this experience for her final portfolio for her master's degree, she posed the following questions: "What is the appropriate balance between teaching individual students and teaching a group? How does a teacher determine how to use what is known about a single student to benefit an entire class of students?" (Duffine, 2001).

Reflecting on this experience, Shana wrote in a journal during the fall, "This project helped me to focus and observe. These are two things that I am not so good at. Through my observations I was able to see things that otherwise I would not." The next day she wrote the following journal entry,

> Since I have some beginning ways of analyzing I am able to more carefully assess students. I was looking over my notes for seminar and I have written [on 9/12/00] "part of observation is to begin with a question"—this is what I have to work on more. I am not just looking for the sake of looking; instead I am trying to discover something. My Descriptive Review helped me to start to form these constructive questions.

Shana began by doubting the usefulness of close observation of individual children. In her words, she had a "conversion experience"; her practice was transformed.

That spring, Shana was a student teacher in a new kindergarten class-room. She was in the midst of teaching a unit on transportation that seemed to be going smoothly. Children were actively engaged in a wide variety of projects and field trips that reflected their questions. One day Shana was caught off guard. As she described this event:

> Each morning two of the students in my class, Lamar and Ahmed, would arrive many minutes prior to their classmates. I made an effort each day to solicit feedback on my teaching and the class's activities from these two students. Both Lamar and Ahmed were eloquent students who were willing to engage in conversation with me. Each day the two students would tell me what they had liked about the day before and we would talk about other things that were happening in their lives. I made a conscious effort to pay close attention to Lamar and Ahmed during these times, as a result of what I knew about the benefits of critically observing children. When Lamar and Ahmed were not talking to me they bantered on topics typical of kindergartners. In light of the fact that I believe that I can learn about children from observing them, I also always kept my ear on their conversations. On this particular day Ahmed and Lamar were looking at a chart that I had posted in the room called "The ABC's of Transportation." The chart had an illustration of a different mode of transportation for each letter of the alphabet. (For example, the letter "C" had a drawing of a car next to it.) As I was writing on our class dry-erase board I overheard a conversation that went somewhat like this:
>
> *Lamar*: Are snowboards transportation?
> *Ahmed*: No they're not. It doesn't have wheels. It needs wheels to be transportation.
> *Lamar*: Right. Like the trolley and the train with wheels.
>
> At this point I needed to intervene. I thought that the students understood what transportation was. I never took into consideration that they would not understand this concept. I panicked! We had been studying land transportation for two and a half weeks. How could they not understand?
> I took a deep breath and turned towards Lamar and Ahmed and asked them what they were talking about. Through a brief conversation the students spoke aloud my greatest fear. Not only did they not understand clearly what transportation was, but also they thought that wheels defined transportation. I quickly thought about what my next move should be. I knew that I needed to clarify the discrepancies that my stu-

dents had. I also realized that two confused students probably indicated a classroom of confused students. Upon consultation with Maria, my classroom mentor, I changed my plan for the morning and decided to begin the school day with a class meeting on the rug. During the group meeting it was confirmed that many students were confused about the meaning of the word transportation and also with other aspects of the curriculum that I had created. As a class we looked at the transportation ABC chart and came up with the theme common to all of the pictures: they all "can take you places." From this point we determined that there were three categories of things that "take you places," land, air, and sea. Therefore we decided "if it takes you places on the ground, it is land transportation." Armed with this information we generated a list of things that "take us places on the ground." At least two of those things, snowboards and feet, do not have wheels. Thus, as a class, we came to a consensus that the different modes of transportation do not necessarily have wheels.

(Duffine, 2001)

Shana described how she literally listened to her students and used their words to inform her teaching decisions and transform her curriculum. Listening, as I conceptualize it, includes both literally hearing students and attending to them across multiple dimensions. In addition to actually hearing students, listening includes noticing a quizzical look that crosses a child's face, getting a sense of the class through noticing and hearing exasperation or puzzlement in their voices, or interpreting words and actions together. Listening might account for information and practices related to the study of a topic such as transportation that is learned outside of school. In addition, teachers might use listening to attend to the silences or moments when conversation is cut short. By listening to their actual words, Shana learned about the misunderstandings of these students—and many of their classmates—about transportation. Rather than simply telling the student the correct information, she used the knowledge gained from two students to construct new knowledge with her class. The two students gave her insight into how and what the class was learning. Unafraid to correct their misconceptions, Shana invited the students to build new knowledge with her. She reflected on what she had learned through listening.

Upon reflection of this incident I realized that I had accomplished what I had wanted to ultimately do. I used my observational skills to focus on a small number of students as Carini suggests.[2] I then used the information that I gleaned from those observations and turned it into a lesson for the entire class. The lesson was "evolutionary" and "developed according to students' needs and teacher and students' interests." The fusion of my purposes in teaching occurred in a brief moment and I was ecstatic. To the outside observer this group lesson on modes of transportation was not momentous, but to me it was an occasion to celebrate. (Duffine, 2001)

Shana celebrated this moment because it represented a transformative moment in her own teaching that was directly connected to her close listening and work with a few students. She went from the particular—a focus on one child and one idea—to a larger understanding of how to teach the whole class. The child study and descriptive review process gave her the tools to begin this venture.

In the fall seminar, we taught student teachers to listen to how and what students knew rather than to seek a particular answer. We also taught them to listen for who students were and what interests, knowledge, and stances they brought to their learning. A focus in our work with student teachers was to help them learn to inquire into their students' understandings (e.g., Ball, 1993; Duckworth, 2001). Mina Shaughnessy (1976, 1977) was one of the first educators to make a powerful case for how much we can learn from the errors students make, reframing error as a window into student understanding. (See also Hull & Rose, 1989, 1990.) We taught our student teachers to listen not only to the individuals in the class—for their proclivities and particular stances toward learning—but also to the class as a group.

Formulating Questions. In the following scene from the fieldwork seminar, I offer one example of how we taught student teachers to construct inquiry questions to guide their investigation of teaching. To introduce this process, we asked student teachers to write down their current beliefs about teaching. We talked about the importance of thinking carefully about their values and beliefs in relationship to educational practice, in order to avoid the pitfall of teaching by enacting techniques. We wanted to encourage student teachers to develop ways to teach based on the practice of listening to students, and supported by their beliefs and understandings about children, their knowledge of learning and teaching, their content knowledge and its relationship to pedagogy (Shulman, 1986, 1987), and an articulation of the purposes of schooling.

After student teachers had written for a short time, we asked them to state their questions aloud so that we could talk about them as a group. Ann and Karol, student teachers at the same nearby urban public school, explained that both of their questions addressed how class size has an impact on classroom management. They had each developed separate questions that related to this topic. Karol asked, "How do you communicate caring while setting limits?" Ann's question was: "How much attention do you give to students with different needs and how much choice can you offer them?" Although neither of these questions was directly about listening, each reflected knowledge about the role of listening to teach.

For the next several minutes, student teachers volunteered their questions. Ralph said that he was interested in why there wasn't more opportunity for play in the classroom. He went on to describe sterile, traditional teaching methods at his school. Nora said her question was about how the "structure of the classroom" has an impact on classroom management. She was a student teacher in a combined classroom with 66 students and two teachers, and she struggled with how to teach such a large group of children. She used the word *structure* to refer to the participant structures or the ways that students and teachers interacted in whole-class and small-group settings. She was running into difficulties with the large group and wondered how to plan activities so that individual students could learn in this setting. Janet volunteered that she was interested in what "good" whole-class instruction looks like and when it is appropriate to teach the entire group rather than work with small groups or individuals. Lucy asked how mixed-grade groupings and detracking affect student learning. Rebecca wondered if inclusion is helpful or harmful to special education students. Annette said that her interest was in how "unstable" or disorganized and chaotic classroom environments affect kids. Elise wondered how you balance your time between your dual roles as disciplinarian and instructor. Finally, Joan asked if team teaching benefits or disadvantages teaching. Each of these questions reflected the concerns student teachers brought to the seminar and their teaching. They also displayed their struggle to learn to listen to their students and to the entire class.

After gathering their questions and writing them on the board, I reminded student teachers that the goal of the project was to examine pedagogy with the underlying question: Given what we know about children, how should we teach? Sarah added that the student teachers should articulate questions that lend themselves to gathering rich, contextual data from the classroom. I suggested that this might mean reworking their questions. For example, I explained that Janet's question about what comprises "good" teaching might be changed to, "What is the range of decisions a teacher makes when teaching a whole class?" I reminded her that she could track how and when teachers in her classroom, including herself, used knowledge based on listening to individual children or to the class as a whole to make decisions. Such questions allow students to listen for and analyze the range of options available to them rather than judging practice. I explained that although Janet might not be able to identify "good" practice in the short time students had for the project, she could certainly document a range of practices. A focus on listening could help her to analyze teachers' decisions at various moments.

Crafting inquiry questions helps student teachers to listen to their students by giving them the tools to acquire an intentional and articulated focus in a fast-paced, polyphonic classroom. In developing a question about orchestrating classroom management, for example, student teachers learn to listen for the subtle changes in the content and style of responses that teachers offer students across multiple categories such as race, class, and gender, as well as the assumptions that undergird those responses.

In this class discussion, the student teachers framed inquiry questions that reflected their insights derived from their current classroom experiences as well as their anticipation of full-time student teaching that spring. Taking an inquiry stance helped the student teachers to listen in a focused manner. Sarah and I used student teachers' explorations of their own interests and questions to teach them how to frame their project to give them a way to inquire into teaching and learning. We used detailed discussions of individual questions to teach the whole group how to reflect on and reframe their own questions. Framing questions was thus one of many tools we gave student teachers for understanding listening to teach. Our goal was to help them use inquiry questions to focus their listening to students, and to document and reflect on their practice. Once student teachers formulated their inquiry questions, we explicitly taught them to analyze their own and their mentors' teaching practices.

Analyzing Teaching Practices

In our teacher education program, we emphasize that pedagogy and curriculum should grow out of a deep knowledge about elementary students combined with knowledge of content and pedagogy. We teach student teachers to reflect constantly on their teaching and the teaching that they observe to make sense of their pedagogical decisions. In order to help them learn to reflect, we explicitly instruct them in how to analyze and critique. A class discussion on John Dewey and progressive education presented one such moment for reflection and analysis.

Rather than promoting particular techniques for teaching, our goal is to introduce student teachers to a range of methodologies, so they can develop ways of teaching that are undergirded by an articulated set of beliefs. We spent a few weeks at the beginning of the term focused on pedagogy, reading Dewey (1938/1963) and critiques of progressive education from a range of perspectives. Student teachers often regarded everything we taught them as "progressive education," and so we used a study of Dewey to complicate this understanding.

We began our second class on progressive education by handing out several note cards, each with a central tenet of progressive education drawn from

Dewey's writing and adapted from a recent book by Perrone (2000), *Lessons for New Teachers*. Each student received a card with one of the principles; four to five student teachers had the same card. Student teachers were asked to form pairs or threesomes with peers who held matching cards. Next, students were asked to take the role of either the "believer" or the "doubter" of their statement and to divide the roles evenly (see Elbow, 1987). The "believers" were instructed to garner arguments in agreement with the statement, whereas the "doubters" were asked to construct a case against the principle. Student teachers chose their roles and wrote their positions. In order to debate these positions, they combined their smaller groups forming groups of four or five who had each received the same card. After the debate, they were asked to rehearse and perform a 2-minute, two-act play, each act representing one side of the issue. Student teachers quickly put together clever plays that drew on and sometimes parodied their classroom experiences. Their performances of the skits drew laughter and applause.

After the performances, we asked the student teachers for feedback on the activity. In particular, we wanted them to articulate how (and whether) the skits had helped them to grapple with principles of progressive education. Student teachers noted the ways in which they were able to look at issues from both sides; they observed the negative light cast on the positions held by the "doubters," particularly in the skits, and they raised questions about the feasibility of enacting these progressive practices, especially in large urban schools.

Next, we asked student teachers to use Dewey, or more general progressive education principles, to critique the way we had set up the discussion and experiences around these ideas. In other words, we gave them a particular frame to analyze our teaching during that class. In order for student teachers to apply this sort of analysis to their own teaching, we felt that it was important to begin with an opportunity for them to critique our class and the choices we made as instructors. Acknowledging the ways in which teachers always balance depth and breadth and the limitations of a quick exercise such as the one we planned for sustained dialogue, we invited the student teachers to offer their views about whether and how this was progressive teaching.

I began by asking,

> What were we trying to do? From a Deweyan or progressive stance, what worked and didn't work about what we asked you to do with these statements? We want you to be able to critique your own teaching. Looking at our class is one way to begin to learn how to do this critique.

The student teachers offered a range of responses. Nora related this question to her own decision-making process as a new student teacher. She explained,

[The issues raised by choosing to use skits for this activity are similar to what] I think about as I'm trying to start to do lessons. Mary and I did a big one last week. [In our planning, our question was] how do you give content but make it entertaining? [In class today] it was definitely more entertaining for people to act out skits, but how do you make sure the nuances can be communicated in a short amount of time?

Student teachers are often inclined to try to make their teaching fun. They have a strong desire to be liked by their students and may remember their own schooling as boring and dull. As a consequence, they often conceptualize teaching as a string of activities. We emphasize again and again the importance of designing teaching according to beliefs and goals. Our use of the skits to interrogate ideas about progressive education enabled Nora and others to examine and articulate their own choices and decisions. Nora described what was lost—the nuances of the various principles—by turning the ideas into short skits. Along with others, she spoke of the stereotyped or shallow notions that came through in the plays. This analysis of the class gave Nora and others new insights into the choices they made as student teachers in their classroom placements.

Joan had been worrying about an interaction she observed in her own classroom. The head teacher's interactions with students and parents around how to prepare students for testing had disturbed her. She used this unsettling experience as the basis for one of her group's skits; they enacted the scene with Joan as teacher. By putting herself in the head teacher's role so that she had to respond to difficult questions raised by students, reassure them, and disclose tricky information to parents, she gained a new perspective on the complexity of responding to students in the moment. As she stated:

The teacher situation [that we acted out] happened in our school. When it happened, I felt really bad and upset by it and left. I couldn't believe that my teacher was acting that way. [But] when I *was* the teacher [in the skit], I found the points valid and I wanted the student to give the right answer. I wanted my class to be successful. I had already met the parents. I had already done the testing. Taking on the role made a huge change for me.

This student teacher and others in the class exhibited a tendency to advocate a middle ground between "progressive" and "traditional" classrooms as a compromise. I challenged this tendency, pushing student teachers to articulate clearly their beliefs about teaching as contextualized by their settings, students, and the expectations of the community. I suggested that this process was more complicated than simply compromising and enacting a little of each methodology. It was important to listen to the values and goals of the community in order to craft teaching practices, and it was also important to choose and defend a consistent set of beliefs. Noting the power of experiencing other teachers' decisions, evident in the doing of the skit, we likened this enactment to strategies they might use to teach their own students. Joan's reflection on her skit led into a discussion about reaching compromises too quickly, and the pitfalls of reaching too quickly for facile solutions.

Mary Jo made the final comment in the conversation. She raised a provocative question about whether this kind of teaching is realistic in large school systems, especially in an era overshadowed by standardized tests. She stated:

> I was thinking about what Group 6 did with sky and grass. In science class we were talking about how much do you let kids make their own assumptions and then when do you have to tell kids facts, when they are going to have to take standardized tests. When do you say, "No, that is not why the sky is blue. The sky is blue because" and get them ready for the test versus fostering their imagination? I'm just throwing it out for people to think about.

Mary Jo addressed the realities of the current climate in the urban school system where she and most of her peers were placed for their student teaching. As in most urban districts, classes in this district were often overcrowded, resources were stretched, and many teachers openly voiced their feelings of discouragement. She used the activity and our invitation to critique and raise questions about how to make the ideas introduced in the university classes relevant to the conditions in the city public schools. We helped the students see how Dewey's (e.g., 1902/1956) stance of "both/and" rather than "either/ or" could help them to see their way out of this dilemma (cf Fishman & McCarthy, 1998). We argued that if they used this notion, they would not have to choose to *either* prepare students for tests or foster their imagination. Rather, they could design curricula for both goals. We did not offer easy answers but raised questions and possibilities. As always, this made some students uncomfortable in the moment. They saw that using this process to reflect and analyze was not necessarily going to lead to answers; more likely, it would lead to more questions.

By inviting critique, we asked students to pay close attention and to listen again to our work together as a class in order to analyze what and how they had learned. Student teachers connected the class activity with their own struggles to plan classes and understand the decisions made by their classroom mentors. They wrestled with whether to make school "fun" or instructive and wondered how to achieve a balance. They described how the activity helped them to understand teaching decisions. Many reflected on their idealistic pictures of how classrooms should function, focusing on the goal of preparing children for standardized tests. Student teachers took this opportunity to think carefully about the structure of the seminar and the limitations and possibilities afforded by that structure.

Further, they were asked to critique the class in a very particular way. We asked student teachers to use the lens of progressive education, or Dewey's beliefs, to analyze *how* we had introduced these ideas to them. We wanted to teach student teachers to critique in specific ways that were grounded in evidence. Our hope was that this process would do more than make the concepts we were teaching seem more concrete. We anticipated that by engaging in a process of critiquing others (in this case their professors), the student teachers would become more self-reflective and better understand the feedback offered to them as student teachers. By carefully planning our classes on the basis of particular ideas and then inviting critique, we engaged student teachers in a dialogue about practice grounded in listening carefully and reflecting on practice.

Encouraging Student Teachers to Become Activists

As a culmination to the discussions about pedagogy, we chose to explore democratic classrooms and the purposes of schooling. Our focusing question for this class was: If we want democratic classrooms, what do we need to tinker with and what do we need to transform in classrooms and schools? (Jewett, personal communication, 8/17/00). We initiated a series of discussions beginning with small-group explorations of the articles assigned for that week (Fraser, 1997; Meier, 1996; Perry & Fraser, 1993). When the class came back together as a large group, I asked the student teachers, "In the context of democratic classrooms or schooling, what do you want to preserve from your current classrooms, what would you like to tinker with, and what will you transform when you are a full-time teacher?"

Joan began the discussion with a story about her work with a young boy in her class who "doesn't appear to know a whole lot but really took us by surprise" by getting every answer correct on an assessment. Excited about his success, she went to the teacher with this news. The teacher ignored this new information and held on to her original understanding of the student, saying "that there are always a few students who never know anything so you just kind of don't bother with them. There are always a few hopeless children."

Joan was astounded. As she explained,

> Those [children who seem to be failing] would be the ones you would really want to work on because they are, you know, clearly a little bit on the lower level. But I just could not believe that a teacher said to me,

"Don't bother with them," and that doesn't seem democratic to me at all. That is something I would definitely transform. Never assuming that any of my students are hopeless or can't do anything.

Joan's analysis reflected our focus on listening to know particular children. She was unwilling to take a deficit perspective and give up on children. One assignment had been for student teachers to write a vignette of a time a student surprised them. Her comments about her classroom reflected her desire to use what she had learned from paying close attention to students to transform classroom practice.

Another student described a science lesson she had recently taught. She explained that the students were "asking a lot of questions and I was letting them lead it and it went over the time that it should have gone. It was longer than it should have been." Afterwards, the Penn mentor—her supervisor—praised her for encouraging students to ask and find answers to their questions. However, the classroom mentor—her cooperating teacher—informed her that the lesson was too long. The student teacher explained, "Allowing their voices to be heard through, yes it took more time, but they probably learned a lot more because of it." She went on to describe the ways that she would use this form of listening to tinker with classroom practice by taking a different stance than that advocated by her classroom mentor.

The conversation continued as student teachers described the ways they would make both small and large transformative changes in the teaching practices they saw in their fieldwork classrooms. For instance, Karen explained that she would rearrange the layout of the room to encourage more group work. Nora suggested that she would devise a schedule and physically arrange her classroom to engage students in conversations about the books.

In their visions for classrooms, student teachers were listening to students, critiquing practice, and imagining new possibilities. They were speculating about the activist stance they might take in their own classroom or school (e.g., Cochran-Smith, 1995, 2000; Ladson-Billings, 1999, 2001). We talked about the role of new teachers in a school and the importance of listening to and learning the school culture before enacting large changes to transform practice. We also discussed the importance of understanding theory as a way to articulate reasons behind changes in their own classroom practices. We suggested that they would be in stronger positions to advocate ways of teaching that matched their own beliefs if they were knowledgeable and first garnered the respect of their colleagues and principals. Thus we framed the notion of taking an activist role based, in part, on listening to students and to colleagues.

Students put these ideas together in their own ways in portfolios at the end of the year. The portfolios give them opportunities to reflect on their experiences and to articulate their own visions of teaching. Drawing on her experiences, Jeanette Kaplan (2001) concluded that a humane education is manifest in and "maintained by the hundreds of intimate conversations between a child and his or her teacher" (p. 6)—what Freire (1970) calls a "permanent relationship of dialogue" (p. 66). She described in detail the conversations that were possible in her urban classroom and informed her own teaching.

> Yes, careful lesson planning and skilled classroom management are integral, even fundamental, to any academically and socially-sound learning environment. I will not forget our investigations into water and clay, our year-long study of Native Americans, our measurement activities, nor our reading of *Holes*. I also hope to remember the lovely, lovely moments when 33 children settled into an industrious buzz. But, I have to admit, while examples of good and even exciting instruction, those things are not what I treasure nor are they what made my relationship with my students so humane this year. What I treasure and looked forward to were our conversations. We talked to each other. We talked before school, after school, during school. We talked about big things—a mother's illness, interracial dating, the dying of a pet—and small things—the tiniest pencil we ever saw, our stomach-aches, and my different rings. We shared books with one another and gave each other hugs. We noticed one another's scratches and bruises. We knew each other. We liked each other. We made our classroom a more humane place to be. (Kaplan, 2001 pp. 6–7)

With the increased emphasis on measuring students' acquisition of content through high-stakes standardized tests, moments for conversations like these, where deep and respectful listening occurs, will disappear. Students like Jeanette found time in their student teaching for a new kind of interaction with students. The seminar gave them the chance to reflect on and articulate these ideas in order to reimagine their practice as classroom teachers the next year. Jeanette concluded her portfolio with this short anecdote and a powerful vision of education.

> As I was putting together my portfolio this week, I received an email from my classroom mentor. She writes, "The kids were so bad today. They said it was because they weren't getting enough attention. See, even they recognize it." For some reason, I am hopeful. We take our cues from our students. Collective recognition will result in collective action and engage us all in a mutual struggle to reclaim our humanity. (Kaplan, 2001, p. 21)

Taking a listening stance in teaching is essential to holding on to this vision of teaching as a struggle to reclaim humanity. Only by listening can teachers truly know—and teach—their students.

DEMONSTRATING LISTENING TO TEACH
IN THE MIDST OF INTERACTION

Each of the foregoing descriptions of how we introduced student teachers to the concept of listening to teach involves student teachers drawing from their own experiences in classrooms to contribute to our discussions. We used student teachers' work in their classrooms and their documentation of these practices as our primary texts for teaching them about children, learning, and teaching. It was relatively easy to design ways of teaching that drew on these experiences. What proved more difficult was to enact this stance by listening to student teachers ourselves and building our interactions on that knowledge. In other words, in order to illustrate the principles of listening we urged student teachers to incorporate into their own teaching, we attempted to enact these ways of listening into our own practice and, further, to make our teaching decisions public. This practice raised a number of tensions and complexities. Each of these complexities was parallel to those faced by classroom teachers.

We often used our own decision-making processes and struggles to design the class as a way to make transparent some of the same tensions student teachers faced in their own classrooms. For instance, with 40 student teachers in the seminar, it was difficult to listen to and hear all of the student teachers without privileging those who were the most articulate about their questions and concerns. We constantly struggled to listen to all student teachers and all perspectives in the classroom. We attempted to point out the ways power was distributed in classroom conversations and dynamics. We made explicit links to similar challenges faced by student teachers in large urban classrooms.

Related to this was our concern about silencing student teachers ourselves and creating a climate devoid of moments when student teachers silenced each other. For instance, we often brought up volatile issues such as race and racism in teaching. At times student teachers, particularly those who were White and had little experience with these discussions, made statements that could be interpreted as racist. We felt a responsibility to correct or at least comment on these statements, and we wanted to do so in such a way that we did not silence the student who made the statement, keeping her from participating in the discussion. Further, as other researchers have noticed, we saw the ways that White student teachers, in particular, avoided conversations about race and, when given the lead in class discussions, often steered us clear of such issues (e.g., Cochran-Smith, 2000; Schultz et al., 2000; Taliaferro, 2001). We constantly worried about when to step in to redirect conversation and when to maintain a respectful distance.

One African American student commented that without more student teachers of color—there were only three African American student teachers and three Asian and Asian American student teachers out of 40 that year—it wasn't fair to have discussions about race. Another African American student wrote that in discussions of race, White student teachers put their peers of color in the position of acting as authorities, taking them out of their role as students and pushing them to become teachers. Further, she explained, this power invested in student teachers of color—as experts about race and about teaching children of color—could be reclaimed at any moment by their White peers. Thus, although student teachers of color might seem to have more power in discussions about race, their hold on the power was tenuous at best and could be lost at any moment (Taliaferro, 2001). We attempted to describe and analyze the distribution of power in our discussions as a class, making these dynamics explicit and public, so that student teachers could learn to listen for and analyze these dynamics in their own classrooms (Schultz et al., 2000). This wasn't easy and there were many times when the conversations fell short.

Like many educators, we struggled to balance our goal of providing student teachers with experiences and information about teaching, particularly in urban contexts, and our desire for the seminar to reflect the questions that arose from their own experiences. We introduced a number of processes, notably the Descriptive Review of a Child, that take time and practice to learn. We openly described the dilemmas we faced as instructors when we made decisions ahead of time about what to teach, in lieu of building our class content solely around student teachers' questions in the moment. Again, these decisions mirrored those our students confronted in their own classroom planning.

We can give student teachers ideas about how to listen to students and a set of practices that support this stance. In the context of a busy classroom, however, listening is multilayered, and responding to students with deep understanding is often difficult. Even when a teacher knows students well and understands many of their questions, it is often difficult to use this knowledge in the complicated context of teaching. The following excerpt illustrates our own experience as teacher educators with the difficulty of listening to and acting on knowledge of students without the opportunity for reflection. This scene highlights the interactive nature of listening in comparison to the more remote stance of observing.

The Challenges of Listening in the Moment

After we worked with student teachers to reframe their own questions for the inquiry into teaching portfolios, we asked them to meet in their school groups to develop a group question for a multimedia project. This culminating project was designed to facilitate collaborative inquiry in a single school. We wanted student teachers to frame this inquiry with the questions of teaching and learning they had developed for their individual projects. Some groups, in which there was agreement about the questions, found this a relatively easy task. Others had more difficulty in reaching consensus about the direction to take in their collective project.

One school, located in a low-income neighborhood with a population that is close to 100% African American, had four student teachers: two White, one African American, and one a native of Singapore. The group had engaged in many conversations about race and discussed the role of middle-class—particularly White, middle-class—teachers in low-income, predominantly African American schools. Whether or not student teachers were matched with classroom mentors in terms of race and class, every one of them struggled with the ways their philosophies of teaching differed from those of their classroom mentors. They all worried about their positions as student teachers in this challenging urban context. For instance, one of the White student teachers, Alice, was placed with an African American teacher whose teaching and classroom management style was relatively authoritarian. Although this student teacher was uncomfortable—as many prospective teachers are—with the yelling and the harsh language she heard from her classroom mentor, she also realized that there was much she could learn from this teacher, who had control over the class and respect from the community. The Asian student teacher, Jocelyn, saw her White mentor struggling with a difficult group of students and wondered how she might tap the students' families and communities for ways to understand classroom management. A third student teacher, Karen, placed with a biracial mentor, worked to understand her own commitment as a White, middle-class female to predominantly low-income and African American urban public schools. An African American student teacher, Rebecca, who was educated mostly in independent schools and raised in low-income and middle-class communities, wanted to understand the style of her African American teacher, who had always taught in public schools. Rebecca consistently raised questions of equity that were painfully apparent to her.

Two of the student teachers, Rebecca and Alice, who are African American and White, respectively, initially took the lead in the discussion of the group inquiry question. Together they designed an inquiry project to compare their own teaching styles with those of their classroom mentors. According to their design, each student teacher and mentor would plan a lesson around the same topic or issue. The plan was for the mentor and the student teacher to teach an identical lesson, to compare how each of them taught the lesson, and then to analyze the results through an examination of student work. It is important to note that this design did not follow the intent of the assignment, which was for students to document their own practice and that of the teachers in the school as it naturally occurred, rather than through an experimental design. Throughout this initial conversation, two group members, Karen and Jocelyn, who are White and Asian, respectively, were silent. Karen, in particular, was clearly agitated and uncomfortable with this plan.

After several minutes, Karen interjected some questions and comments that were critical of the project's experimental design. She noted that there were too many intervening factors that could influence the outcome of the experiment. Anxious to avoid conflict, Alice suggested that they regroup and each come up with five or six possible research questions. In other words, when Alice was faced with a conflict, her initial solution was to abandon the collaboration in order for each student to go her own way. Rebecca had stronger feelings about the project she and Alice had just designed. She defended the idea, saying: "Listen, listen to me. Say you give a writing assignment. Think about how students responded. A lot of different themes come out." She was invested in conducting this experiment and liked the idea. Karen reiterated her point. After several tense exchanges between the two student teachers, Karen concluded that she felt Rebecca was trying to convince her of something rather than trying to work with her. "I may not want to do the I teach, she teaches thing. There are so many things that influence what happens." There was silence. The group had reached an impasse. Karen had articulated an opposing point of view, and they were at a loss to find a middle ground. Each held on tightly to her position.

When student teachers work in small groups, Sarah and I circulate to answer questions and help to focus or move along the conversation. At times we simply listen to where each of the discussions is going so that we can gather those themes together later in the class. Other times we take a more active role in the conversation. Just as the group reached this point in their discussion, I walked over to check on their progress. I had not heard their prior conversation.

Appealing for my help, Alice described their experimental project to me. Rather than immediately responding that they could not set up an experiment, I asked, "Is that really what you want to do?" Without hesitation, and before anyone else could respond, Karen answered "No." At the time, I did not realize that by my question, I had inadvertently supported Karen's position over that of her peers. With my straightforward question meant to help the students to explore possibilities, I had shifted the balance of power.

I continued, "What is something you are *really* interested in?" Jocelyn, who had been relatively silent up to this point, offered that she was interested in "how classroom management translates onto the playground." Rebecca added that she was interested in "how classroom management affects learning." Knowing that many of the student teachers in the group had questions about classroom management and the opportunities for students to learn in their classrooms, I suggested to Rebecca that she reframe her question so that it was stated in terms that did not imply a causal relationship. I suggested that they might look at questions such as: "How do teachers make decisions about classroom management across classrooms? What kinds of decisions do teachers make?"

Karen listened carefully and thought about how they might work together as a group to look at their own teaching decisions. She suggested a new angle, offering the idea that as a group they focus on social class. She stated her own interest in looking at how the different socioeconomic background of each group member is reflected in her teaching.

There was an uncomfortable pause in the conversation as each student reflected on her different perspectives and interests. Moments later, breaking the silence, I suggested that if it were too hard for the group to come up with a single guiding question that was inclusive of all their interests, they could develop a more general question that would elicit description of their school contexts. Another possibility I offered was for the group to find a common thread to connect their individual questions. These comments echoed advice I had given other groups that afternoon. Working from my guidelines, Alice suggested that they inquire into how teachers direct lessons to all learners. Karen responded that "in general, in your first year all that you think about is classroom management issues." Alice asked her how they would frame a question about this topic, and the following exchange transpired between the two student teachers:

> *Karen*: Well that and interactions with parents worry me.
> *Alice*: What do you think about what we have learned?
> *Karen* (interrupting): It is most important to come up with a topic. We can work with the words.
> *Alice* (apparently disregarding Karen's point): We can say—
> *Karen* (in an attempt to broaden the conversation): Rebecca, I want to make sure that you are not getting left out.
> *Rebecca*: It is too soon for me to decide [on a topic].
> *Karen*: Could you throw out ideas?

The students brainstormed various solutions. I glanced at my watch and noticed the class period was almost over. With the question or topic unresolved, I called the whole class back together for closing announcements and instructions.

On one hand, when I entered the group's discussion, I widened the conversation to include more of the participants, and for a brief time there was more evidence of collaboration in the group's talk. With my questions I attempted to redistribute the power. On the other hand, in my quick analysis and contribution to the discussion, it was not apparent how my comments were shaped by my understanding of these student teachers and some of their struggles in the classroom. Each of the student teachers was struggling in different ways with personal issues about who they were as teachers in their challenging contexts. I knew many of their stories, yet it was difficult in a group conversation to use this knowledge in quickly formulating my response to the group. Although I knew some of the ways that the tensions and dynamics played out in this group, in the split second of composing a response to them, which in this instance began with a question, I found it difficult to use that knowledge. Although at first my question allowed more voices to be added to the conversation, later it seemed to narrow the scope of the conversation and each student's participation. Initially it may have promoted more listening; later the student teachers seemed less willing to listen to each other. Given the hundreds of interactions between teachers and students, it is often difficult to ensure that each interaction is infused with the knowledge we have gleaned from listening closely to students. As a teacher with many students and many decisions and interactions during each class, I often find it difficult to use what I know in each interaction with them. This mirrors the challenges student teachers face when enacting the ideas about listening we teach in our program.

Maintaining Independent Ideas in Collaborative Inquiry

In this example, the student teachers enacted the three processes described in this chapter: They struggled to formulate a question, looked for ways to analyze the teaching in their classrooms, and began to imagine their roles as activist teachers. One of the many challenges I faced as their teacher was not only to listen to each student but also to find ways for all voices in the group to be heard and respected. I needed to be aware of the power I held in this conversation as well as the power dynamics among the students. In my questions, I both opened up and shut down conversation. My interaction with the group was based on questions that allowed me to listen to students. Yet even with my questions, I did not create a context for each student to participate fully in the conversation.

The group eventually found a way to listen to each other and build on each other's ideas. During the final class of the semester, and after many conversations, they presented their group project that used a single question to unite their individual investigations. Their question, placed in the center of a poster, read: "How do we blend different voices to form authentic relationships that will enable urban public school students to succeed?" Each of the four students addressed a different form of listening in her presentation. Each individual question was written and illustrated in a separate quadrant on hands, each cut from a different color of construction paper. The hands symbolized the diversity of students in their school, their individuality as group members, and their coming together in agreement and collaboration.

Karen opened the presentation by explaining that an interest in relationships was common to each of the group members' investigations. Specifically, Alice was interested in how a teacher can try to reach every child regardless of his or her learning style by forming an individual relationship with that child. Rebecca explained that she wanted to learn about the structure of the curriculum and how it frames the overall questions in a classroom. Jocelyn's focus was on the interaction between teachers and parents and the larger community. Finally, Karen explored classroom management issues. Pointing to the hands on the edge of the poster cut out of different shades of brown construction paper, Karen concluded, "On the surface [our school] is not very diverse. It is almost completely low-income and African American. But really, once you get to know your kids, they are all really different."

The student teachers found a way to listen to each other in order to construct a common question. However, this listening did not mean compromise, and they each held on to the autonomy of their own investigations. The four hands and four quadrants reflected their unique interests and perspectives. The central question and image of the hands reflected collaboration and their ability to listen and learn from each other. In addition, their individual questions embodied their understanding of the content of the seminar. Each question was about a different form of listening and reflected their interpretation of how they were learning to teach. This final project illustrated one way student teachers translated ideas about listening to teach into a collaborative inquiry project about their school.

LISTENING WITH THE EAR, THE MIND, AND THE HEART

The two most common ways of describing listening to teach are in terms of content or building curriculum around students' interests (e.g., Calkins, 1986; Levy, 1996; Meier, 1996; Skilton-Sylvester, 1994) and understanding the meanings students bring to their statements and problem solving (e.g., Ball, 1993, 1997; Duckworth, 2001). The forms of listening that are the foundation for our teacher education program include these important ideas and add to them the notion of listening to who children are—their particularities and the larger contexts of their lives—and also to the elements of classroom interactions, including rhythm, balance, and silence. A fundamental purpose of this book is to suggest a deeper, more nuanced understanding of listening.

The vignettes of teaching in this chapter illustrate the power of the conception of listening to teach to transform student teachers' ideas about teaching and teacher education. First, in their exploration of listening to teach, student teachers reframed their knowledge of their roles as teachers and their understanding of how to teach. Through repeated reflection and analysis of the difficult questions in their classrooms, they learned to take an activist stance in their teaching, enacting solutions rather than simply naming problems. As new teachers they learned to enter their classrooms with questions instead of searching for ready-made answers in texts or programs. When teachers rely on listening to students to fashion pedagogy and curriculum, teachers are nearly always changed.

Second, listening to teach reframes student teachers' notions about learning *how* to teach. In their work in the classroom with their instructors, mentors, and peers, they extended their understanding of where to look for support and resources in learning to teach. Student teachers understood that their knowledge of pedagogy and content must be braided with knowledge garnered from listening closely to students.

Learning to teach is a complicated process, especially in urban settings where schools are underfunded and teachers are under tremendous pressure to improve test scores and teach mandated curricula. In these conditions, new teachers are often overwhelmed. It is difficult for them to listen to students and their families or guardians. Researchers have recently identified the ways in which children and adolescents who grow up in difficult situations are resilient (e.g., Ward, 2000). Our task as teacher educators is to develop and support resiliency in student teachers, helping them to see their inner strengths and resources, pointing them to networks or groups of teachers who support each other's practice, and teaching them to listen closely to their students as a guide to their teaching. This listening is complicated to teach in part because we must listen closely to student teachers at the same time that we introduce these ideas to them. The challenge is not only to add student teachers' questions and concerns to our syllabi but also to adapt our interactions or teaching decisions in order to use the pedagogy we advocate in our teaching. This kind of teaching requires that we take the same kinds of risks and make ourselves vulnerable in the same ways that we ask of student teachers in their classrooms. Ultimately, it requires a focus not only on content but on our moment-to-moment transactions with students, so that we can imagine ways to teach that respect each student in the class, whether that class is made up of kindergartners or advanced graduate students. It suggests that we provide openings and a curriculum that is porous.

The Chinese character for "listen" is comprised of three radicals.[3] The radical for ear is on the left. At the top right is the radical for head, mind, or brain (depending on how it is translated). At the bottom right is the radical for heart. Taken together, the three radicals make up the ideogram "listen." There is a connection between the way this word or idea is represented in Chinese and the philosophical stance toward listening that it suggests. The ear is the receptacle for hearing; the sounds are interpreted by the heart and mind. Listening is more than simply hearing or receiving sounds through the ear. Listening to teach suggests receiving information through the heart and mind in order to understand, to learn, and to act. Teaching students to participate in pluralistic democratic communities means being present in the moment and responding and interpreting with both the heart and mind.

Classrooms are often sites of "blooming buzzing confusion" (James, 1890). A critical challenge for teachers is to make sense of the confusion in order to establish the conditions for teaching and learning to transpire. One response to the cacophony that often characterizes classrooms is for the teacher to impose order, demanding silence and compliance. Trends toward standardization reinforce such moves. Some schools and districts have mandated school uniforms as a way to create order. One of the rationales for this requirement is that students will take school more seriously if they focus on academic subjects rather than clothes. Uniforms impose order. Another response to the complexity of schools, especially larger urban schools, is to mandate standardized curriculum. The belief is that equality will result if everyone is taught the same material in the same way. Acknowledgment of the variabilities posed by individual students, teachers, and the local context is blurred in favor of a focus on material and method that remain constant. Differences, in effect, are erased. A third way to control the confusion of classrooms is through an overlay of scripted lessons. These scripts are imposed without regard to context or individuals, on the assumption that a predictable sequence of activities or questions and responses will lead to learning.

I propose an alternative response to the complexity and inherent confusion of schools: to listen closely to students in order to craft pedagogy and curriculum that reflect and build on their lives. The framework presented in this book outlines four ways of conceptualizing listening that are useful for interpreting and teaching students in the "blooming buzzing confusion" of a classroom. Taken together, these practices comprise a stance toward teaching that shifts the dynamics of a classroom and provides teachers with a way to continue learning from their teaching throughout their careers. Listening to teach provides teachers with knowledge of how to respond to students in the moment and also profoundly enriches teachers' interpretive frameworks so that they can make sense of the worlds students bring into the classroom.

The framework for listening to teach is useful for teachers in "suburban" classrooms where progressive or constructivist methods often hold sway, and it is useful for teachers who are in school districts that strictly mandate the use of structured, prescriptive methods or curriculum. There is growing bipartisan support for legislation like the *No Child Left Behind Act of 2000* (U.S. Department of Education, 2000), which relies on yearly high-stakes standardized testing. A listening stance is, if anything, more critical in classrooms where there is pressure to increase test scores and drill children in phonics. Whatever the pedagogy or material, teachers cannot simply deliver material as if individual children do not exist. Even if the structure of the school day and the content of the teaching are predetermined, it is incumbent on teachers to learn who their students are and tailor the teaching to *those* students. This book provides a framework for doing just that.

It is often overwhelming for teachers to confront the complexity of a classroom. Classrooms in California, for instance, can have 32 students who speak 29 languages. It is impossible to pay attention to every aspect of classroom life at one time. The notion of listening to teach helps a teacher to focus on and make sense of the activity and interactions. In listening to know particular children, teachers are able to listen for the voices of individual students as a way to understand both how to teach those students and how to teach other students in the class. A focus on particulars gives a teacher insight into the whole, beginning with a deep understanding of individuals. A focus on the humanity of students foregrounds students' voices and their particularized contributions.

When teachers listen for the rhythm and balance of a group, they gain a sense of the whole based on the knowledge of the particular and an ability to grasp the larger picture. In confronting a complex classroom, teachers can listen for its pulse, or rhythm and balance, to learn how and when to respond to the class as a whole. By teaching students what it means to be part of a group, listening and responding to each other, teachers work toward pluralistic democratic community.

Listening for the social, cultural, and community contexts of a complicated classroom implies listening to what is beneath and beyond the surface. In order to make sense of their busy and complicated classrooms, teachers can listen to students in the moment across multiple dimensions. This listening includes paying attention to all that the students bring to the classroom from their outside lives. I suggest that teachers listen to the voices that are loud and those that are silent, the perspectives that define the classroom group and those that are missing. Listening for what is absent helps teachers to understand what is present. The silence defines and frames the sound. The notion of listening for the larger contexts of students' lives and for the silences suggests teaching toward possibilities: teaching toward what might be rather than what is.

In place of silencing the cacophony of a classroom and imposing order on top of it, I suggest that teaching involves improvisation. Jazz musicians draw on multifaceted knowledge in order to improvise, adhering to a structure and within that structure creatively producing new forms. This is an apt metaphor for teaching.[4] Like teaching, playing jazz involves moment-to-moment decisions, interpretation, and improvisation. It suggests going beyond a script or a score and creating new music or knowledge in the moment. Jazz musicians are not born knowing how to improvise seamlessly with the music. It's a slow process that—like teaching—takes many years of playing and listening.

In *The Black Atlantic*, Gilroy (1993) posits that jazz "symbolizes and anticipates (but does not guarantee) new non-dominating social relationships" (p. 79). Rather than following a single score, jazz musicians improvise in a coordinated way through juxtaposition and contrast (Gilroy, 1993). According to this metaphor, diversity, disagreement, and conflict are viewed as resources rather than as modes of engagement that must be avoided (Schultz et al., 2000). Likewise, the "blooming buzzing confusion" of classrooms presents opportunities and possibilities. Fearful of failure, teachers and administrators often seek harmony and simple answers that lead to uniformity. In contrast, I propose a framework for listening to teach in order to provide an approach to teaching that deepens interactions and understanding in the moment and across a lifetime.

James Baldwin (1985) wrote in his "A Talk to Teachers":

> The purpose of education, finally, is to create in a person the ability to look at the world for himself or herself, to make his own decisions, to say to himself this is black or this is white, to decide for himself whether there is a God in heaven or not. To ask questions of the universe, and then to live with those questions, is the way he achieves his identity. But no society is really anxious to have that kind of person around. What society really, ideally, wants is a citizenry that will simply obey the rules of society. If a society succeeds in this, that society is about to perish. (p. 326)

As a society we need to consider whether our education system should be geared toward teaching students to follow directions or whether we are committed to teaching youth to become actively engaged in questioning and participating in shaping a pluralistic democratic society. Education that provides students with the capacity to look at the world on their own terms begins with close listening. It implies creating contexts for all students to become actively engaged in each aspect of classroom life so that they can, in Greene's words (1988), "think forward to the future, dream, and reach beyond" (p. 3). For the past 100 years, educators, parents, and politicians have debated what and how teachers should teach and what and how children should learn. As we enter a new century in which classrooms are filled with students whose diverse backgrounds are often different in many ways from those of their teachers, we will need to envision fundamentally different ways of conceptualizing the teaching and learning transaction. Locating students at the center of teaching, using their stories to inform our decisions, is one place to begin.

Notes

Chapter 3

1. Lynne has written about her own classroom frequently over the years. This chapter is built on my research in Lynne's classroom, our discussions together, and the many articles she has authored (cf. Strieb, 1985, 1992, 1993, 1995, 1999).

2. The text of this conversation is drawn from a transcript of the conversation typed by Lynne during the actual conversation and field notes taken by the author. It is supplemented by numerous conversations and close readings of the text with Lynne and members of PTLC.

Chapter 4

1. Another version of this chapter appears in *Research in the Teaching of English* (Schultz, 2002).

2. There were another ten students, five males and five females, whom I observed and interviewed periodically in order to make the sample more inclusive of the range of students in the high school.

3. Lensmire (2000) makes a similar point in a discussion of Graves's (1983) notion of following the child's meaning in writer's workshop.

Chapter 5

1. Later Patti Buck and Tricia Niesz joined as ethnographers and spent a few days a week documenting classroom, cafeteria, hallway, and after-school activities. They participated in the focus groups, conducted interviews, and initiated a writing group. Their work has been essential to the ideas in this chapter.

2. The actual racial breakdown of the school reflected the ratio achieved by each school in the district under the desegregation order. Approximately 75% of the students were White, 20% to 25% of the students were students of color, and most of these were African American. In addition to African Americans, the group of students of color included Asian Americans and South Asian or Indian students. Students who called themselves "Spanish" were mostly Puerto Rican and identified as both Black and White. There were also a number of multiracial students.

3. These portraits were written in collaboration with Tricia Niesz and Patti Buck (Schultz et al., 1999).

4. This group consisted of four African American students (three girls and one boy), two Asian American students (both girls, one who identified as Indian and the other as Japanese American), and three White students (two boys, who spoke during the discussion, and one girl who did not).

5. We have edited the transcripts for this manuscript so that they are easier to read. The symbol ( ) designates that a word or phrase was unintelligible. Descriptive information is placed inside parentheses; for example, (silence) indicates that the speaker's voice trailed off. Words inside brackets were implied but not explicitly stated. They were added to the transcript for clarification. The following abbreviations indicate the racial identities students chose for themselves: (B) = Black or African American, (W) = White, (L) = Latino/a, (I) = Indian, (A) = Asian/Pacific Islander.

6. The students in this group included four African American students—three girls and one boy, five White students—two girls and three boys, one South Asian girl; and a biracial girl who was White and Puerto Rican. Portions of this focus-group meeting have been analyzed elsewhere (Schultz et al., 2000).

7. We have identified students by the categories they chose for themselves when they signed permission slips for the study.

8. Fine, Weis, Powell, and Wong (1997); Frankenberg (1993), Schultz (1997a, 1999), and others have noted the tendency for Whites to strategically slip in and out of whiteness, often using ethnicity to do so.

9. Although it is likely that opportunities also varied by gender and along other lines of difference, these variables were not the focus of our data collection or analysis for this particular project.

Chapter 6

1. Dewey was not always comfortable with the Progressive Education movement and at times separated himself from it. Still, his ideas are most often associated with this movement.

2. This reference is to Himley (2000), a core text in our seminar.

3. I am grateful to Helen Duffy for pointing this out and offering this explanation.

4. Thanks to Bryan Brayboy, who brought this to my attention.

References

Abu El-Haj, T., & Schultz, K. (1998). *Twenty years of reflection and action: Lessons from an inquiry-based urban professional development group*. Grant funded by the MacArthur/Spencer Professional Development Research and Documentation Program.

Anzaldúa, G. (1987). *Borderlands/borderlands/la frontera: The new mestiza*. San Francisco: Aunt Lute Books.

Bakhtin, M. (1981). *The dialogic imagination* (C. Emerson & M. Holquist, Trans.). Austin: University of Texas Press.

Baldwin, J. (1985). A talk to teachers. In *The price of the ticket: Collected nonfiction, 1948–1985* (pp. 325–332). New York: St. Martin's.

Ball, D. L. (1993). With an eye on the mathematical horizon: Dilemmas of teaching elementary school mathematics. *Elementary School Journal, 93*(4), 373–397.

Ball, D. L. (1997). What do students know? Facing challenges of distance, context, and desire in trying to hear children. In B. J. Biddle, T. L. Good, & I. F. Goodson (Eds.), *International handbook of teachers and teaching* (pp. 769–818). Boston: Kluwer Academic.

Ball, D. L., & Cohen, D. K. (1999). Developing practice, developing practitioners: Toward a practice-based theory of professional education. In L. Darling-Hammond & G. Sykes (Eds.), *Teaching as the learning profession: Handbook of policy and research* (pp. 3–32). San Francisco: Jossey-Bass.

Banks, J. A. (1984). *Teaching strategies for ethnic studies* (3rd ed.). Boston: Allyn and Bacon.

Banks, J. A. (1994). *Multiethnic education: Theory and practice* (3rd ed.). Boston: Allyn and Bacon.

Bartolomé, L. (1994). Beyond the methods fetish: Toward a humanizing pedagogy. *Harvard Educational Review, 62*(2), 173–194.

Bates, D., Chase, N., Ignasiak, C., Johnson, Y., Zaza, T., Niesz, T., Buck, P., & Schultz, K. (2001). Reflections: A middle school play about race relations. In J. Shultz & A. Cook-Sather (Eds.), *In our own words: Students' perspectives on school* (pp. 127–148). Lanham, MD: Rowman Littlefield Press.

Berlin, I. (1996). *The sense of reality: Studies in ideas and their history*. New York: Farrar, Straus, and Giroux.

Bransford, J. D., Brown, A. L., & Cocking, R. R. (Eds.). (1999). *How people learn: Brain, mind, experience, and school*. Washington, DC: National Academy Press.

Buchanan, J. (1994). Teacher as learner: Working in a community of teachers. In

175

T. Shanahan (Ed.), *Teachers thinking, teachers knowing* (pp. 39–52). Urbana, IL: NCTE-NCRE Press.

Bullough, R., & Gitlin, A. D. (2001). *Becoming a student of teaching: Linking knowledge production and practice.* New York: Routledge.

Calkins, L. M. (1994). *The art of teaching writing* (2nd ed.). Portsmouth, NH: Heinemann. (originally published in 1986)

Camitta, M. (1993). Vernacular writing: Varieties of literacy among Philadelphia high school students. In B. Street (Ed.), *Cross-cultural approaches to literacy* (pp. 228–246). New York: Cambridge University Press.

Carini, P. F. (1982). *The school lives of seven children.* Grand Forks, ND: North Dakota Study Group on Evaluation.

Carini, P. F. (1986). Building from children's strengths. *Journal of Education, 168*(3), 13–24.

Carini, P. F. (2000, April). *How to have hope: Play's memorable transiency.* Talk delivered at the Miquon Institute, Miquon School, Miquon, PA.

Carini, P. F. (2001). *Starting strong: A different look at children, schools and standards.* New York: Teachers College Press.

Cazden, C. B. (1988). *Classroom discourse: The language of teaching and learning.* Portsmouth, NH: Heinemann.

Cazden, C. B. (2001). *Classroom discourse: The language of teaching and learning* (2nd ed.). Portsmouth, NH: Heinemann.

Clark, C. M. (1988). Asking the right questions about teacher preparation: Contributions of research on teacher thinking. *Educational Researcher, 17*(2), 5–12.

Clifford, J. (1986). Introduction: Partial truths. In J. Clifford & G. Marcus (Eds.), *Writing culture: The poetics and politics of ethnography* (pp. 1–26). Berkeley: University of California Press.

Cochran-Smith, M. (1995). Uncertain allies: Understanding the boundaries of race and teaching. *Harvard Educational Review, 65*, 541–570.

Cochran-Smith, M. (2000). Blind vision: Unlearning racism in teacher education. *Harvard Educational Review, 70*(2), 157–190.

Cochran-Smith, M., & Lytle, S. L. (1999). Relationships of knowledge and practice: Teacher learning in communities. In A. Iran-Nejad & C. D. Pearson (Eds.), *Review of research in education* (pp. 249–305). Washington, DC: American Educational Research Association.

Coleman, J. (1966). *Equality of educational opportunity.* Washington, DC: U.S. Office of Education.

Cushman, E., & Emmons, C. (2002). Making contact zones real. In G. Hull & K. Schultz (Eds.), *School's out!: Bridging out-of-school literacies with classroom practice* (pp. 203–232). New York: Teachers College Press.

Daly, M. (1973). *Beyond God the Father: Toward a philosophy of women's liberation.* Boston: Beacon Press.

Darling-Hammond, L. (1998). Education for democracy. In W. C. Ayers & J. L. Miller (Eds.), *A light in dark times: Maxine Greene and the unfinished conversation* (pp. 78–91). New York: Teachers College Press.

Darling-Hammond, L., French, J., & Garcia-Lopez, S. P. (Eds.). (2002). *Learning to teach for social justice.* New York: Teachers College Press.

Delgado, R. (1995). Legal storytelling: Storytelling for oppositionists and others: A plea for narrative. In R. Delgado (Ed.), *Critical race theory: The cutting edge* (pp. 60–70). Philadelphia: Temple University Press.

Delgado Bernal, D. (2002). Critical race theory, Latina critical theory and critical race-gendered epistemologies: Recognizing students of color as holders and creators of knowledge. *Qualitative Inquiry, 8*(1), 105–126.

Delpit, L. (1986). Skills and other dilemmas of a progressive Black educator. *Harvard Educational Review, 56*, 379–385.

Delpit, L. (1988). The silenced dialogue: Power and pedagogy in educating other people's children. *Harvard Educational Review, 58*, 280–298.

Delpit, L. (1995). *Other people's children: Cultural conflict in the classroom.* New York: The New Press.

Dewey, J. (1902). The school as social centre. *National Education Association Journal of Proceedings and Addresses*, 373–383.

Dewey, J. (1944). *Democracy and education.* New York: The Free Press. (Original work published 1916)

Dewey, J. (1956). *The child and the curriculum.* Chicago: University of Chicago Press. (Original work published 1902)

Dewey, J. (1963). *Experience and education.* New York: Macmillan. (Original work published 1938)

Dewey, J. (1980). *Art as experience.* New York: Perigree. (Original work published 1931)

Duckworth, E. (1987). *"The having of wonderful ideas" and other essays on teaching and learning.* New York: Teachers College Press.

Duckworth, E. (Ed.). (2001). *Tell me more: Listening to learners explain.* New York: Teachers College Press.

Duffine, S. (2001). Unpublished master's portfolio, University of Pennsylvania, Philadelphia.

Dyson, A. H. (1997). *Writing superheroes: Contemporary childhood, popular culture, and classroom literacy.* New York: Teachers College Press.

Dyson, A. H. (1999). Coach Bombay's kids learn to write: Children's appropriation of media material for school literacy. *Research in the Teaching of English, 33*(4), 367–402.

Eisenhart, M. (2001). Changing conceptions of culture and ethnographic methodology: Recent thematic shifts and their implications for research on teaching. In V. Richardson (Ed.), *The handbook of research on teaching* (4th ed., pp. 209–225). New York: Macmillan.

Elbow, P. (1987). *Embracing contraries: Explorations in learning and teaching.* Oxford: Oxford University Press.

Ellison, R. (1952). *The invisible man.* New York: Signet Books.

Engelmann, S., & Carnine, D. (1991). *Theory of instruction: Principles and applications.* Eugene, OR: ADI Press.

Erickson, F. (1982). Classroom discourse as improvisation: Relationships between academic task structure and social participation structures in lessons. In L. C. Wilkinson (Ed.), *Communicating in the classroom* (pp. 153–181). New York: Academic Press.

Erickson, F. (1984). School literacy, reasoning, and civility: An anthropologist's perspective. *Review of Educational Research, 54*(4), 525–546.

Erickson, F. (1987). Transformation and school success: The politics and culture of educational achievement. *Anthropology and Education Quarterly, 18*(4), 335–383.

Erickson, F. (1995). The music goes round and round: How music means in school. *Educational Theory, 45*(1), 19–34.

Erickson, F. (1996). Going for the zone: The social and cognitive ecology of teacher–student interaction in classroom conversations. In D. Hicks (Ed.), *Discourse, learning, and schooling* (pp. 29–62). New York: Cambridge University Press.

Erickson, F. (1997). Culture and society in educational practices. In J. A. Banks & C. A. McGee Banks (Eds.), *Multicultural education: Issues and perspectives* (3rd ed., pp. 32–60). Boston: Allyn and Bacon.

Fecho, B. (2000). Critical inquiries into language in an urban classroom. *Research in the Teaching of English, 34*(3), 368–395.

Fiering, S. (1981). Commodore School: Unofficial writing. In D. H. Hymes (Ed.), *Ethnographic monitoring of children's acquisition of reading/language arts skills in and out of the classroom.* Final Report to the National Institute of Education, Philadelphia, PA.

Figes, E. (1986). *The seven ages.* London: H. Hamilton.

Finders, M. J. (1997). *Just girls: Hidden literacy and life in junior high.* New York: Teachers College Press.

Fine, M. (1987). Silencing in public school. *Language Arts, 64*(2), 157–174.

Fine, M. (1991). *Framing dropouts: Notes on the politics of an urban high school.* Albany: State University of New York Press.

Fine, M., Weis, L., & Powell, L. (1997). Communities of difference: A critical look at desegregated spaces created for and by youth. *Harvard Educational Review, 67*(2), 247–284.

Fine, M., Weis, L., Powell, L. C., & Wong, L. M. (Eds.). (1997). *Off white: Readings on race, power, and society.* New York: Routledge.

Fishman, S. M., & McCarthy, L. (1998). *John Dewey and the challenge of classroom practice.* New York: Teachers College Press.

Fletcher, R. (1996). *A writer's notebook: Unlocking the writer within you.* New York: Avon Books.

Fordham, S. (1991). Peer-proofing academic competition among Black adolescents: "Acting White" Black American style. In C. Sleeter (Ed.), *Empowerment through multicultural education* (pp. 69–93). Albany: State University of New York Press.

Fordham, S. (1993). Those loud Black girls: (Black) women, silence, and gender "passing" in the academy. *Anthropology and Education Quarterly, 24*(1), 3–32.

Fordham, S. (1996). *Blacked out: Dilemmas of race, identity, and success at Capital High.* Chicago: University of Chicago Press.

Fordham, S., & Ogbu, J. U. (1986). Black students' school success: Coping with the burden of "acting White." *The Urban Review, 18*(3), 176–206.

Foster, M. (1997). *Black teachers on teaching.* New York: New Press.

Foucault, M. (1977). *Discipline and punish: The birth of the prison.* (A. M. Sheridan-Smith, Trans.). Harmondsworth, England: Penguin.

Frankenberg, R. (1993). *The social construction of whiteness: White women, race matters*. Minneapolis: University of Minnesota Press.

Fraser, J. W. (1997). *Reading, writing and justice: School reform as if democracy matters* (pp. 93–128). Albany: State University of New York Press.

Freire, P. (1970). *Pedagogy of the oppressed*. New York: Herder and Herder.

Freire, P. (1973). *Education for critical consciousness*. New York: Seabury Press.

Gay, G. (2000). *Cultural responsive teaching: Theory, research, and practice*. New York: Teachers College Press.

Gee, J. P. (1996). *Social linguistics and literacies: Ideology in discourses* (2nd ed.). London: The Falmer Press.

Gee, J. P. (2000). The new literacy studies: From "socially situated" to the work of the social. In D. Barton, M. Hamilton, & R. Ivanic (Eds.), *Situated literacies: Reading and writing in context* (pp. 180–196). London: Routledge.

Geertz, C. (1973). *The interpretation of cultures*. New York: Basic Books.

Giddens, A. (1979). *Central problems in social theory*. Berkeley: University of California Press.

Gilmore, P. (1983). Spelling "Mississippi": Recontextualizing a literacy event. *Anthropology and Education Quarterly, 14*(4), 235–256.

Gilmore, P., & Glatthorn, A. A. (Eds.). (1982). *Children in and out of school: Ethnography and education*. Washington, DC: Center for Applied Linguistics.

Gilroy, P. (1993). *The Black Atlantic: Modernity and double consciousness*. Cambridge, MA: Harvard University Press.

Graves, D. (1983). *Writing: Teacher and children at work*. Portsmouth, NH: Heinemann.

Greene, M. (1988). *The dialectic of freedom*. New York: Teachers College Press.

Greene, M. (1993). Diversity and inclusion: Towards a curriculum for human beings. *Teachers College Record, 95*, 213–221.

Greene, M. (1995). *Releasing the imagination: Essays on education, the arts, and social change*. San Francisco: Jossey-Bass.

Guinier, L., & Torres, G. (2002). *The miner's canary: Enlisting race, resisting power, transforming democracy*. Cambridge, MA: Harvard University Press.

Gutiérrez, K., Baquedano-López, P., Alvarez, H. H., & Chiu, M. M. (1999). Building a culture of collaboration through hybrid language practices. *Theory Into Practice, 38*(2), 87–93.

Heath, S. B. (1983). *Ways with words: Language, life, and work in communities and classrooms*. Cambridge, England: Cambridge University Press.

Heath, S. B. (1994). The project of learning from the inner-city youth perspective. In F. A. Villarruel & R. M. Lerner (Eds.), *Promoting community-based programs for socialization and learning* (pp. 25–34). New Directions for Child Development, No. 63. San Francisco: Jossey-Bass.

Heath, S. B. (1996). Ruling places: Adaptation in development by inner-city youth. In R. Jessor, A. Colby, & R. A. Shweder (Eds.), *Ethnography and human development: Context and meaning in social inquiry* (pp. 225–251). Chicago: University of Chicago.

Heath, S. B. (1998a). Living the arts through language plus learning: A report on community-based youth organizations. *Americans for the Arts Monographs, 2*(7), 1–19.

Heath, S. B. (1998b). Working through language. In S. M. Hoyle & C. T. Adger (Eds.), *Kids talk: Strategic use of language use in later childhood* (pp. 217–240). New York: Cambridge University Press.

Heath, S. B., & McLaughlin, M. W. (1993). *Identity and inner-city youth: Beyond ethnicity and gender.* New York: Teachers College Press.

Hicks, D. (2002). *Reading lives: Working-class children and literacy learning.* New York: Teachers College Press.

Himley, M. (with Carini, P. F.). (Eds.). (2000). *From another angle: Children's strengths and school standards.* New York: Teachers College Press.

Himley, M. (Ed.). (2002). *Prospect's descriptive processes: The child, the art of teaching, and the classroom and school.* North Bennington, VT: The Prospect Center.

Hogan, D. (1990). Modes of discipline: Affective individualism and pedagogical reform in New England, 1820–1850. *American Journal of Education, 99,* 1–56.

Hollins, E. R. (1996). *Transforming curriculum for a culturally diverse society.* Mahwah, NJ: Lawrence Erlbaum.

hooks, b. (1994). *Teaching to transgress: Education as the practice of freedom.* New York: Routledge.

Hull, G., & Rose, M. (1989). Rethinking remediation: Toward a socio-cognitive understanding of problematic reading and writing. *Written Communication, 6,* 139–154.

Hull, G., & Rose, M. (1990). "This wooden shack place": The logic of an unconventional reading. *College Composition and Communication, 41,* 287–298.

Hull, G., & Schultz, K. (2001). Literacy and learning out of school: A review of theory and research. *Review of Educational Research, 71*(4), 575–611.

Hull, G., & Schultz, K., (Eds.). (2002). *School's Out!: Bridging out-of-school literacy with classroom practices.* New York: Teachers College Press.

James, W. (1890). *Principles of psychology.* New York: Holt.

Kanevsky, R. D. (1993). Descriptive Review of a Child: A way of knowing about teaching and learning. In M. Cochran-Smith & S. L. Lytle (Eds.), *Inside/outside: Teacher research and knowledge.* New York: Teachers College Press.

Kaplan, J. L. (2001). *I will learn from you: Making education humane.* Unpublished master's portfolio, University of Pennsylvania, Philadelphia.

Kohl, H. (1994). *"I won't learn from you" and other thoughts on creative maladjustment* (pp. 1–32). New York: New Press.

Kondo, D. K. (1990). *Crafting selves: Power, gender, and discourses of identity in a Japanese workplace.* Chicago: University of Chicago Press.

Ladson-Billings, G. (1994). *The dreamkeepers: Successful teachers of African-American children.* San Francisco: Jossey-Bass.

Ladson-Billings, G. (1998). Just what is critical race theory and what's it doing in a nice field like education? *Qualitative Studies in Education, 11*(1), 7–24.

Ladson-Billings, G. (1999). Preparing teachers for diversity: Historical perspectives, current trends, and future directions. In L. Darling-Hammond & G. Sykes (Eds.), *Teaching as the learning profession: Handbook of policy and research* (pp. 86–123). San Francisco: Jossey-Bass.

Ladson-Billings, G. (2000). Racialized discourses and ethnic epistemologies. In N. K. Denzin & Y. S. Lincoln (Eds.), *Handbook of qualitative research* (2nd ed., pp. 257–277). Thousand Oaks, CA: Sage.

Ladson-Billings, G. (2001). *Crossing over to Canaan: The journey of new teachers in diverse classrooms.* San Francisco: Jossey-Bass.

Ladson-Billings, G., & Tate, W. F. (1995). Toward a critical race theory of education. *Teachers College Record, 97*(1), 47–68.

Lee, C. D. (1993). *Signifying as a scaffold for literary interpretation: The pedagogical implications of an African American discourse genre.* Urbana, IL: National Council of Teachers of English.

Lee, C. D. (2000). *The cultural modeling project's multimedia records of practice: Analyzing guided participation across time.* Paper presented at the annual meeting of the American Educational Research Association, New Orleans, LA.

Lensmire, T. (1994). *When children write: Critical re-visions of the writing workshop.* New York: Teachers College Press.

Lensmire, T. (2000). *Powerful writing, responsible teaching.* New York: Teachers College Press.

Levinson, B. A., & Holland, D. C. (1996). The cultural production of a person: An introduction. In B. Levinson, D. Foley, & D. Holland (Eds.), *The cultural production of a person: Critical ethnographies of school and local practice* (pp. 1–54). Albany: State University of New York Press.

Levy, S. (1996). *Starting from scratch: One classroom builds its own curriculum.* Portsmouth, NH: Heinemann.

Lorde, A. (1984). *Sister/outsider: Essays and speeches.* New York: The Crossing Press Feminist Series.

Luttrell, W. (1997). *Schoolsmart and motherwise: Working-class women's identity and schooling.* New York: Routledge.

Lytle, S. L., & Cochran-Smith, M. (1992). Teacher research as a way of knowing. *Harvard Educational Review, 62,* 447–474.

Macedo, D. (1994). *Literacies of power: What Americans are not allowed to know.* Boulder, CO: Westview Press.

Mahiri, J. (1998). *Shooting for excellence: African American and youth culture in new century schools.* New York: Teachers College Press.

McDermott, R. P. (1987). The explanation of minority school failure, again. *Anthropology & Education Quarterly, 18,* 361–367.

McDermott, R. P. (1993). The acquisition of a child by a learning disability. In S. Chaiklin & J. Lave (Eds.), *Understanding practice: Perspectives on activity and context* (pp. 269–305). New York: Cambridge University Press.

McDermott, R. P., & Gospodinoff, K. (1979). Social contexts for ethnic borders and school failure. In A. Wolfgang (Ed.), *Nonverbal behavior* (pp. 175–195). New York: Academic Press.

McDermott, R. P., & Varenne, H. (1995). Culture as disability. *Anthropology & Education Quarterly, 26*(3), 324–348.

Mehan, H. (1979). *Learning lessons.* Cambridge, MA: Harvard University Press.

Meier, D. (1996). *The power of their ideas: Lessons from a small school in Harlem.* Boston: Beacon Press.

Meier, D. (2002). *In schools we trust: Creating communities of learning in an era of standardization*. Boston: Beacon Press.

Moje, E. B. (2000). "To be part of the story": The literacy practices of gangsta adolescents. *Teachers College Record, 102*(3), 651–690.

Moll, L. C. (1992). Bilingual classroom studies and community analysis: Some recent trends. *Educational Researcher, 21*(3), 20–24.

Moll, L. C., & Diaz, S. (1987). Change as the goal of educational research. *Anthropology & Education Quarterly, 18*, 300–311.

Moll, L. C., & Greenberg, J. B. (1990). Creating zones of possibilities: Combining social context for instruction. In L. C. Moll (Ed.), *Vygotsky and education: Instructional implications and applications of sociohistorical psychology* (pp. 319–348). New York: Cambridge University Press.

Morrison, T. (1993). *Lecture and speech of acceptance, upon the award of the Nobel Prize for literature*. New York: A. A. Knopf.

Niesz, T. (2000). *Voices of critique: Challenging silences and conformity at a post-desegregated middle school*. Talk delivered at the Ethnography in Education Forum, Philadelphia, PA.

Nieto, S. (1994). Lessons from students on creating a chance to dream. *Harvard Educational Review, 64*(4), 392–426.

Nieto, S. (1999). *The light in their eyes: Creating multicultural learning communities*. New York: Teachers College Press.

Nieto, S. (2000). *Affirming diversity: The sociopolitical context of multicultural education* (3rd ed.). New York: Longman.

Olsen, T. (1978). *Silences*. New York: Delacorte Press.

Ortner, S. B. (1994). Theory in anthropology since the sixties. In N. B. Dirks, G. Eley, & S. B. Ortner (Eds.), *Culture/power/history: A reader in contemporary social theory* (pp. 372–411). Princeton, NJ: Princeton University Press.

Paley, V. G. (1986). On listening to what children say. *Harvard Educational Review, 56*(2), 122–131.

Parker, L. (1998). "Race is . . . race ain't": An exploration of the utility of critical race theory in qualitative research in education. *Qualitative Studies of Education, 11*, 43–55.

Parker, L., Deyhle, D., & Villenas, S. (1999). *Race is . . . race isn't: Critical race theory and qualitative studies in education*. Boulder, CO: Westview Press.

Perrone, V. (1991). *A letter to teachers*. San Francisco: Jossey-Bass.

Perrone, V. (2000). *Lessons for new teachers*. Boston: McGraw-Hill.

Perry, T., & Fraser, J. W. (1993). Reconstructing schools as multiracial/multicultural democracies: Toward a theoretical perspective. In T. Perry & J. W. Fraser (Eds.), *Freedom's plow: Teaching in a multicultural classroom* (pp. 3–24). New York: Routledge.

Philadelphia Teachers' Learning Cooperative. (1984). On becoming teacher experts: Buying time. *Language Arts, 6*(7), 731–736.

Phillips, S. (1992). Acquisition of roles for appropriate speech usage. In R. Abraham & R. Troike (Eds.), *Language and cultural diversity in American education*. New York: Prentice-Hall.

Resnick, M. (1996). Making connections between families and schools. In J. Check, A. Peterson, & M. Ylvisaker (Eds.), *Cityscapes: Eight views from the urban classroom* (pp. 115–132). Berkeley, CA: National Writing Project.

Reyes, M. de la Luz. (1992). Challenging venerable assumptions: Literacy instruction for linguistically different students. *Harvard Educational Review, 62*, 427–446.

Rich, A. (1979). *On lies, secrets and silence: Selected prose, 1966–1978*. New York: W. W. Norton.

Roosevelt, D. (1998). *Fragility and endurance in children's writing and teaching as acts of attention*. Unpublished doctoral dissertation, Michigan State University, East Lansing.

Rosaldo, R. (1989). *Culture and truth: The remaking of social analysis*. Boston: Beacon Press.

Rose, M. (1995). *Possible lives: The promise of public education in America*. New York: Houghton Mifflin.

Rowe, M. B. (1986). Wait time: Slowing down may be a way of speeding up. *Journal of Teacher Education, 37*, 736–741.

Rukeyser, M. (1973). Kathe Kollwitz. In J. Goulianos (Ed.), *By a woman writt* (pp. 373–378). New York: Bobbs-Merrill. (Originally published 1962)

Schultz, K. (1991). *"Do you want to be in my story?": The social nature of writing in an urban third- and fourth-grade classroom*. Unpublished doctoral dissertation, University of Pennsylvania, Philadelphia.

Schultz, K. (1994). "I want to be good; I just don't get it": A fourth-grader's entrance into a literacy community. *Written Communication, 11*(3), 381–413.

Schultz, K. (1996). Between school and work: The literacies of urban adolescent females. *Anthropology and Education Quarterly, 27*(4): 517–544.

Schultz, K. (1997a). Crossing boundaries in research and teacher education: Reflections of a White researcher in urban schools and communities. *Qualitative Inquiry, 3*(4), 491–512.

Schultz, K. (1997b). "Do you want to be in my story?": Collaborative writing in an urban elementary school classroom. *Journal of Literacy Research, 29*(2), 253–287.

Schultz, K. (1999). Identity narratives: Stories from the lives of urban adolescent females. *Urban Review, 31*(1), 79–106.

Schultz, K. (2002). Looking across space and time: Reconceptualizing literacy learning in and out of school. *Research in the Teaching of English, 36*(3), 356–390.

Schultz, K., & Buchanan, J. (1990). *"Rad" Magazine and "Jason and the Golden Chain": The social nature of writing in a third–fourth-grade classroom*. Paper presented at the Ethnography in Education Research Forum, University of Pennsylvania, Philadelphia.

Schultz, K., Buck, P., & Niesz, T. (2000). Democratizing conversations: Discourses of "race" in a post-desegregated middle school. *American Education Research Journal, 37*(1), 33–65.

Schultz, K., & Davis, J. E. (1996). *After desegregation: Students and teachers talk about "race" and relations in post-desegregated schools*. Proposal funded by the Spencer Foundation, Chicago, IL.

Schultz, K., Niesz, T., & Buck, P. (1999). *"Everyone wants to be standard White":* *Invisible dimensions of girls' leadership in a post-desegregated middle school.* Paper presented at the annual meeting of the American Anthropological Association, Chicago, IL.

Shaughnessy, M. (1976). Diving in: An introduction to basic writing. *College Composition and Communication, 27*(3), 234–239.

Shaughnessy, M. (1977). *Errors and expectations.* New York: Oxford University Press.

Sheets, R. H. (2000). Advancing the field or taking center stage: The White movement in multicultural education. *Educational Researcher, 29*(9), 15–21.

Shulman, L. (1986). Those who understand: Knowledge growth in teaching. *Educational Researcher, 15*(2), 4–14.

Shulman, L. (1987). Knowledge and teaching: Foundations of the new reform. *Harvard Educational Review, 57,* 1–22.

Shuman, A. (1986). *Storytelling rights: The uses of oral and written texts among urban adolescents.* New York: Cambridge University Press.

Shuman, A. (1993). Collaborative writing: Appropriating power or reproducing authority. In B. Street (Ed.), *Cross-cultural approaches to literacy* (pp. 247–271). New York: Cambridge University Press.

Skilton-Sylvester, P. (1994). Elementary school curricula and urban transformation. *Harvard Educational Review, 64* (3), 309–331.

Slavin, R. E., & Madden, N. A. (1999). *Success for All/Roots & Wings: 1999 summary of research on achievement outcomes.* Baltimore: Johns Hopkins University, Center for Research on the Education of Students Placed at Risk.

Sleeter, C. E. (1991). *Empowerment through multicultural education.* Albany: State University of New York Press.

Street, B. V. (1993a). (Ed.). *Cross-cultural approaches to literacy.* New York: Cambridge University Press.

Street, B. V. (1993b). The new literacy studies: Guest editorial. *Journal of Research in Reading, 16*(2), 81–97.

Street, B. V. (1995). *Social literacies: Critical approaches to literacy in development, ethnography, and education.* London: Longman.

Street, B. V. (2001). Literacy "events" and literacy "practices": Theory and practice in the "New Literacy Studies." In K. Jones & M. Martin-Jones (Eds.), *Multilingual literacies: Comparative perspectives on research and practice* (pp. 17–30). Amsterdam: John Benjamins.

Strieb, L. Y. (1985). *A Philadelphia teacher's journal.* Grand Forks, ND: North Dakota Study Group on Evaluation.

Strieb, L. Y. (1992). When a teacher's values clash with school values: Documenting children's progress. In J. Andrias, R. Kanevsky, L. Strieb, & C. Traugh, *Exploring values and standards: Implications for assessment.* New York: NCREST, Teachers College.

Strieb, L. Y. (1993). Visiting and revisiting the trees. In M. Cochran-Smith & S. L. Lytle (Eds.), *Inside/outside: Teacher research and knowledge* (pp. 121–130). New York: Teachers College Press.

Strieb, L. Y. (1995). *Everybuddy plays with me.* Unpublished manuscript.

Strieb, L. Y. (1999). Communicating with parents: One teacher's story. In J. W. Lindfors & J. S. Townsend (Eds.), *Teaching language arts: Learning through dialogue*. Urbana, IL: National Council of Teachers of English.

Style, E. (1988). *Curriculum as window and mirror: Listening for all voices*. Oak Knoll School Conference Proceedings. Summit, NJ: SEED.

Sullivan, A. M. (2000). Notes from a marine biologist's daughter: On the art and science of attention. *Harvard Educational Review, 70*(2), 211–227.

Taliaferro, L. (2001, March). *Teachers on race: Discussion of race in teacher education*. Talk at the Ethnography in Education Forum, Philadelphia, PA.

Thompson, A. (1998). Not the color purple: Black feminist lessons for educational caring. *Harvard Educational Review, 68*(4), 522–554.

U.S. Department of Education. (2000). *No Child Left Behind Act of 2000*.

Valdés, G. (1996). *Con respeto: Bridging the distances between culturally diverse families and schools*. New York: Teachers College Press.

Varenne, H., & McDermott, R. P. (1999). *Successful failure: The school America builds*. Boulder, CO: Westview Press.

Vygotsky, L. S. (1962). *Thought and language* (E. Hanfmann & G. Vakar, Eds. and Trans.). Cambridge, MA: MIT Press.

Vygotsky, L. S. (1978). *Mind in society: The development of higher psychological processes*. Cambridge, MA: Harvard University Press.

Walker, V. S. (1996). *Their highest potential: An African American school community in the segregated South*. Chapel Hill: The University of North Carolina Press.

Walkerdine, V. (1991). *Schoolgirl fictions*. London: Verso.

Ward, J. V. (2000). Raising resisters: The role of truth telling in the psychological development of African-American girls. In L. Weis & M. Fine (Eds.), *Construction sites: Excavating race, class, and gender among urban youth* (pp. 50–64). New York: Teachers College Press.

Weis, L., & Fine, M. (Eds.). (2000). *Construction sites: Excavating race, class, and gender among urban youth*. New York: Teachers College Press.

West, C. (1993). *Race matters*. Boston: Beacon Press.

Wenger, E. (1999). *Communities of practice: Learning, meaning, and identity*. New York: Cambridge University Press.

Index

187

About the Author

KATHERINE SCHULTZ is associate professor of education in the Graduate School of Education at the University of Pennsylvania. A former teacher and principal, she currently offers courses on literacy in the elementary school, urban education, gender and education, and teacher education. She coedited the volume *School's Out: Bridging Out-of-School Literacies With Classroom Practice* with Glynda Hull, published by Teachers College Press. Her current research projects include ethnographic research on literacy practices that cross the boundaries of school and communities and a historical account of a collaborative professional development group of teachers that have met continuously for over 24 years.